Tour Guiding Research

MIX
Paper from
responsible sources
FSC® C014540
www.fsc.org

ASPECTS OF TOURISM

Series Editors: **Chris Cooper** (*Oxford Brookes University, UK*), **C. Michael Hall** (*University of Canterbury, New Zealand*) and **Dallen J. Timothy** (*Arizona State University, USA*)

Aspects of Tourism is an innovative, multifaceted series, which comprises authoritative reference handbooks on global tourism regions, research volumes, texts and monographs. It is designed to provide readers with the latest thinking on tourism worldwide and push back the frontiers of tourism knowledge. The volumes are authoritative, readable and user-friendly, providing accessible sources for further research. Books in the series are commissioned to probe the relationship between tourism and cognate subject areas such as strategy, development, retailing, sport and environmental studies.

Full details of all the books in this series and of all our other publications can be found on http://www.channelviewpublications.com, or by writing to Channel View Publications, St Nicholas House, 31-34 High Street, Bristol BS1 2AW, UK.

ASPECTS OF TOURISM: 62

Tour Guiding Research

Insights, Issues and Implications

Betty Weiler and Rosemary Black

CHANNEL VIEW PUBLICATIONS
Bristol • Buffalo • Toronto

Library of Congress Cataloging in Publication Data
A catalog record for this book is available from the Library of Congress.
Weiler, B. (Betty)
Tour Guiding Research: Insights, Issues and Implications/Betty Weiler and Rosemary Black.
Aspects of Tourism: 62
Includes bibliographical references and index.
1. Tours guides (Persons)—Research. 2. Tourism—Research. I. Black, Rosemary, 1955-II. Title.
G154.7.W45 2015
910–dc23 2014018930

British Library Cataloguing in Publication Data
A catalogue entry for this book is available from the British Library.

ISBN-13: 978-1-84541-468-9 (hbk)
ISBN-13: 978-1-84541-467-2 (pbk)

Channel View Publications
UK: St Nicholas House, 31-34 High Street, Bristol BS1 2AW, UK.
USA: UTP, 2250 Military Road, Tonawanda, NY 14150, USA.
Canada: UTP, 5201 Dufferin Street, North York, Ontario M3H 5T8, Canada.

Website: www.channelviewpublications.com
Twitter: Channel_View
Facebook: https://www.facebook.com/channelviewpublications
Blog: www.channelviewpublications.wordpress.com

The policy of Multilingual Matters/Channel View Publications is to use papers that are natural, renewable and recyclable products, made from wood grown in sustainable forests. In the manufacturing process of our books, and to further support our policy, preference is given to printers that have FSC and PEFC Chain of Custody certification. The FSC and/or PEFC logos will appear on those books where full certification has been granted to the printer concerned.

Typeset by Deanta Global Publishing Services Limited.
Printed and bound in Great Britain by Short Run Press Ltd.

Contents

Tables and Figures

Tables

Acknowledgements

We would like to acknowledge the support we received from many individuals and organisations without whom this book would not have been completed.

Firstly, thank you to all the great tour guides we have met, been on tour with, trained and otherwise worked with over the years. Thanks to your passion and your professionalism, you have made us think, smile, laugh, cry and take action. You have made a difference in our lives as well as the lives of many others, and you have been the inspiration for us to start – and to finish – this book.

Our sincere thanks go to Hannah Murphy. Thank you so much for your helpful editing and constructive feedback – your thoroughness and attention to detail were a great help. A big thank you also to Monica Torland, for your thorough analysis based on our Endnote© database reported in Chapter 1, and for your input and feedback on many other aspects of this book.

We appreciate the constructive feedback of both the anonymous reviewer and Channel View's Aspects of Tourism series editors on an earlier version of the manuscript. We are especially grateful to Elinor Robertson (our publishing editor) – you have been wonderful to work with, and your assistance with and enthusiasm for the manuscript always came when we really needed it.

We also acknowledge the institutional support of Southern Cross University and Charles Sturt University and the schools (Tourism & Hospitality Management and Environmental Science) in which we work. Thank you to our many colleagues both within and outside these schools and institutions – too many to name but you know who you are – and thank you in particular for the many great photo and anecdotal contributions.

Finally, our deepest and sincerest thanks to Betty's son Daniel and our respective partners Brian and Ken, not only for their support during the writing of this book, but also for their sustained belief in us. We promise to make up for all that lost time together on weekends and evenings.

1 The Historical and Political Context and Scope of Tour Guiding Research

Introduction to and Aim of the Book

Tour guides can be found at every tourism destination, and nearly everyone both within and outside the tourism industry is familiar with the term and the persona of a 'tour guide'. Few, however, fully understand what a tour guide does and what constitutes 'tour guiding'.

Whether employed by tour operators, resorts, lodges, attractions, theme parks, museums, protected area management agencies, zoos, visitor centres or self-employed, tour guides are often viewed by other stakeholders as an important part of, and sometimes as the key player in, the tourism product and experience. However, it is only quite recently that scholars and researchers have turned their attention to the subject of tour guides and tour guiding. The earliest book on the phenomenon of tour guiding appears to be E.A. Mills' (1920) *Adventures of a Nature Guide*; however, the earliest scholarly publication, Valene Smith's call for trained tour guides, was published much later in the *Professional Geographer* in 1961. Some 50 years on, it is timely and appropriate to undertake a critical review of the scholarly literature on tour guides and guiding.

Prior to Cohen's (1985) seminal paper on the role of the tour guide, published in *Annals of Tourism Research*, there were fewer than a dozen published papers on tour guides or guiding. However, conceptual and empirical papers have gradually found their way into conference proceedings, edited books and scholarly journals, so that there are now close to 300 published papers that focus specifically on some aspect of tour guides or tour guiding. The majority of these are empirical studies which, together with the conceptual literature, provide a substantial body of work from which to consider, reflect on and speculate about tour guiding as a phenomenon of interest.

Many scholars have argued that the tour guide plays a pivotal role in the experience of visitors or tourists who join a guided tour, potentially making or breaking the tour and the experience. Researchers acknowledge the instrumental role of the guide in ensuring that the tour runs smoothly and is a safe, logistical success, but increasingly emphasise the many mediatory and interpretive aspects of guiding. This in turn has drawn attention to the importance of the communicative competency of guides, including the application of best practice principles in interpretation and intercultural communication. The guide's role in fostering sustainability has also come under scrutiny, particularly in influencing and monitoring visitors' behaviour in contexts such as ecotourism and nature-based tourism and in delivering messages that impact post-visit attitudes and behaviour. Research has also begun to explore and measure the influence of these and other aspects of guiding on visitor satisfaction. In part to maintain and improve satisfaction but also to contribute to sustainability, the academic literature on tour guiding has examined the strengths and weaknesses of guide training and education initiatives and has evaluated training approaches that can further enhance the performance of tour guides. Finally, professional associations, professional certification, licensing and codes of practice have been researched for their potential to achieve quality assurance outcomes and to ensure that guides are recognised and rewarded for achieving these outcomes.

These and other themes provide the structure for this book. The aim of the book is to provide an authoritative, state-of-the-art review of the scholarly literature on tour guiding theory and practice to stimulate further research on tour guiding by social scientists across a range of disciplines and to foster quality tour guiding practice.

Specifically, this book seeks to:

- explore how tour guiding theory and practice from a range of disciplines have evolved over time and what factors have contributed to this;
- critically examine tour guiding research, methods, findings to date and research gaps;
- consolidate and synthesise the knowledge base on tour guiding and foreshadow how current and future trends and issues might impact on tour guiding research and practice in the 21st century.

As such, the book draws on the published literature on tour guiding, which in recent years has grown in both depth and breadth. The studies reviewed in this book cover a wide range of contexts in which guided tours are conducted, ranging from city streets to heritage and wildlife tourism attractions, from high-end tourist lodging establishments to national park campgrounds, and from highly developed destinations to very remote ones in both developed and developing countries.

Within the tourism literature, terms such as 'tour guide', 'tourist guide', 'tour leader', 'tour manager', 'tour escort' and 'courier' are sometimes used synonymously. The literature and industry terminology indicates that the use of these terms varies from country to country, region to region, between the public and private sectors and also within the tourism industry itself. In this book, a tour guide is defined as a person, usually a professional, who guides groups (and sometimes individuals) around venues or places of interest such as natural areas, historic buildings and sites, and landscapes of a city or a region; and interprets the cultural and natural heritage in an inspiring and entertaining manner, in the language of the visitor's choice (adapted from the European Federation of Tourist Guide Associations [EFTGA]). It must be acknowledged, however, that the World Federation of Tourist Guide Associations (WFTGA) and the EFTGA consider the designation of 'tour guide' as inappropriate, unflattering and a misnomer, as the term can refer to a book, a brochure (Pond, 1993) or a robotic tour guide (Tomatis *et al.*, 2002: 1). This is why the term 'tourist guide' rather than 'tour guide' is used extensively throughout Europe and the United Kingdom, defined as 'a person who guides visitors in the language of their choice and interprets the cultural and natural heritage of an area, [and who] normally possesses an area-specific qualification usually issued and/ or recognised by the appropriate authority' (WFTGA, 2013). Much of this book, as will become evident, is relevant to others who work beyond such site- or area-specific guiding, such as tour guides, managers, leaders and escorts who move between destinations. In this book, the term 'tour guiding' is used to refer to the work undertaken by all of these people.

A tour guide is a professional who guides groups around venues or places of interest such as natural areas, historic buildings and sites and interprets the cultural and natural heritage in an inspiring and entertaining manner. *Credit*: Anne Bottomley (Sydney city guide)

Elements common to all such tour guides are that they generally lead and manage groups who are normally non-captive in a communicative sense (they don't have to pay attention) but are often captive in a physical sense (it is difficult for individuals to leave the tour or for the tour to discharge the guide) (see for example Macdonald, 2006 and others). Guided tours also typically involve direct experiences of phenomena (as opposed to virtual experiences such as via technology and mass media). For most guided tours there is one guide per group, there is opportunity for the guide to adjust his or her content and style to the group, and there are options for two-way communication and other forms of involvement/interaction by group members. Variations to the norm and different types of guided tours are discussed later in this chapter.

Overview of Tour Guiding Research and Scholarship

The theoretical and empirical research assembled for this book provides for the first time an overview of tour guiding research and scholarship over the past 50 years. This section first presents the methods used to undertake a review of the literature that forms the basis of this book. It then provides a snapshot of that research viewed as an aggregate, including where the research was published, the authors' locations and disciplinary perspectives, the tourism genre in which the studies were undertaken, the study locations and the methods used.

Methods for researching, delimiting and writing about tour guides and guiding

The scholarly body of literature on which this book is based was identified using search engines such as Google Scholar together with library databases such as CAB Abstracts and leisuretourism.com, searching mainly for peer-reviewed journal papers and book chapters focused on tour guiding and tour guides. Some peer-reviewed conference papers, textbooks, doctoral-level theses and grey literature, such as government reports, were uncovered in searches and if accessible they were included. However, articles appearing in professional (non-peer-reviewed) publications such as tour guiding newsletters, magazines and internal government/ organisational publications, as well as information conveyed via websites and in electronic media such as promotional and training videos/DVDs were not systematically searched.

Thus, this book's focus and most of its analysis of tour guiding research and practice are limited primarily to what has been reported in the academic literature. A database was created of journal articles, books, book chapters, conference papers, doctoral theses and research reports published over the past 50 years. Some of these were studies examining broader aspects of tourism such as sustainable tourism, visitor communication/ interpretation, customer service/satisfaction, tourism marketing and tourism/destination management, with tour guides or guiding forming only a part of the overall study or paper, but most (280) were tour guide/ guiding focused. The detailed content of some publications that could not be obtained electronically is not reported in this book, although hard copies or PDFs were collected and reviewed for approximately 90% of the articles that were tour guiding focused. Eight books were identified that focus on tour guiding, nearly all of which are textbooks or manuals written *for* tour guides (both prospective and current) rather than books *about* guides and guiding. Two of these are particularly notable for their depth and breadth of focus (Pastorelli, 2003; Pond, 1993); the remaining are much shorter and narrower in focus.

Some anomalies were identified and subsequently excluded from the book using this search method, but are worth mentioning. Literature on interpretation and visitor communication delivered by non-personal and non-guided media is largely outside the scope of this book (for recent examples, see Kang and Gretzel [2012] on podcast tours and Chu *et al.* [2012] and Wolf *et al.* [2013] on Global Positioning System-triggered multimedia guided tours), and this includes research about guidebooks (sometimes referred to as 'tour guides') (Peel *et al.*, 2012). Another line of enquiry outside the book's focus is research reporting on the development and testing of electronic 'tour guides'. First appearing in the academic literature in the late 1990s, Davies (1998) and others report on handheld, computer-based (smartphone) hardware and software applications developed as non-guided tour guiding services for visitors. Some of these city-focused guides are described as 'interactive', but this simply means that they incorporate user data to customise the service to each visitor with no interface with a human being. Similarly, there is some literature on the development of interactive robotic tour guides for use in museums and similar environments, designed to give visitors a 'pre-defined tour' (Tomatis *et al.*, 2002: 1). Since none of these are about personal (human) tour guides, they have been excluded. Finally, Edelheim (2009) suggests that his work focuses on tour guiding, but the term is used as an analogy for something else (in this case a classroom teaching tool).

In what outlets is research being published?

As already noted, 280 papers were identified that focus specifically on tour guides or tour guiding, and most of these (91%) have been published since 1990. In the literature search process, only one edited book (Black & Weiler, 2003) was uncovered that is devoted specifically to the scholarship of tour guiding.

However, recently a small but dedicated group of mainly European-based tour guiding researchers, scholars and practitioners has met biennially to present and produce papers focused on tour guiding. Entitled the International Research Forum on Guided Tours (http://irfgt.org/about-irfgt-2), these have taken place in Halmstad, Sweden, in 2009, Plymouth, UK, in 2011 and Breda, the Netherlands, in 2013 (Mykletun, 2013). Some of these papers have been published in conference proceedings and some, together with other research, have been published as special theme issues of the *Scandinavian Journal of Hospitality and Tourism*:

- Vol. 12 No. 1 (2012) 'Guided tours and tourism';
- Vol. 13 No. 2 (2013) 'Performing guided tours'.

This journal is not the only one in which tour guiding research is becoming more prominent. There have been 146 papers on tour guides or guiding published in scholarly journals. Of these, three tourism journals, *Annals of Tourism Research*, *Journal of Sustainable Tourism* and *Tourism Management*, have together published 43 papers on tour guides and tour guiding. An examination of trends over time revealed that the publication of tour guiding research in journals has grown exponentially in the past two decades, particularly in comparison to tour guiding research published as book chapters, which has actually declined (see Figure 1.1). Other trends over time relating to the specific research themes of this book are discussed in later chapters.

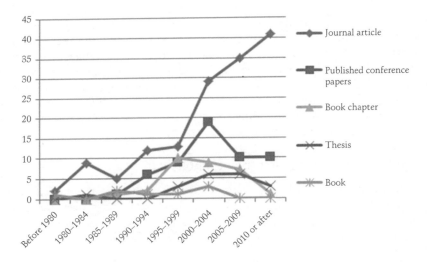

Figure 1.1 Trends in publication of tour guiding research (note: 2010–2013 reflects publications as at 30 June 2013)

Who is undertaking tour guiding research?

An analysis of authors whose institutional affiliation was stated in the publications identified (265 papers) revealed that 82 (32%) were based in Australia, 54 (21%) in the United States, and just under 30 (approximately 10%) in each of the United Kingdom, Europe (other) and China/Hong Kong/Taiwan. However, this does not take into account researchers who have authored multiple publications, so that in reality the spread of authors may be more even across Australia, the United States, the United Kingdom, Europe and China/Hong Kong/Taiwan. Most authors (82%) are based at universities. There were fewer than 10 papers by authors based in all other countries (including only two based in all of Africa, and six based in all of Latin/South America). As only English-language literature was searched, this description of the geographic distribution of authors may not reflect the full range of scholarly research being undertaken on tour guiding, particularly in Europe and Asia where researchers may be inclined to publish their work in non-English-language outlets. Some studies reported in this book cite non-English-language tour guiding references, particularly European and Chinese authors, but the majority of the work cited in the 280 papers was published in English.

The disciplinary perspective of researchers provides another lens, albeit an imprecise one, with which to view who is undertaking research on tour guiding. Evidence of disciplinary focus is not always self-evident, but on the basis of the affiliations of the 25 most prolific authors in the database (who collectively authored 120 of the 280 publications) it is clear that human geography, environmental studies, business/marketing/management, sociology, anthropology, communication/language studies, psychology and environmental education figure prominently in tour guiding research. These same disciplines are evident in the journals in which researchers publish, along with others such as conservation/biology, cultural studies and of course leisure, recreation and tourism studies. The disciplines of economics, political science, law, medicine, history and most of the physical sciences do not appear to be influencing research on tour guides and tour guiding. Obvious trends over time are not particularly apparent, although in the past decade the number of studies bringing theory and scholarship from disciplines outside of tourism studies to the investigation of the phenomenon of tour guiding has increased. The chapters in this book provide examples of the application of disciplinary theory to the study of particular aspects of tour guides and guiding, and these are revisited in the conclusion to identify theoretical areas of relative neglect and therefore research opportunity.

As with the disciplinary influence on tour guiding scholarship, the following overview of the type of tourism within which tour guiding has been researched, the geographic location of the research and the methods used by researchers provides a bird's-eye view of research to date. Once again, the limitations of the database – that is, papers published mainly in the English-language academic literature – need to be acknowledged.

Tourism genre

Encompassed in the term 'tour guide' as defined for this book are many types of guides working across a wide range of environments and settings. Guided tours can be categorised using a number of different criteria, including purpose, settings and environments (Black & Weiler, 2005; Pond, 1993), subject matter, length, types of clients and activity, reflecting the heterogeneity of the guiding industry. Unfortunately, there is no agreed-upon typology of guided tours based on these or any other characteristics. For the purposes of the book, a number of types of guiding can be viewed as aligning with well-known tourism genres and settings (see Table 1.1). This

Table 1.1 Tourism genres, settings and corresponding types of tour guiding

Tourism genre	Setting	Type of tour guiding
General or mass tourism	Any (vary from one hour to day tours)	Generalist tour guiding
Group/package tours	Any (usually extended and overnight tours)	Tour escorting/ extended tour guiding/driver guiding
Nature-based tourism	Natural environments both land and marine based, including wildlife attractions such as zoos (vary from one hour to day and overnight tours)	Nature-based/ecotour guiding
Adventure tourism	Natural environments, both land and marine based (day and overnight tours)	Adventure guiding
Heritage/cultural tourism	Heritage and historic sites Heritage attractions and museums Indigenous sites and host communities (vary from one hour to day tours)	Heritage interpreting/ guiding
City/urban tourism	Cities, towns, shopping areas, tourist attractions, industrial sites (vary from one hour to day tours)	City guiding

typology aims to reflect a contemporary picture of tour guiding; however, it is important to acknowledge that an individual tour guide does not necessarily work in just one genre nor undertake just one type of guiding. It is difficult to group some guides into specific categories as their roles and responsibilities are complex and may vary with a number of variables, such as site, season or employer.

The diversity of guides in this typology reflects a number of factors, such as the increasing segmentation and specialisation of the tourism sector (Douglas *et al.*, 2001; Hawkins & Lamoureux, 2001), changing visitor/tourist motivations and demands (Jones, 1999), the increasing demand for tourism professionals (particularly guides) (Hawkins & Lamoureux, 2001) and the recognition that guides play a key role in the visitor experience.

The type or genre of tourism within which the research on tour guiding was undertaken could be ascertained for 259 of the publications. Of these, 54 (21%) could be considered as either focusing on tour guiding in general or mass tourism, or on a mix of tour guiding contexts. Nature-based tourism was the context for more than a third (35%) of the papers, followed by heritage/cultural tourism (21%) and adventure tourism (10%). While acknowledging the potential for bias in the data set (as a result of the authors' own predilections for nature-based tour guiding research), the rigour and objectivity with which the literature search was conducted suggest that this distribution is an accurate reflection of research to date. In particular, tour guiding in the context of group/package tours (6%) and urban tourism (5%) seems to be relatively under-researched.

Study location

Tour guiding takes place in every geographic region of every country in the world and, according to Zillinger *et al.* (2012: 1), 'Guided tours can be found at more or less all places where tourism exists'. However, the study locations of the research reviewed in this book are not evenly distributed across the globe. Of the 280 studies analysed, 215 were empirical studies, of which 191 reported a geographic location for the research. Of these, 47 (25%) were undertaken in Australia, with the majority of the remainder being undertaken in China/Hong Kong/Taiwan (17%), the United States (12%), Europe (excluding the United Kingdom) (11%), Asia (excluding China, Hong Kong and Taiwan) (9%) and Latin/South America (7%). Ten studies (5%) were undertaken in multiple locations. Fewer than 10 studies were undertaken in any other single country, region or continent and, perhaps surprisingly, only three studies were undertaken in the United Kingdom (see Figure 1.2). A more nuanced examination of the geographical distribution of research on tour guiding is provided in the individual chapters of this book.

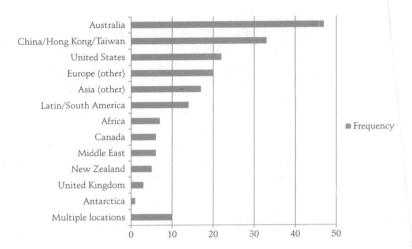

Figure 1.2 Study location of empirical research on tour guides and tour guiding, 1979–2013 (*n*=191)

Study method

There has been a notable diversity in the methods used by researchers to investigate tour guides and tour guiding. A number of publications are, or course, conceptual or do not report methods (26%). Those that are empirically based are fairly evenly spread in their use of qualitative (77 studies), quantitative (51 studies) and mixed methods (53 studies). Like much of tourism research, surveys are a widely used method of data collection by tour guiding researchers, with 99 studies reporting the use of some sort of survey of visitors, operators, guides and/or other stakeholders. The majority of these (70) report using on-site or field-based surveys, as opposed to mail, telephone or online surveys. Interviews (93 studies) are used frequently, with most (74) being face-to-face, semi-structured or structured interviews. Observation, including participant observation (69 studies), is also frequently used to collect data. Methods used much less frequently include case studies, ethnography, focus groups, document analysis, textual/diary/narrative analysis and visual/photo analysis. More methodological details about many of the studies reviewed for this book are included in the individual chapters.

The Context of Tour Guiding

In reviewing the literature for this book, it became apparent that the broader context of tour guiding has been somewhat neglected. For example, while some authors include a brief history of tour guiding in their papers (summarised in this section), none have undertaken a critical historical analysis of the phenomenon of tour guiding. Nor have there been investigations of the international context of tour guiding, for example how global trends such as technology or climate change have or are impacting on tour guides and tour guiding. The potential relationships between these trends and tour guiding practice are revisited in the book's conclusion.

History and evolution of guided tours

Guiding is probably one of the world's oldest professions, with early historical accounts referring to pathfinders and cicerones, who were antecedents of the contemporary guide (Pond, 1993). In the 5th century BC, Herodotus, an extensive traveller and writer, depended not only on guides but also more specifically on guides who spoke his language (Herodotus trans., 1972). Although Herodotus was critical of some guides, they were essential 'at a site such as Olympia, where there was a ... forest of statues ... the accumulation of hundreds of dedications ... a tourist was helpless without a guide' (Casson, 1974: 265).

According to Cohen (1985), the origins of the modern tour guide were in the 17th and 18th centuries with the advent of the 'Grand Tour'. This new form of tourism emerged as a direct outcome of the quest for learning that followed on from the Renaissance period. British male aristocrats were encouraged to travel as part of their education (Cohen, 1985; Holloway, 1994). This form of tourism involved visiting the major cultural centres of Europe accompanied by a tutor or guide and frequently took three or more years. These tours were the predecessor of the modern study tours that are most often organised by educational institutions and led by expert guides (Morse, 1997).

The 19th century saw the development of group pleasure travel through the initiatives of Thomas Cook, who was the tour guide/tour manager of many of these excursions. According to Hall (1995), Cook's concept of group travel, together with improved transportation and other social and technological developments, marked the start of mass tourism. This development brought with it the need for service personnel in all aspects of the tourism industry, including hotels, restaurants, tour operations, attractions and transport services. These personnel included tour guides who were responsible for escorting groups and individuals, and interpreting the natural and cultural heritage of the area. Thus was the birth of the modern tour guide, and as such Cook is sometimes referred to as the 'patron saint of modern tour guides' (Pond, 1993).

In the early 20th century, nature guides like Enos Mills (1920) were leading visitors through the North American wilderness and laying the foundations for the profession of interpretation (Regnier et al., 1994). According to Reigner et al. (1994: 2), Mills did not believe his only role was to guide people through the wilderness safely: 'A nature guide is not a guide in the ordinary sense of the word, and is not a teacher. At all times, however, he [sic] is rightfully associated with information and with some form of education. But nature guiding as we see it, is more inspirational than informational'.

Guiding is one of the world's oldest professions, with nature guides of the early 20th century laying down the foundations for national park interpretation. *Credit*: Graeme Burgan (Phillip Island Nature Park)

The first national park guides in the United States were soldiers at Yellowstone National Park who gave tours of the thermal features and so-called 'cone talks' (Chittenden, 1979). The first licensed guides in the United States, according to Pond (1993), were guides who escorted friends and relatives around the battlefield of Gettysburg. Licensing of these guides started in 1915 under the War Department and continues today under the National Park Service. These guides are renowned for being professional and well trained.

In recent decades, guided tours have been viewed as a means of visiting a destination or experiencing a place economically, efficiently and safely, particularly for inexperienced travellers (Schmidt, 1979). Guided tours are often stereotyped as being highly choreographed experiences involving passive group members who have little or no say in the tour itinerary and style (Zillinger *et al.*, 2012). Many guided tours today continue to be offered as predefined experiences, appealing to some visitors who want a safe, cheap and quick way to 'see the sites and sights'. They may be particularly attractive when visiting a destination or undertaking an activity for the first time, or when going somewhere (such as Antarctica) or doing something that requires specialist transportation, equipment or skills (such as whale watching). Sometimes a guided tour is the only way to experience a site or destination, for example one cannot swim with wild dolphins or visit the Galapagos Islands without a guide, and Chinese visitors cannot travel outside China on an approved destination status (ADS) tour without a local guide (Black, in press).

However, as tourism has become a more globalised phenomenon, contemporary guided tours have developed into diverse, multifaceted, context-specific and adaptable products, offering benefits beyond safety and convenience. For example, individuals and groups of visitors can arrange a personalised guided tour by hiring a taxi-driver guide, and tour clients can plan their own itineraries and choose their own guide as part of a personal, business or conference trip. Guided tours can have opt-in and opt-out segments, for example guided coach-based tours may include optional shopping or walking tours. The educational component of a tour can also be variable and can be customised to particular market segments and even to individuals, using technology such as smartphones and headsets that allow individuals to listen (or not listen) to commentary, choose the commentary language and in some cases interact with the content. Finally, tour clients can choose a guided tour not to buffer but to facilitate engagement and a more authentic experience with a destination, its environment and its host population (Black, in press).

Importantly, guided tours are now differentiated in terms of both product and market, ranging from very inexpensive to very expensive, and catering to first-time through to very experienced travellers.

New forms of guided tours are emerging that are co-creations between tourism operators, guides and clients (Jonasson, 2011), a topic that is revisited in Chapter 8. With the introduction of technology such as wireless internet, Geographic Information Systems and Global Positioning Systems there is now a blurring between guided and non-guided tours as visitors move between one and the other during their holiday.

The social, cultural and political context and nature of tour guiding

In addition to moving with the times, guided tours are embedded in the social, cultural and political contexts in which they occur, and thus may look very different from one destination to the next. According to Zillinger et al. (2012: 3), up to the present 'the phenomenon of guiding has been connected to a variety of questions through its intimate relations to innovation, politics and economy, social interactions and power relations, culture and indigenous tourism and local versus global'. A number of studies examining the political, social and cultural contexts of guiding at specific sites and destinations are reviewed in this section. While the tour guiding literature has given relatively little attention to these contexts, they are acknowledged as important. The role that individual tour guides sometimes choose to play, either consciously or unconsciously, as political instruments is discussed more fully in Chapter 2.

An early study into the *political context and politicising of tour guiding by government* was Mitchell's (1996) investigation of tour guides as vehicles for the creation of the government's desired image of Malta. Mitchell's ethnographic study revealed the role of guides as being less about communication and more about promotion. Guides were trained and more or less compelled (via compulsory licensing) to present images of Malta that 'perpetuate national claims to European-ness' (Mitchell, 1996: 203). These included privileging cultural and social elements of the past such as food, architecture, modes of transport and religion that depict Malta's links to Europe, thereby promoting its inclusion in the European Union.

Although such highly politicised tour guiding policies and practices may be relatively rare, they exist elsewhere. Direct force by policing and law enforcement, and indirect force through mechanisms such as training and licensing, can influence and create uniformity in the way that guides arrange their tours, select objects and places of interest, and deliver their tours.

At least two in-depth studies of guiding (Bras, 2000; Dahles, 2002) confirm this to be the case in Indonesia. Dahles (2002), in her study of tour guiding in Indonesia under Suharto's New Order regime, revealed the use of Indonesian tour guides by government policies to extol particular state ideologies. Guides were government trained to present an official authorised narrative. For fear of losing their jobs, guides kept visitors away from the 'backstages' of undesirable aspects of a destination, so guides played an important role in constructing local identity and limiting opportunities for visitors to meet local people. The Suharto government also regulated tour guiding through licensing, certification, training, pay and benefits. For example, the content of training focused on state ideology, national culture, history, language, defence and national security. Finally, tours were marketed and managed in ways that controlled how guides could conduct their tours and the content of their commentaries. The government-sanctioned 'ideal' guide was more of an information giver than an interpreter (see Chapter 2), with guides operating standardised and carefully staged tours with little or no consideration of the needs and interests of visitors (see discussion of Salazar [2005] in Chapter 2).

A case study by Bras (2000) of a designated 'traditional' village, now an open-air museum in Lombok, Indonesia, exemplifies the tension between the Indonesian provincial and national governments with respect to national and local identity, with the national government promoting tourism as a strategy to unify and modernise the country and present a standardised Indonesian Javanese culture. Bras (2000) found that the official trained guides presented a static, simplified image of the local Lombok culture that conformed to the needs of the provincial government, contrasting with the local informal village guides' representation of contemporary village life using personal biographies.

In separate studies in another part of the world, both Bowman (1992) and Sizer (1999) note the differences in perspectives of Palestinian and Israeli guides. While guides in Israel are, in theory, free to construct and modify their narratives depending on the group, the Israeli government influences the actions and commentary of the guides in subversive and indirect ways. Bowman (1992) found that Israeli guides are privileged through regular training offerings, while Palestinian guides have limited access to training and licenses. Both types of guides have to tailor their commentaries and tours to accommodate the nationalist vision to what visitors want to see and hear. The Israeli guides build up sympathy for their cause in their commentaries and the places they take visitors, portraying Palestinians as dangerous terrorists, in part to increase the dependency of visitors on Israeli guides. They avoid the Palestinian areas and contact with Palestinian people. As one Israeli guide said in Bowman's (1992) study:

> What they see they see because I point it out ... They're dependent on you to create their experience for them. This creates an enormous dependence of all kinds, and when this is coupled with the fact that they're Christian and you're Jewish – and most [guides] are chauvinistic – you get to the point that the Christian is seeing the holy land through a Jew ... This has political implications. Israel needs public sympathy very badly, especially in Europe and America. How do you get through to them [travellers from Europe and North America]? Give them an Israeli guide: we'll sneak propaganda in through the back door ... (Bowman, 1992: 123)

In contrast, the Palestinian guides are limited in how they can present their points of view and that of Palestine. If they talk about the politics of the region, they may be reported and lose their licence, so they tend to veil their Arabic or Palestinian identities. In contrast to the Israeli guides, they try to expose visitors to the Palestinian areas, though, like the Indonesian guides, they avoid making any commentary for fear of losing their licence. Even so, this exposure to the Palestinian point of view is not well regarded by the Israeli authorities and increasingly there are fewer licensed Palestinian guides as they are edged out by limiting their access to training opportunities through high fees, the enforcement of prerequisites and delivery in Hebrew only.

In a more recent study, Gelbman and Maoz (2012) look at the Island of Peace, an unofficial tourist site promoting peace on the border of Israel and Jordan. An analysis of Jewish-Israeli tour guide commentaries, interviews and participant observation revealed that the guides' narratives were not around peace but generally around conflict and war and presented the Jordanians as 'backward' and stubborn. According to the authors, the guides fail to take advantage of the potential of the site to promote peace and reconciliation between the two nations. They suggest that guide training and a more professional and neutral approach by the guides would assist in meeting this potential.

Huang and Weiler (2010), whose study had a less explicit focus on policy and politics, noted the narrow range of guide roles incorporated by the Chinese government's tour guide training and licensing programmes. Tour guides play the role of 'folk ambassadors' in China's foreign affairs and are trained and monitored to deliver an acceptable political standpoint and accurate information about the country's national policies and regulations. Training content is influenced largely by the China National Tourism Authority's (CNTA) view of tour guides' roles, which is based more on political ideology than on what visitors want or what research has identified as quality guiding practice. Thus, training is used as a political tool to emphasize tour guiding business knowledge and skills, to highlight elements of professional ethics, and to update guides on policies and regulations. Moreover, 'socialist ideology and political correctness overwhelm other selection criteria in China's awards-for-excellence schemes' (Huang & Weiler, 2010: 853). However, Huang and Weiler (2010) argue that this is not unique to China, as any quality assurance system is embedded in its political and social context, which necessarily directs and limits its scope and emphasis.

Lastly, Yamada's (2011) investigation of ecotourism policy in Japan represents an isolated example of research focused on the contribution of government policy to tour guiding's environmental roles and practices. It is clear from Yamada's research that guides are seen as an instrument for implementing ecotourism policy in Japan, and in particular for controlling what visitors are exposed to, understand and even feel about Japan's natural environments: 'Guiding is viewed as facilitation of conservation and environmental education' (Yamada, 2011: 143). Yamada argues that the Japanese government's policies regarding the roles of guides have helped to build the image of guides as value adding to ecotourism and have contributed to improved tour guide training and quality guiding.

In summary, tour guides are used as political instruments by some governments to influence visitor experiences and present a specific image of a country. As will be illustrated in Chapter 2, guides can also consciously direct a tour to strategically impact visitors' views and experiences, and thus they cannot be viewed as benign, apolitical, unbiased and a-cultural mediators of visitor experiences. According to Mitchell (1996: 199) '... experiences of [a country's environment, people,] history and culture [can be highly] mediated by guides'.

Language and Terminology Used in This Book

A number of key terms used throughout the book are defined in this section; in some cases, an expanded discussion of certain terms is provided in later chapters.

The terms 'tourist'/'visitor'/'client'/'customer'/'participant' have been used in the book as per the original study author's usage, but the terms are often used interchangeably, as these groups of people have similar needs and expectations when it comes to tour guides and tour guiding. Generally, the authors use 'visitor' to capture the findings of multiple studies, as it is a term that encompasses but is not limited to tourists. The word 'audience' is not used, as tour participants are more than just listeners and require a guide to do more than just present information and entertain them; they require a person who is ideally professionally trained to lead them safely and in a sustainable manner while performing a range of roles including communication, interpretation and mediation.

As previously mentioned, a 'tour guide' is a person, usually a professional, who guides groups or individual visitors or tourists around venues or places of interest such as natural areas, historic buildings and sites, and landscapes of a city or a region; and who interprets the cultural and natural heritage in an inspiring and entertaining manner. In many studies the term 'tour guide' is used even though the guides may be working in a specific setting, for example in a city. The term 'generalist guide' is used in the book to identify guides who do not specialise in a particular tourism environment, setting or genre. The term 'specialist guide' is used for guides who work in very specific settings and thus may require specialist knowledge and skills, such as heritage, adventure, ecotour or nature guides. It is acknowledged that there are subtle differences between all these terms and the use of certain terms often reflects the different tourism genres, guiding settings, countries and employing organisations. However, irrespective of the term used to refer to the tour guide, this book is relevant to all tour guides and guiding stakeholders.

Specialist guides such as heritage, adventure, ecotour and nature guides work in specific settings and may require specialist knowledge and skills. *Credit*: Rosemary Black (Antarctic tour guide)

'Interpretation' is a term used extensively in the book and is defined as engagement with tourists/visitors in ways that provoke them to think about and connect with natural and cultural heritage, including places, sites, people, artefacts and natural and historical events, and that foster a sense of care and stewardship among tourists/visitors. Interpretive guiding is therefore the application of the principles of interpretation in a guiding context in order to achieve one or more outcomes such as enhancing the visitor experience; improving visitor satisfaction; increasing visitor awareness or understanding; and influencing attitudes, behavioural intentions and behaviours.

The World Tourism Organisation (WTO, 2013) defines sustainable tourism as 'tourism that takes full account of its current and future economic, social and environmental impacts, addressing the needs of visitors, the industry, the environment and host communities'. In keeping with this definition, this book uses the term 'sustainability' in relation to tour guiding to incorporate ecological, economic, social and cultural dimensions, sometimes referred to as the four pillars of sustainability.

The terms 'accreditation' and 'certification' are sometimes used synonymously across studies. An individual tour guide who has attained a certain level of competence and proficiency (e.g. knowledge and skill), usually determined by way of an examination or a series of on-the-job assessments, is said to be a certified or accredited guide. In this book, the term 'certification', or more accurately 'professional certification', is used.

Finally, the term 'performance' is used in the book in two contexts. First, in Chapter 3 it refers to the dramaturgical techniques used in guiding such as theatre or storytelling. The second use of the term 'performance' appears in Chapters 5 and 7, where the term refers to a guide's execution of his or her roles and tasks. This is often in relation to visitors' or sometimes other stakeholders' expectations regarding those specific roles as well as their level of satisfaction with the guide's work. It is also used in relation to the use of quality assurance mechanisms; that is to maintain or enhance role performance.

Overview of the Book

Based on the results of the literature search described at the outset of this chapter, the most prominent topics that appear in the published literature on tour guiding over the past 50 years were identified and systematically reviewed, reduced and refined to develop six themes that make up the six main chapters of the book. Each of these six chapters is based on between 41 and 86 papers published for the most part in peer-reviewed journals, but also as book chapters and in published conference proceedings. Some doctoral theses, textbooks and government reports are also included. Nearly all are either conceptual papers or empirically based studies and, because some studies cross over more than one of the six themes, they may be discussed and cited in more than one chapter. Nor are the themes themselves mutually exclusive, and thus there is some cross-referencing between chapters.

Each chapter overviews the literature on the chapter's theme, presented either chronologically (where there is a notable trend in the research), geographically (for example, where there is a story to tell about research conducted in a particular region of the world or in developing versus developed countries) or using other sub-themes that capture both the diversity and focus of the research. Due to the volume of research and the thematic structure of the book, some very good individual studies on tour guiding have been excluded from the main chapters of this book. In some cases, conceptually isolated, yet important, research studies have been included in the 'emerging themes' section of the final chapter.

Each of the chapters presents highlights of the methods and findings of many studies, using examples where appropriate. It was not possible to present detailed results of all studies so the reporting is, in many cases, brief and selective. The aim is to provide sufficient detail to build a picture of the research theme as a basis for identifying implications for practice and avenues for further research. Key references on each chapter's theme are identified at the end of each chapter; in some cases these are seminal papers and in others they are more recent papers that present a strong empirical study or convey an important current perspective on the subject matter. In selecting these, consideration was given to their geographic and tourism genre context and to their availability either online or through electronic journal collections generally accessible through university libraries. Topics and areas that have been neglected by scholars and researchers are identified within each chapter, and in the concluding chapter of the book.

Chapter 2 examines the multiple and complex roles and role dimensions of tour guiding, including the tour guide as social and cultural mediator. Chapter 3 focuses on the role of the guide as communicator and interpreter and presents research, theory and practice relating to interpretation, performance, storytelling and intercultural communication. The four pillars of sustainability are used as a framework in Chapter 4 to examine theory, research and practice relating to guides' contribution to sustainability. Chapter 5 reviews visitors' expectations of and satisfaction with their guides and guided experiences. In Chapters 6 and 7, issues of quality assurance in guiding are examined. Chapter 6 examines training, education and professional development as tools for quality assurance, and explores the strengths and weaknesses of approaches to training in both developed and developing countries, while Chapter 7 focuses on current findings regarding the use of professional associations, professional certification, licensing and codes of practice as mechanisms for quality assurance in tour guiding practice. Chapter 8, the final chapter, presents the key findings from the previous chapters and explores, both theoretically and empirically, future directions in tour guiding, including trends and contemporary issues in society and in tourism, and the implications for research, scholarship and practice.

2 The Multiple and Complex Roles of the Tour Guide

From the very earliest published literature on tour guiding to the present, scholars have observed that the role of the guide is multifaceted and that identifying all the roles required of a professional guide, let alone ensuring that these roles are performed to the satisfaction of a range of stakeholders, is a challenge for practicing guides and researchers alike (Pond, 1993; Welgemoed, 1993). The purpose of this chapter is to explore the multiple and complex roles that are associated with tour guiding from the perspective of a number of scholars, as well as from the perspective of various stakeholders based on published research findings. This includes perceptions of the relative importance of these roles and, in some cases, how well guides perform these roles. This chapter begins with a review of two key frameworks that have sought to capture the multiplicity of roles played by tour guides, including the origin, application, refinement and current status of each framework in the tour guiding literature. Rather than re-presenting these frameworks in their original form, this section focuses on their commonalities, particularly the role dimensions or spheres of guiding, based on studies that have applied these frameworks. This is followed by a thematic presentation of other research relating to tour guiding roles. Sub-themes include key studies and findings regarding the roles played by guides in developing countries versus developed countries, the mediatory role of the guide and the sociopolitical and cultural roles of individual guides. Chapter 3 takes a more in-depth look at the suite of communication roles played by tour guides, including interpretation and intercultural communication, while other roles performed by guides in relation to sustainability are covered in Chapter 4.

The role of the guide is multi-faceted, requiring flexibility and the ability to problem-solve. *Credit*: Brian Alston (Willis's Walkabouts)

Frameworks that Capture the Multiple Roles of a Guide

One of the earliest published papers in the field of tour guiding is Cohen's (1985) sociological perspective on the interrelationships between the guide and tour participants. His paper, entitled 'The tourist guide: The origins, structure and dynamics of a role', presents a conceptual framework of the various roles and functions of the tour guide as a basis for comparative studies of guiding in a range of environments. This framework grew out of his work on jungle guides and, to some extent, town guides in Thailand (Cohen, 1982). Based on observation and participant observation of some 25 trekking guides and interviews with half of these guides plus their managers, Cohen (1982) 'tested' his role framework and refined it for later publication in the tourism literature. This section of the chapter provides a brief overview of and subsequent applications and extensions to Cohen's (1985) framework.

According to Cohen (1985), guides play both pathfinding and mentoring roles, the former being the geographic way-finding role associated with traditional guiding, and the latter being a more modern, complex and heterogeneous role which can range from spiritual advice to educational tutelage. He allocates the multiplicity of roles played by the guide to two spheres, which he labels the *leadership* and *mediatory* spheres of guiding. According to Cohen, each of these has an outer- and an inner-directed aspect; that is, each has tasks directed outside the tour group and tasks directed within the group, creating four major components or roles played by guides. Cohen uses these to identify four key guiding roles: the *instrumental*, *social*, *interactional* and *communicative* roles of the guide. Cohen's mapping of these four roles in relation to his two spheres of guiding (leadership and mediation) is captured in Table 2.1.

Table 2.1 The spheres of tour guiding and the roles of a generalist guide

Sphere 1: Leadership sphere (group focused)	Instrumental role of the guide (Role 1) (navigating, providing physical access, shepherding the group)	Social role of the guide (Role 2) (entertaining, managing tension and group dynamics, maintaining group morale)
Sphere 2: Mediatory sphere (individual focused)	Interactionary role of the guide (Role 3) (go-between, facilitating engagement with locals and local services)	Communicative role of the guide (Role 4) (informing, mentoring, interpreting)

Source: Adapted from Cohen (1985: 17).

As illustrated in Table 2.1, roles associated with the leadership sphere are largely oriented towards group/tour management, while those associated with the mediatory sphere are oriented towards enhancing the experience of individual group members. Cohen (1985: 15) considers the guide's communicative role as being the essence of what makes a quality professional guide, with interpretation being 'the distinguishing communicative function of the trained tour guide' (see Chapter 3). Other researchers and scholars have focused on the broader mediatory roles of the guide (see the 'The Mediating Role of the Guide' section in this chapter), which Cohen labels as the interactionary role of the guide.

While Cohen's (1985) 'inner-directed' and 'outer-directed' perspectives helped inform the development of his original four-cell framework identifying the various components of a tour guide's roles, this distinction has been abandoned by subsequent researchers, who have instead focused on Cohen's individual roles and role spheres as depicted in Table 2.1. This is also true of applications of Weiler and Davis's (1993) extension of Cohen's framework to nature/ecotour guiding, discussed in more detail later in this chapter.

Cohen's (1985) framework is based on applying sociological concepts and dimensions to tour guiding, with limited empirical testing, which may be regarded as a limitation of the framework. Hillman (2003) and others are critical of the applications and extensions of Cohen's framework in the literature as being largely descriptive representations of a guide's roles and performance (e.g. Mitchell, 1996), a point returned to later in this chapter. Regardless, Cohen's seminal work on tour guiding roles has served as an important and useful foundation for further discussion and exploration of the dimensions associated with these roles, how these change over time and how they vary in different contexts.

Numerous authors, beginning in the 1980s (Almagor, 1985), have referred to Cohen's work and/or have undertaken to inventory, or have otherwise tried to capture, the diverse roles played by tour guides. Generally, however, early papers (pre-2001) on tour guiding roles were largely atheoretical and unempirical in their approach. Black and Weiler's (2005) review of 12 of these studies over a period of 22 years (1979–2001) identified the following 10 key roles that are expected of guides (in descending order of frequency of mention): (1) interpreter/educator, (2) information giver, (3) leader, (4) motivator of conservation values/role model, (5) social role/catalyst, (6) cultural broker/mediator, (7) navigator/protector, (8) tour and group manager/organiser, (9) public relations practitioner/company representative and (10) facilitator of access to non-public areas. Most of the authors of these studies acknowledge, however, that 'the number [and relative importance] of roles vary depending on ... the tour setting, the type of group and their needs and interests, and the employer's and industry's expectations of the guide' (Black & Weiler, 2005: 26–27).

Leading, navigating and protecting the group are important roles played by tour guides. *Credit*: Betty Weiler (Limpopo Eco Operations, South Africa)

Comprehensive lists and inventories of roles are often presented in textbooks and resources aimed at novice tour guides (Pond, 1993), but the lengthiness of these lists, the inconsistency in terminology and the lack of mutual exclusivity in specifying the various roles make them impractical for research, as well as for practical outcomes such as quality assurance and assessment of guide performance. While it may be considered an oversimplification of the roles of a tour guide for some purposes, the conciseness of Cohen's (1985) conceptual framework has made it attractive to researchers and scholars and led to it continuing to be widely cited.

One notable limitation of Cohen's (1985) framework, and indeed most research on stakeholder expectations and perceptions of role performance (discussed in a later section of this chapter and in Chapter 5), is a preoccupation with the needs of the visitor and inadequate attention to other stakeholders such as those associated with the destination (local, regional and national), industry, individual business/organisation, host population or natural environment. Cohen's framework provides limited insight into the positive (or negative) contributions of tour guiding to host communities, environments and destinations. In part due to the growth in ecotourism and nature-based tourism in the late 1980s, Cohen's framework came under scrutiny as failing to acknowledge the role of the guide in ensuring an environmentally and culturally responsible visitor experience.

In an effort to make theoretical sense of tour guiding roles in relation to all stakeholders, particularly in the context of ecotourism and nature-based tourism, Weiler and Davis (1993) developed a framework (see Table 2.2) depicting the roles of the nature-based/ecotour leader/ guide. Informed by a survey of tour operators and a content analysis

Table 2.2 The spheres of tour guiding and the roles of a nature-based/heritage tour guide

Sphere 1: Tour management (focus on group)	'Organiser' (Role 1)	'Entertainer' (Role 2)
Sphere 2: Experience management (focus on individual)	'Group leader' (Role 3)	'Teacher' (Role 4)
Sphere 3: Resource management (focus on host environment)	'Motivator' (Role 5)	'Nature/heritage interpreter' (Role 6)

Source: Adapted from Weiler and Davis (1993).

of tour brochures, they proposed that an ecotour guide's multiple roles could be subsumed under not two but three spheres, each of which (like Cohen) included two distinct roles. The first and second spheres – tour management and experience management – are adaptations of Cohen's (1985) original theoretical framework (leadership and mediation, respectively). As in Cohen's framework, the first sphere (*tour management*) focuses on pathfinding and organising (Role 1) and managing and entertaining (Role 2), while the second sphere (*experience management*) focuses on leading, mediating and fostering engagement (Role 3) and informing and mentoring (Role 4). Thus, the first sphere focuses on the group, while the second sphere focuses on the needs of individuals within the group. Weiler and Davis added a third sphere – *resource management* – which focuses on the needs of host communities and environments. In this sphere, the guide plays a key role in motivating and managing visitors' on-site behaviour to minimise adverse effects on the natural and cultural environment (Role 5), as well as fostering longer-term understanding, appreciation and conservation of those environments, mainly through heritage and nature interpretation (Role 6).

Although informed by a fairly limited analysis of guides and guided tours in Australia, Weiler and Davis's (1993) framework became a point of departure for subsequent papers (Ballantyne & Hughes, 2001; Gurung et al., 1996) and also served as a theoretical framework for at least four empirical studies (Haig & McIntyre, 2002; Howard et al., 2001; Pereira & Mykletun, 2012; Randall & Rollins, 2009). For example, Gurung et al.'s (1996) survey of 117 Nepalese tour and trekking guides revealed that interpretation (Role 6) is, according to these guides, their most important role but is typically underperformed due to inadequate training. Howard et al. (2001), on the basis of interviews with Australian indigenous guides and observations of selected tours, confirmed the relevance of all six of Weiler and Davis's tour guiding roles to indigenous tours and identified specific and multiple examples of guides performing all of these roles. They give some evocative examples of the guides' role as both a teacher and an interpreter:

Guides frequently used Paakintji language when describing animals and plants. Examples were provided of how English words have been derived, often through mispronunciation, from Paakintji (e.g. Mulga for Malka). Aboriginal concepts were explained to tourists by use of analogies, metaphors and similes that the tourist could understand. Examples of this include likening Mutawintji to a cathedral ... One guide likened smoking ceremonies to the use of incense by Catholics, and another referred to the engraving as *archives of our people*. These comparisons bring Aboriginal culture into a familiar context to the visitor. (Howard *et al.*, 2001: 34)

Haig and McIntyre (2002) and Randall and Rollins (2009) undertook to operationalise Weiler and Davis's (1993) framework and assess tourists' perceptions of the relative importance and/or performance of each guiding role. In Haig and McIntyre's (2002) study, tourists rated all six roles identified by Weiler and Davis (1993) as important; however, the role of entertainer (Role 2) was viewed as notably less important by tourists on ecotours (in comparison to the ratings by tourists staying at an ecotourism resort). Using 12 rating items, Randall and Rollins (2009) obtained tourists' perceptions of both role importance and guides' performance of the six roles. Tour clients rated guides as performing well on all six roles, which is commendable given that guides are often required to perform multiple roles simultaneously and sometimes these roles conflict (Arnould & Price, 1993). Of course, tourists judge the guide mainly based on the performance of tasks they can see, and in relation to their own tourist experience (see Chapter 5).

It bears noting that Cohen (1985) and Weiler and Davis (1993) developed their frameworks as heuristic tools rather than as testable theoretical models. While some researchers (e.g. Pereira & Mykletun, 2012; Randall & Rollins, 2009) have used Weiler and Davis's framework as a basis to develop indicators for measuring role performance, in some cases these efforts have met with limited success, particularly when trying to capture visitors' perspectives. This is partly because of the difficulty of labelling a guide's roles in ways that clearly distinguish one role from another, especially through the eyes of the visitor. Moreover, visitors simply cannot always see (and may not care about) the guide's performance of his or her roles when categorised in this way.

Ballantyne and Hughes (2001) and Weiler (1999) also considered the *perceptions of different stakeholder groups* such as operators, guides, residents and expert assessors *regarding the importance and/or performance of guides' roles.* The results of these and other studies indicate that some destination and protected area managers, operators and guides underestimate the importance of the mediating/mentoring roles of the guide (Roles 3 and 4), and judge the provision of information as more important than roles such as good interpretation (Role 6), the delivery of minimal impact messages (part of Roles 5 and 6) and influencing visitors' attitudes and behaviours (Role 6) (Ballantyne & Hughes, 2001; Weiler, 1999). The mediation role of the guide is dissected later in this chapter, while the guide's interpretive role is the subject of Chapter 3. Overall, the results of research on tour guiding roles have been mixed, are not widely generalisable and are largely inconclusive other than to confirm that the three role spheres and the six roles identified by Weiler and Davis (1993) (see Table 2.2) are seen as important by most operators, guides and visitors. Most of these studies have called for wider investigation of and further refinement in measuring both role importance and guide performance, particularly outside the nature-based ecotourism sectors.

Poudel *et al.* (2013: 47) quite rightly criticise elements of both of these tour guiding role frameworks as 'ambiguous', noting that 'it is unclear what the functions of tour guides are under each role'. One of the purposes of their study was to empirically derive the role spheres of tour guides. Based on roles identified in a range of previous studies, they developed a 12-item scale for measuring the perceived importance of a guide's multiple roles, and administered it to trekkers in the Himalayas. Factor analysis produced three spheres that largely aligned with the three spheres identified by Weiler and Davis (1993) (see Table 2.2), which Poudel *et al.* labelled instrumental, social and educational. Trekkers were significantly more likely to rate instrumental (tour management) as the most important role sphere, followed by the educational (resource management) and then the social (experience management) spheres.

In a recent operationalisation of Weiler and Davis's (1993) three spheres of tour management, experience management and resource management, Pereira and Mykletun (2012) argue for the addition of a fourth sphere, the economy, to acknowledge that the role of the guide extends beyond benefiting natural environments to fostering social and economic outcomes for destinations. Further examination of their expanded version of the framework is called for; however, it is suggested here that the addition of the term 'destination' to the third sphere (resource management) of Weiler and Davis's (1993) framework may achieve the same objective. A refined set of spheres that is intended to apply across all guiding contexts is presented in Table 2.3.

In summary, both Cohen's (1985) and Weiler and Davis's (1993) conceptual frameworks have stood the test of time in drawing attention to both the diversity of guiding roles that are common to all contexts and types of tour guiding, and the specialist roles that ecotour/nature guides are required to perform. With the widespread adoption of sustainable tourism as an ideology, it is timely to acknowledge the importance of the destination/resource management sphere of guiding for all types of guides and in all contexts in which guides work. While specific guiding practices undertaken by a guide, such as a guide's use of heritage/nature interpretation

Table 2.3 The three key spheres of tour guiding and the roles of a contemporary tour guide

Sphere 1: Tour management	Instrumental roles focused on organising and managing the group
Sphere 2: Experience management	Mediatory roles focused on facilitating individuals' engagement and learning
Sphere 3: Destination/resource management	Interpretive and role-modelling roles focused on the sustainability of host environments, communities and destinations

Source: Based on Cohen (1985), Weiler and Davis (1993), Pereira and Mykletun (2012) and Poudel *et al.* (2013).

or social/cultural mediation, will not always sit entirely within just one of these spheres, the three spheres serve to collectively capture the key role dimensions of tour guiding.

Roles Played by Tour Guides in Developing Countries

Aside from research that classifies and clarifies the guide's various roles, there are a number of lines of research enquiry regarding tour guiding roles. For example, case studies have explored both the 'eco' and the more generic *roles of guides in developing countries*, including Botswana (Almagor, 1985), Nepal (Gurung *et al.*, 1996; Poudel *et al.*, 2013), several Latin American countries (Pereira & Mykletun, 2012; Weiler & Ham, 1999), Indonesia (Cole, 1997; Dahles, 2002; Salazar, 2005), Madagascar (Ormsby & Mannle, 2006) and Thailand (Cohen, 1982; Hounnaklang, 2004). Collectively, these studies have produced important findings about the roles of guides that seem particularly relevant to developing countries, notably that guiding in these countries is a means of livelihood that may help to reduce poverty (Shephard & Royston-Airey, 2000). Also, as already noted, Pereira and Mykletun (2012) identify contribution to the economic sustainability of a destination or region as a key sphere of a guide's role. Moreover, when earning a living is a priority, there may be less attention to the destination/resource management sphere. Guides may fear that delivering conservation messages and monitoring visitor behaviour may offend visitors and risk jeopardising the economic sustainability of their tours. On the other hand, there is increasing evidence (Kayes, 2005) that Western visitors, including those to developing countries, appreciate and even expect these kinds of messages and are disappointed when guides do too little of this (see Chapter 4). This suggests that quality assurance initiatives such as those examined in Chapter 7 may be needed to ensure that guides perform these roles well, especially in a developing country context.

It must be acknowledged that there are examples of high-level role performance among guides in some developing countries. In their study of guiding in Madagascar, Ormsby and Mannle (2006) conducted individual and group interviews with park staff, non-government organisation (NGO) staff, guides and local residents. Their findings illustrate the roles that some guides play in explaining the benefits of parks and delivering other conservation messages to local residents (see Chapter 4). The guides are also active in making connections with people in the villages and directing tourist dollars to these areas, which has the added effect of building local support for protected areas and tourism.

Roles Played by Tour Guides in Developed Countries

As Shephard and Royston-Airey (2000: 331) note, 'the roles and ethos of … guides have diverged in developed and developing countries'. Empirical research on the *roles of guides in developed countries* include Australia (Ballantyne & Hughes, 2001; Haig & McIntyre, 2002; Hillman, 2004; Howard *et al.*, 2001; Scherrer *et al.*, 2011; Weiler & Richins, 1990; Yu & Weiler, 2006), Canada (Randall & Rollins, 2009), Greece (Giannoulis *et al.*, 2006; Gilg & Barr, 2006; Giovannetti, 2009; Skanavis & Giannoulis, 2009), Hong Kong (Ap & Wong, 2001; Mak *et al.*, 2011), Japan (Yamada, 2011), New Zealand (Boren *et al.*, 2007), Taiwan (Chang, 2006), the United Kingdom (Hounnaklang, 2004; Shephard & Royston-Airey, 2000) and the United States (Ham & Weiler, 2003; Sharpe, 2005). Several of these studies have focused on interpretation, quality assurance or training – issues that are discussed in greater detail in other chapters. The following paragraphs highlight findings relating to one particular theme that is prominent in the research with respect to the roles played by guides in developed countries: the guide's role in managing visitor behaviour and impacts, especially in protected areas.

In contrast to research on tour guiding in developing countries, a common theme evident in research conducted in developed countries is the central *role of the guide as a tool for visitor management* in protected areas and remote locations. For example, Boren *et al.* (2007) empirically demonstrated that the presence of a guide had a positive impact on the pro-environmental behaviour of wildlife tourists in New Zealand. This study was also able to demonstrate that groups led by a guide have less negative impact, in this case less disruption to the natural behaviour of seals, than non-guided groups. The guide's role in this regard is not only to role model responsible behaviour but also to monitor and sometimes control visitor behaviour, to help protect natural and cultural heritage resources and sites as well as to reduce risk associated with on-site visitor behaviour. Such roles have been acknowledged in the tour guiding literature for at least 20 years (Thomas, 1994) but research documenting their efficacy is relatively recent. Other research relating to the guide's effectiveness in the visitor management role in both developed and developing countries is discussed in Chapter 4. Research on role performance in relation to quality service and the satisfaction of Chinese tourists is discussed in Chapter 5.

Guides manage their groups to help protect resources and sites and reduce risk to visitors. *Credit*: Deborah Che (Kansas Underground Salt Museum tour)

Other Specialist Roles Played by Guides in Both Developing and Developed Countries

A small number of specialist guiding roles have been researched in both developed and developing countries, building up a body of knowledge that may transcend these contexts.

For example, there are studies that have investigated the guide as an *ethical and moral leader, mentor and role model*. Cohen *et al.* (2002) undertook in-depth interviews, focus groups and a questionnaire-based survey of nearly 1000 Israeli and international guides of youth study tours. Like all guides, these madrichs (informal counsellor-guides) are required to play multiple roles, but their responsibilities as informal mentors and role models are highlighted by the researchers as distinguishing the madrichs from other types of guides. However, while acknowledging the unique market served by these guides, a review of the guiding literature suggests that mentoring and role-modelling are, in fact, also characteristic behaviours of nature and adventure guiding (see Chapter 4). Role-modelling of appropriate social and cultural attitudes and behaviours are also often part of mediation, as highlighted by Cole (1997) and Gurung *et al.* (1996) in the next section of this chapter.

The role of the tour guide as both an enabler and a manager of *risk* has been touched on by only a few researchers (Carr, 2001; Johnson, 2001;

Scherrer *et al.*, 2011; Wang *et al.*, 2010) and is worthy of more research attention, particularly given the changing contexts in which tour guides are now working, as highlighted in Chapter 1. Some of these studies focus on the importance of the guide's role in minimising risk, particularly in natural environments. For example, in their study of cruise-based tours in the Kimberley, a remote natural area in North Western Australia, Scherrer *et al.* (2011) found considerable variability among guides in terms of their application of knowledge and skills to managing risk. The researchers observed a number of preventable injuries due to inappropriate or inadequate visitor management practices by the guides. Some of these were attributed to operational decisions beyond the control of the guides (e.g. group size) and others were attributed to poor practices in staff recruitment and training, which tend to prioritise other tasks that guides are required to perform as crew members in addition to tour guiding and visitor management.

On the other hand, Wang *et al.* (2010) view risk through the eyes of a Taiwanese tour leader, using qualitative and quantitative methods to identify quite a considerable range of perceived risks which, based on data reduction analysis, they grouped into tour leaders' self-induced risk (due to negligence), tourist-induced risk (e.g. visa problems) and exogenous risk (e.g. accident). The latter two they report as far more prevalent than risk due to negligence.

Collectively, these studies confirm that the work of a tour guide cannot be captured in a single one-size-fits-all list of roles. Holloway (1981) and Cohen (1982) both noted more than 30 years ago that the role of the guide is a marginal occupational role that is not institutionalised or ritualised, but is subject to the guiding context, the visitors participating in a tour and the guides themselves. Thirty years later, this situation remains unchanged, whereby the roles of a guide are still variable and contestable, and continue to be defined not only by visitors' expectations, but also by other stakeholders such as host communities, tourism operators and protected area managers (Weiler & Ham, 2001). Viewing tour guiding as involving three common role spheres – that is, instrumental (tour management), mediatory (experience management) and interpretive/ sustainability (destination/resource management) – may provide a more useful lens with which to assess guide performance and identify the strengths and weaknesses of tour guiding in particular contexts than a shopping list of roles does. However, the use of common role spheres may also present challenges in that tour guiding tasks do not always fit neatly into these spheres (Macdonald, 2006). It is also evident that research findings about a tour guide's roles often cannot be widely generalised and, as a result, our understanding of the relationships between the roles performed by guides and the consequences or outcomes of these for visitors and other stakeholders is limited.

The Mediating Role of the Guide

This section of the chapter reviews the considerable body of research on the mediating/brokering role of the guide. This provides an appropriate platform from which to examine an individual guide's social, cultural and political roles, the subject matter of the final section of this chapter.

Some 30 years ago, Cohen (1985) suggested that there was evidence of a shift in the role of tour guides from being one primarily of leadership (pathfinding) to a more eclectic set of roles including mediation. Even prior to Cohen, scholars such as Holloway (1981) were drawing on sociological theories to argue the importance of a guide's role as a mediator between hosts and tourists. With the widespread availability of guidebooks and electronic media for information gathering and navigation, tour guiding may be shifting even further from traditional way-finding, and in some contexts, mediation may be the key reason for employing a guide (McGrath, 2007). This section reviews some of the key studies focusing on the guide as mediator. Research focusing on a related topic, the application of intercultural communication theory to tour guiding, is covered in Chapter 3.

Most, if not all, visitor experiences are highly mediated by both personal (human) and non-personal (often self-directed) media (Jennings & Weiler, 2006). These can range from pre-visit communication such as travel documentaries, guidebooks, websites and other marketing tools, through to on-site communication, facilities and infrastructure such as signs, visitor centres, podcasts and special events, through to post-visit communication such as newsletters and social media pages. In addition to tour guides and others who are formally employed to act as mediators, there are many who informally mediate, such as taxi and bus drivers, local residents, restaurant and retail staff, and friends and relatives. Like all mediators, tour guides can mediate in ways that enhance or detract from a visitor's experience as well as facilitate or inhibit positive outcomes for destinations and host communities (Jennings & Weiler, 2006).

In this book, the terms 'mediator' and 'broker' are used interchangeably to include any active attempts by a guide to mediate the experience, mainly in relation to social and cultural outcomes. The actions of the guide may range from decisions about where and when to access a site, community or destination, to verbal communication, to role-modelling, to intervening and controlling what visitors see, hear and do. Cohen (1985) distinguishes between the social mediation and cultural brokerage roles of the guide. According to Cohen, social mediation involves acting as a go-between, linking visitors to the local community, facilitating access to tourist sites and facilities and ensuring that the host environment is non-threatening for the visitor, while cultural brokerage involves connecting visitors with host cultures on an intellectual (cognitive) level. Other authors (Cole, 1997) have acknowledged and examined the mediating role of tour guides without distinguishing between social and cultural mediation. This section of the chapter examines the roles of both social and cultural mediation and their collective contribution to the visitor experience and other outcomes.

A substantial body of literature is emerging on cultural brokering/mediating by tour guides. Tour guides are considered by some to be the quintessential intercultural mediators of the tourism industry (Scherle & Kung, 2010; Scherle & Nonnenmann, 2008). The latter paper, which is mainly about the identity of a tour guide, acknowledges the roles played by guides in mediating not only between tourists and destinations, but especially between host communities. In the former paper, the authors offer a number of quotes from tourists to illustrate the guide's role as a mediator, of which two are included here:

> The tour guide stopped spontaneously in a village, chatting briefly with the people; then we were allowed to walk through the village together and even to visit two houses. Everything happened in a good, relaxed atmosphere and with much laughter, on the part of the Indians and on our part. (Scherle & Kung, 2010: 16)
>
> Towards evening there was music and dance … other population groups besides traders and farmers came. Our guide continually drew our attention to little peculiarities in the guests' relations with each other that we wouldn't have noticed ourselves. Along with this, wonderful local cuisine and drinks, everything served and prepared for the normal inhabitants – just wonderful! (Scherle & Kung, 2010: 16)

Holloway (1981) too identified the role of 'cultural broker', a focus that has been pursued by a number of other researchers (Cohen, 1985; Gurung et al., 1996; McGrath, 2007; Mitchell, 1996; Pearce et al., 1998; Scherle & Nonnenmann, 2008). Macdonald (2006) provides a useful historical review of early research focused on the role of cultural broker, noting that most authors assume a gulf of understanding and a certain lack of empathy between the culture of the visitor and the visited. Generally, the term 'broker' suggests action that bridges this divide, mainly as a means to enhance the experience of the visitor.

In contrast, there has been much less research focusing on the social (as opposed to the cultural) mediatory role of the guide (Jensen, 2010; Macdonald, 2006) and no research has focused on the guide's role in mediating within tour groups. Moreover, Jensen (2010) argues that, to date, subsuming social mediation by guides under intercultural communication and cultural brokering (making sure visitors from other cultures understand and get a good experience) has had the effect of privileging the visitor's perspective at the expense of the host communities. Notwithstanding Jensen's concern, studies on social mediation and cultural mediation/brokering are highly interrelated both conceptually and methodologically and thus the findings are presented collectively here. The focus here is on the guide's role in facilitating cultural/social access, interaction and understanding on the part of the visitor. The perspective of the host community is presented as part of sustainable tourism and tour guiding (Chapter 4).

It is useful to somewhat disaggregate the phenomenon of mediation when considering the findings of previous research. Macdonald (2006), arguing that mediation is more complex than what is captured in Cohen's (1985) definitions, distinguishes between *communicative* mediation (influencing how visitors understand a site or destination) and *interactional* mediation (influencing how, where, when and with whom visitors interact with host people and environments). Weiler and Yu (2007: 15) categorise cultural mediation into three domains or areas of influence: mediating physical *access*, mediating cognitive/affective access or *understanding* via the provision of information (roughly equivalent to Macdonald's communicative mediation) and mediating social access by facilitating the opportunity for *encounters* (roughly equivalent to Macdonald's interactional mediation). Finally, McGrath (2007) highlights *emotional access* (empathy for host people/communities/cultures) as a fourth area that tour guides can influence as part of their mediatory role. This can include empathy for historical people and cultures. Each of these classification schemas is based on in-depth research with tour guides and visitors in different but mainly intercultural or heritage guiding contexts, teasing out the domains of the guide's role as mediator. Drawing on all of these schemas, the following four domains provide a framework within which to examine the research that has been undertaken to date on the mediatory role of tour guides:

- mediating/brokering physical access;
- mediating/brokering encounters (interactions);
- mediating/brokering understanding (intellectual access);
- mediating/brokering empathy (emotional access).

Mediation can, of course, both facilitate and inhibit visitor access and a positive experience across all these domains. Some of the research reviewed in this section examines how guides actively block or mediate negatively between visitors and the host communities and environments they visit.

A number of the studies that have focused on cultural brokering/ mediation are conceptual with limited empirical findings (e.g. Holloway, 1981), or have undertaken fieldwork on a small scale such as in one specific guiding context, using qualitative methods within a constructivist paradigm (e.g. Cole, 1997; Macdonald, 2006). Nonetheless, collectively they provide rich illustrations of the mediatory role of the guide, including the physical access, encounter, understanding and empathy domains of influence.

The distinction flagged in Chapter 1 between mediation and interpretation is worth making here; that is, that 'interpretation' is both a role in itself and a collection of techniques for mediation, particularly for helping visitors to understand and feel empathy towards objects, persons, sites or environments. As will be seen in the following section, the bulk of the research on mediation has been on the use or non-use of communication, particularly interpretation, in order to facilitate understanding. The strategic use of tour guides to influence on-site behaviour and change post-visit attitudes and behaviours might also be considered as mediation; however, these are considered separately in Chapter 4.

Domain 1: Mediating/brokering physical access

Macdonald (2006) and Weiler and Yu (2007) acknowledge the role of guides in brokering physical access to places and spaces. In an early study of adventure guides, Arnould *et al.* (1998) outline how guides provide a 'cocoon of civilization' through which visitors can experience the wilderness:

> We prepare them with equipment, food, shelter, all the basic necessities that we have in the civilized world – we teach them how to utilize those things that we give them, so they don't have a reason to be afraid of the wilderness … (Arnould *et al.*, 1998: 94)

Guides play an important role in staging the experience, including channelling and controlling visitors to be in the right place at the right time. They do this not only by physically manoeuvring tour groups but also by what Arnould *et al.* (1998) refer to as communicative staging; that is, by controlling what and how they present and interpret to visitors. In what MacCannell (1976) calls staged authenticity, guides can: focus on the 'front stage', they can introduce visitors to real and authentic backstages in response to visitors' desire for authenticity or they can construct a pseudo 'backstage' that gives visitors the impression of authenticity. In other words, tour guides can mediate physical access by not only providing opportunities to see and experience elements of the local environment, heritage and culture, but also by determining what is not revealed to visitors (Holloway, 1981).

In a cross-cultural context, Howard *et al.* (2001) observed and interviewed indigenous tour guides in one national park in regional Australia. The indigenous guides played a role in mediating (limiting) physical access to sites through the use of both communication and role-modelling. Guides can also broker physical access by providing visitors with opportunities to use all of their senses to appreciate the host culture and share and experience local stories, music and food (Weiler & Yu, 2007).

Domain 2: Mediating/brokering encounters

Both Macdonald (2006) and Weiler and Yu (2007) also stress that the mediatory role of the guide involves brokering interactions between a group and host communities, for example by providing language interpretation and facilitating two-way communication. Guides can also limit visitors' interactions with local people by drawing a group's attention inwards towards the guide rather than outwardly directing it to the host community (Holloway, 1981; Cohen, 1985). Tour guides can passively or actively mediate encounters between visitors and host communities, among tour group members and between visitors and staff working in hotels and tourist attractions. Guides can act as go-betweens and language brokers in these situations and may also act as a role model for appropriate environmental, social and cultural behaviour (Gurung *et al.*, 1996; Weiler & Yu, 2007). For example, Cole (1997) contrasted commercial tour leaders with anthropologists acting as cultural brokers on one Indonesian island. She concluded from her ethnographic case study observations of both types of guides that only those with anthropological 'training' had adequate cultural understanding to both enhance the cross-cultural experience of visitors and minimise negative sociocultural impacts through communication and role-modelling of appropriate behaviour towards host communities. The anthropologist-trained tour leaders thus played a role of mediating encounters with local residents. Tour leaders who lacked cultural understanding were unwilling and/or unable to do so.

Domain 3: Mediating/brokering understanding

The most researched domain of mediation is the guide as a broker of understanding (Macdonald, 2006; Weiler & Yu, 2007) or intellectual access (McGrath, 2007). Tour guides can mediate understanding by using information and enrichment as a tool for conveying the significance of a place or site (Ap & Wong, 2001; Bras, 2000; Hughes, 1991). Often they use their multilingual skills, which visitors and hosts often lack, in order to bridge communication gaps. They also use a variety of interpretive communication strategies such as analogies, personal references and anecdotes and non-verbal communication such as artefacts to create meaning and facilitate memorable experiences. Macdonald (2006) draws on media theory to examine the mediatory roles played by walking tour guides of the former Nazi party rally grounds in Nuremberg. Based on interviews with guides, analysis of guiding scripts and participant observation as both a guide and a tour member, her case study elucidates the 'negotiated and sometimes even contested' (Macdonald, 2006: 123) nature of guides' mediation. Many of the techniques used by the guides to foster understanding and appreciation of the site are well-known interpretive techniques such as asking questions, making comparisons to objects familiar to the group and using props (e.g. photos from the past).

Similarly, Howard *et al.* (2001) concluded in their case study of indigenous guides that the guides played a role in mediating access to information (understanding) not only through their use of interpretive techniques and role-modelling, but also by challenging stereotypes and visitors' misconceptions about Aboriginal culture. The guides' cultural brokering role revolved largely around communicating and interpreting local cultural values, both those of the site and those of Aboriginal society more generally.

Indigenous guides play a brokering role by communicating and interpreting local cultural values of the site and of Aboriginal society more generally. *Credit*: Venture North Safaris – Arnhem Land NT

There are also studies that demonstrate the role of guides as negative mediators, in the sense of inhibiting rather than fostering understanding. In the small but heritage-rich city of Yogyakarta, Indonesia, Dahles (2002) found little evidence of guides using cultural mediation to enhance the visitor experience. Dahles attributes this to the political regime at the time, which led to tour guides being trained and directed to present a specific political commentary to tourists that promoted the government's views. The guides' performances were thus both staged and routinised, limiting and thus negatively mediating understanding. A similar conclusion was drawn by Mitchell's (1996) ethnographic case study of Malta, although presented in a more favourable light. In an in-depth case study that analysed the training and practice of 10 tour guides using multiple data sources and methods, Mitchell demonstrates the critical role played by these guides in creating and perpetuating positive images of Malta with the express purpose of supporting the country's application for accession to the European Union (EU). The role played by these guides is specifically designed to promote images of a modern and highly European Malta and Maltese culture, the latter in part by presenting archaeological and heritage sites and linking these to present-day Europe. Thus, a visitor's understanding of Malta's heritage and culture is highly mediated by the guides.

A final example of the negative mediation of understanding is McGrath's (2007) critique of tour guiding of archaeological sites in Peru. She notes that the predominant type of guiding is the transfer of knowledge rather than cultural mediation or understanding. McGrath also bemoans the separation of cultural and nature guiding and, like Kohl (2007), suggests that the role of the guide in developing countries needs to mature to being a facilitator and broker of multiple meanings rather than the more traditional 'show-and-tell' role currently played by guides in many of these countries.

Domain 4: Mediating/brokering empathy

The domain of mediation that is least developed conceptually is that of empathy or emotion. McGrath (2007: 376) suggests that the guide's role as mediator needs to help visitors 'get under the skin' of visited areas rather than just providing physical and intellectual access. Modlin et al. (2011), in their case study of a southern US plantation house museum, provide an evocative illustration of how the emotional connection facilitated by museum guides can lead to empathy for some (in the case of their study, White American landowners) historical figures and sectors of society. Modlin et al. (2011) observed how guides use interpretive techniques such as storytelling to create not only cognitive but also affective connections with the former plantation owners. However, through selectivity in their narrative content and in how and where they move visitors through the site, they actually fail to create empathy for the enslaved community. Similar to mediating understanding, the mediation of empathy is heavily reliant on a guide's skills in interpretation; thus, Chapter 3 covers more about the mediation of understanding and empathy.

The final section of this chapter explores how individual guides differ in the ways and the extent to which they actively filter and bias what, when, where and how visitors experience a destination and thus how they mediate the experience, whether intentionally or not.

The Sociopolitical and Cultural Roles of a Guide

According to Modlin et al. (2011), much of the tour guiding literature tends to take a functional view of tour guides, which they see as problematic, particularly with respect to the guide's role as mediator or broker of the visitor experience. As already noted, Cohen's (1985) model has preoccupied researchers' investigations of tour guide roles and has privileged the perspectives of the visitor and the tour group at the expense of the wider context. However, Christie and Mason (2003) argue that guides are not apolitical, unbiased and a-cultural and suggest that there should be more recognition that guiding is not value free. They promote the concept of transformative guiding that encourages guides to critically self-reflect on their assumptions about the world (see Chapter 6). Other authors such as Dahles (2002) argue that the traditional and benign conceptualisation of tour guides as cultural mediators fails to capture guides' capacity to function as political actors. Still others contend that, while Dahles' (2002) work is important in recognising the larger politics of tour guiding and the government control of guides, it does not fully acknowledge the guides' agency in shaping the meanings that visitors gain from sites and destinations (Macdonald, 2006).

An individual guide can play a key part in either affirming or potentially challenging traditional or current perspectives on controversial issues like climate change, slavery or apartheid. For example, Hanna et al. (2004) found that docents (volunteer guides) improvise and add to standard narratives drawing on their own experiences and ideas, thus functioning as 'creative storytellers' who may challenge or question popular discourses about people, places and perspectives. Salazar (2006: 848) also observed that guides' narratives 'are not closed or rigid systems, but rather open systems that are always put at risk by what happens in actual encounters [with visitors]'. As mentioned earlier, in a case study of volunteer guides working in one plantation house in Louisiana, Modlin et al. (2011) found that the guide's narratives privileged the planter-class family and either ignored or misrepresented the slaves, leading to further marginalisation which the authors term 'affective inequality'. Guides exercise their agency by using selected facts and stories, performance and emotion, all of which are influenced by their own background, life experiences and political interests, in order to configure, arrange and present their narrative (for more about narrative and storytelling see Chapter 3).

Guiding has also been explored through the theoretical lens of glocalisation. Salazar (2005) studied a select group of guides based in Yogyakarta, Indonesia, in the post-Suharto period, where there has been a relaxation of government control of guides and a loosening of regulations in the guiding industry. Using an in-depth ethnographic study, he explored how, through their daily practices, the guides present and actively deconstruct local culture for a diverse global market and how this process is transforming culture. Salazar found that the guides' (re)construction of an authentic, exotic and mythologised image of Yogyakarta is actually being changed and fragmented by globalisation. The guides use a variety of glocalisation strategies during their village tours, for example they tend to downplay their English skills and international experiences and avoid using their mobile phones because they think that is what visitors want to see and experience.

Overend (2012) and others (Hallin & Dobers, 2012; Salazar, 2006) have noted the role of individual guides in selecting and presenting specific places as part of a tour on behalf of the tourist. In this sense, tourists who choose to go on a tour are accepting the guide's decisions and selections and trust that the guide will deliver accurate information through information and stories (see also Chapter 3). Hallin and Dobers (2012) illustrate this in their investigation into the relation between place and its presentation. Their comparative discourse analysis of two different guided tours of Stockholm supports Overend's (2012) proposition that the guide and the guided tour have the power to select what is or is not seen or experienced by the tourist and thus, whether intended or not, that the guide's role is inherently political.

Implications for Research

The literature on tour guiding roles, role spheres, domains of mediation and the expectations and performance of roles by various stakeholders has attracted considerable research attention and has had some influence on advancing the profile and broadening the scope of what tour guides do. However, Macdonald (2006: 122) is critical of 'taxonomically dissecting tour guide work into discrete elements', suggesting instead an approach that emphasises the interrelationships between the elements. Aloudat (2010) is similar in noting the roles of the guide as being broad-ranging, dynamic and overlapping. Their point is well taken – the roles of a guide are seldom distinct and research investigating the interplay between roles in different contexts is non-existent. Aloudat goes further in suggesting the need for research to examine the role of the guide beyond the guided tour experience, for example as promotional agents for the destination.

While the roles of the tour guide have been explored quite extensively in the literature, particularly from a sociological perspective, there is scope for drawing more explicitly on theory from other disciplines such as organisational behaviour and consumer behaviour/marketing to progress this focus. For example, the extent to which guides are recruited, trained and empowered to deal with variations in role expectations and performance would be a fruitful avenue for further research, as would an examination of the impact of changing visitor expectations, industry trends (such as increased travel from new and emerging markets) and increased threats (such as litigation and terrorism) on tour guides' roles.

In addition, research has been largely confined to nature, heritage and adventure tourism contexts with an emerging focus on city-based guides, particularly their roles as mediators and particularly in Europe. In the meantime, tour guiding has continued to expand due to the number and breadth of guided tours and guiding contexts (e.g. theme parks, educational/ industrial sites, shopping tours, events) now available. How tour guiding roles are changing, and how they may be different in new and/or niche areas of the industry such as pro-poor tourism, philanthropic tourism, volunteer tourism and dark tourism, are topics that have not attracted the attention of researchers to date. Even large, well-established sectors of the tourism industry such as business tourism and events seem to have paid little attention to the role of the guide.

Some excellent research is emerging around the general topic of mediation by tour guides, yet there is still a fairly low level of understanding as to what visitors expect and why they do or do not use tour guides as mediators. This body of research is also dominated by a focus on mediation of understanding, with more research needed on mediation of physical access, encounters (interactions) and affect (empathy). With so many and varied interactions in a visitor experience, it is difficult to identify and describe the nature of mediation, let alone quantify and evaluate its contribution to the experience and to sense-making.

This review provides some evidence of the potential and actual mediation undertaken by tour guides; however, the outcomes of mediation for both the visitor and the visited are seldom fully captured in research. The areas that can be influenced by mediation and the mechanisms of mediation, including those used by, or of potential use to, tour guides, are complex and poorly understood. What skills and techniques are most effective for each type of mediation and with which markets? Studies on cultural mediation to date have also provided little insight into what visitors want or expect by way of cultural mediation. How do visitors view the relative importance of physical, interactional, intellectual and emotional mediation? These questions have yet to be answered in research on the social/cultural mediation of tour guiding.

Implications for Tour Guiding Practice

Documentation and analysis of the roles played by guides have served numerous purposes (Black, 2002; Black & Weiler, 2005). They have underpinned the development of the competencies required by a guide to undertake these roles, such as group management, communication, presentation and leadership skills, each of which is associated with underpinning knowledge. These in turn have formed the building blocks of training programmes (see Chapter 6). Guiding roles have also informed other quality assurance schemes such as codes of ethics, guide certification programmes and the tools developed within these programmes for assessing and enhancing performance (see Chapter 7). Tour guiding roles also provide a basis for critically examining existing training and other quality assurance mechanisms. For example, Huang and Weiler (2010) found that the focus of China's quality assurance system was on a limited number of tour guiding roles and tended to overlook those most critical to harnessing the guide as a vehicle for sustainable tourism. They note that, in China, training and reward schemes are based not on empirical research but on the knowledge and biases of individuals in positions of authority. This points to the need for Chinese (and probably other) government recognition and reward schemes to be updated in order to ensure that the guide's performance as a role model, advocate, mentor, interpreter, cultural broker and environmental monitor meets the expectations of visitors and other stakeholders.

Moreover, the tourism industry could be far more proactive in how it markets and manages specific tour guiding roles, such as what guides do as formal and informal mediators, which may in turn contribute to better quality control for all concerned. Very few tourism operators, let alone other stakeholders in the industry, are transparent and proactive in, for example, communicating what roles they expect their guides to play and how they recruit, train and reward their guides in their performance of these roles. Finally, an individual guide has the capacity to broker experiences that may have considerable impact on both the individual visitor and the group. Guides themselves may need to become more cognizant and self-reflective about the impact of their role performance on visitors and other stakeholders, as well as the impact of their communication and actions in relation to other mediators.

Chapter Summary

This chapter has examined the multiple and complex roles and role spheres of tour guiding, including the tour guide as a social and cultural mediator. The following is a summary of some of the key findings in this body of literature.

The key roles played by guides fall into one of three spheres: instrumental (tour management), mediatory (experience management) and interpretive/sustainability (destination/resource management). Generally, there has been a shift from guides playing largely an instrumental role to playing multiple roles.

While visitors and other stakeholders agree that an array of specific guiding roles is important, they differ in their views of the relative importance and performance of individual roles. Research has uncovered differences in perceptions depending on the background of the visitors and the guiding context (e.g. location and type of tour).

Some studies have identified differences in the relative importance of roles between developed and developing countries. For example, guiding as a means of earning a living and improving one's standard of living may eclipse the performance of other roles. In developed countries, particularly in protected areas, the roles of the guide in role-modelling, managing and monitoring visitors' on-site behaviour may take precedence.

In virtually all guiding contexts, guides can mediate or broker visitors' physical access, encounters, understanding and empathy, but most research has focused on the guide's use or lack of use of interpretation to mediate understanding. The guide's role as a mediator in each of these domains can be positive as well as negative; that is, the guide can facilitate but can also constrain access, encounters, understanding and empathy.

Beyond the functional view of the roles of a tour guide that has dominated research, in practice each guide and each tour can be quite different, and there can be interplay, overlap and even conflict between the various roles. As such, individual guides can have considerable social, cultural and political agency in how they play out their roles. Thus, despite the structure and formal labelling of guiding roles, as presented in this chapter, it is important to acknowledge that numerous scholars, beginning with Cohen's (1982) first paper on jungle guides and continuing to the present, have cautioned against taking an overly prescriptive approach to specifying the roles of a tour guide. Moreover, Cohen's description of guiding as a marginal occupational role some 30 years ago is largely still true today. The fact that guides continue to undertake their work in a non-institutionalised, unregulated work environment gives them considerable scope and flexibility in practice. While for many guides this is what makes the work appealing, it does make it difficult to determine what is a satisfactory or exemplary role performance (see Chapter 5) and to embed quality assurance mechanisms that regulate and reward good tour guiding practice (see Chapter 7).

In the Black and Weiler (2005) study described earlier, the one role that was seen as important in all the studies reviewed was that of interpreter. Providing engaging experiences while delivering important messages through nature and heritage interpretation is the role that has received the most research attention in the literature, particularly in the ecotour guiding literature (Black & Weiler, 2013). The communicative role of the guide, including interpretation and intercultural communication, is the focus of Chapter 3.

Key references

(1) Poudel, S., Nyaupane, G.P. and Timothy, D.J. (2013) Assessing visitors preference of various roles of tour guides in the Himalaya. *Tourism Analysis* 18, 45–49.
(2) Howard, J., Thwaites, R. and Smith, B. (2001) Investigating the roles of the Indigenous tour guide. *Journal of Tourism Studies* 12 (2), 32–39.
(3) Boren, L., Gemmell, N. and Barton, K. (2007) The role and presence of a guide. Preliminary findings from swim with seal programmes and land-based seal viewing in New Zealand. In M. Lück, M.L. Miller, A. Graupl, M.B. Orams and J. Aujong (eds) *Proceedings of the 5th International Coastal and Marine Tourism Congress. Balancing*

Marine Tourism, Development and Sustainability (pp. 366–380). Auckland: Auckland University of Technology.

(4) Macdonald, S. (2006) Mediating heritage: Tour guides at the former Nazi party rally grounds, Nuremberg. *Tourist Studies* 6 (2), 119–138.

(5) Modlin, E.A., Alderman, D.H. and Gentry, G.W. (2011) Tour guides as creators of empathy: The role of affective inequality in marginalizing the enslaved at plantation house museums. *Tourist Studies* 11, 3–19.

(6) Scherle, N. and Nonnenmann, A. (2008) Swimming in cultural flows: Conceptualising tour guides as intercultural mediators and cosmopolitans. *Journal of Tourism and Cultural Change* 6 (2), 120–137.

3 Tour Guides as Interpreters, Storytellers and Intercultural Communicators

Nearly everyone who researches and writes about tour guides and tour guiding highlights the importance of the communicative role of the guide. The purpose of this chapter is to present theory and research findings relating to the use of communication in the context of tour guiding, particularly the theory and practice of interpretation and intercultural communication as they apply to tour guiding. This chapter begins by defining communication as it is used in the tour guiding literature. Included is a review of the few studies that have examined the communication competence of tour guides in a broad sense. This is followed by defining and reviewing the very extensive body of literature focused on interpretation and interpretive guiding, widely accepted as the primary means by which a tour guide communicates with visitors not only to enhance the experience, but also to achieve other outcomes of benefit to visitors and other stakeholders. A brief overview of the newly emerging research area of the guide as performer, storyteller and narrator is then provided. This chapter finishes with a review of research on intercultural communication competence in the context of tour guiding. A more in-depth examination of interpretation, persuasive communication and role-modelling as tools for managing visitors and fostering sustainability is provided in Chapter 4.

Defining and Measuring the Communication Competence of Tour Guides

Communication and the effective use of a suite of communication tools seem to be key to tour guiding, yet one has to search hard to find a tour guiding text or research paper that actually defines communication or communication competence in the context of tour guiding. According to Steiner and Reisinger (2004: 122), 'early communication scholars defined communication mechanistically as a process of conveying information from one person to another ... illustrated as a one-way, two-way or circular process involving a sender, receiver, medium and message'. Oschell (2009), drawing on Spitzberg and colleagues' (e.g. Spitzberg & Cupach, 1984) extensive work on communication competence, notes that communication competence is the perceived effectiveness and appropriateness of a person's communication in a given context, in order to achieve interpersonal objectives such as disseminating information or mediating conflict: 'In the context of commercially guided trips, guides must communicate in a way that is perceived as competent by their clients in order to successfully inform, educate, and gain compliance' (Oschell, 2009: 15). Other conceptualisations of communication define it as being a 'symbolic, interpretive, transactional, contextual process in which people create shared meanings' (Lustig & Koester, 1993: 25), a definition that is reflected by Arnould et al. (1998), discussed below, and in some of the more recent qualitative work being undertaken by researchers such as Bryon (2012) and Jonasson and Scherle (2012) examined later in this chapter.

Leclerc and Martin (2004), like many researchers studying human behaviour, advocate a behavioural-cognitive approach to the study of tour guide communication. Their approach is underpinned by an assumption that individuals (i.e. visitors) have expectations about what comprises communication competency, and these expectations are used by these individuals to judge the communication of others (i.e. guides) as being effective or competent.

A few researchers have tried to dissect, operationalise and measure the elements of effective or competent communication in the context of tour guiding. Ryan and Dewar (1995) developed a modified version of a communication competency scale based on Spitzberg and Hurt's (1987) work, consisting of 43 seven-point (very poor to excellent) rating items, but each of the 43 items in their scale was analysed independently, with no attempt to factor analyse or otherwise identify groupings that capture specific dimensions of a person's communication. Supervisory staff used the scale to conduct 28 evaluations of volunteer guides at a national historic park, which proved to be a useful diagnostic tool for the guides but not necessarily a valid and reliable measure of communication competence. Since then, Leclerc and Martin (2004) have reported that research conducted in a Western (mainly American) context has identified four distinct dimensions of communication competence: non-verbal behaviours (e.g. eye contact), topic/content behaviours (e.g. sharing information about oneself), conversational management behaviours (e.g. asking questions) and wider-context macro behaviours (e.g. being polite). Their study used a somewhat simplified set of these dimensions – non-verbal communication, verbal communication and traits – employing four sub-scales to measure non-verbal communication, three sub-scales to measure verbal communication and one scale to measure traits. In their study of visitor perceptions of the relative importance of communication competence in tour guides, each of these dimensions was measured using multiple individual measurement items, in the form of a communication competence scale that consisted of 31 seven-point scale items. Four hundred and forty-one American, French and German tourists from 11 tour groups were asked to rate their perceptions of the importance of these dimensions of communication competence to tour guiding (Leclerc & Martin, 2004). With the exception of the traits scale, the American respondents rated a guide's competence of greater importance than the European respondents did.

Leclerc and Martin (2004) did not report the importance of each of the dimensions of communication to tour guiding in relation to the other dimensions, and few other studies have investigated the communication competence of tour guides. However, a similar study was undertaken by Oschell (2009) using another of Spitzberg's theoretical frameworks (Spitzberg & Cupach, 1984), the relational model of communication competence. This model posits communication competence as consisting of knowledge (knowing what behaviour is best suited for a given situation), skill (having the ability to apply that behaviour in the given context) and motivation (having the desire to communicate in a competent manner). According to Oschell (2009: 16), the communicative efforts of guides are more likely to be perceived by clients as appropriate and effective and to achieve desired outcomes if the guide is seen to have the relevant knowledge, skill and motivation. Oschell (2009) developed a scale to measure white-water rafters' perceptions of the levels of motivation, knowledge and communicative skills exhibited by their guide as well as his or her overall communication competence. The results from her survey of 343 respondents were used to validate a scale for use in a nature-based guiding context. Perhaps not surprisingly, guides who were perceived as motivated, knowledgeable and skilled in communicating were more highly rated in terms of communication competence. Of particular relevance here is that the guides' skills were seen as the strongest predictor of perceived communication competence. Notwithstanding the behaviour-cognitive focus of the methods and instrument of Oschell's (2009) study, the scale with some minor modifications is applicable to other guiding contexts.

Finally, Dioko et al. (2013) provide an interesting sociolinguistic analysis of the communication techniques used by Chinese tour guides with their English-speaking tourists. In-depth interviews conducted with 24 experienced guides, eight from each of three well-established tourism destinations in China (Guilin, Beijing and Shanghai), revealed that guides often use sophisticated verbal communication techniques, some of which are considered interpretive techniques (discussed in the next section of this chapter). For example, guides are fond of using proverbs (often based on Confucian philosophy) to introduce a delicate subject:

In Guilin dialect, we would say: as the forest expands, all kinds of birds swarm in. You may meet any type of people. Some people are friendly in nature but their personality is unbearable. So I will not say people from this place are friendlier, or people from the other are less friendly. I don't see it. I think this is a common human feature in everyone. (Dioko *et al.*, 2013: 35)

Chinese guides also used metaphors, analogies, similes and humour to support and maintain China's traditional social, political and economic order and sometimes to criticise it (see also the discussion in Chapter 2 about the sociopolitical and cultural roles of the guide):

Beijing is like Washington in the US and Shanghai is like New York in the US, so local residents will surely be proud of their own cities. (Dioko *et al.*, 2013: 38)

You may think Yangshuo is beautiful because you haven't been there before, but I think it's much worse than 10 years ago, just like a countryside girl who goes to a big city, neither traditional nor modern. (Dioko *et al.*, 2013: 40)

With the exception of research on interpretation (which has largely focused on self-guided media, although there is a growing body of research that includes face-to-face interpretation/tour guiding), these are the only published studies on guides' communication competencies. The next sections of this chapter focus on communication as a tool to enhance the visitor experience via interpretation. This includes a developing body of research on interpretation for Chinese-speaking tourists/visitors and the use of particular interpretive communication techniques (e.g. drama, storytelling and narration). In the final section of the chapter, research on intercultural communication is examined.

Defining Interpretation and Interpretive Guiding

Of all the roles performed by tour guides, it is interpretation that has attracted the most attention of tour guiding authors and researchers. This section of the chapter revisits and expands on the definition of interpretation introduced in Chapter 2. This is followed by a brief chronological/historical perspective on the place of interpretation in tour guiding as reported in the academic literature. This leads to articulation of the principles of interpretation and reporting of research investigating their application to tour guiding, a matter that is often promulgated but less often critically examined by tour guiding researchers.

Cohen (1985), Pond (1993) and other authors state unequivocally that interpretation is the primary means by which a guide communicates with visitors. There are probably a number of interrelated reasons for this. Interpretation is an area that potentially offers much to tour guiding, including enhancing both the visitor experience and visitor satisfaction (see Chapter 5), contributing positively to visitor attitudes and behaviour, serving as a management tool for protected area managers, achieving the goals that local residents and communities have for tourism and contributing to tourism and destination sustainability (see Chapter 4). It can also make the practice of tour guiding more enjoyable and satisfying for the guide. By comparison, other roles identified in Chapter 2, such as tour logistics and group management, and even other communicative roles such as giving directional information and customer service, while important, offer less scope for value-adding by tour guides. Many of these roles can be challenging, but most are easier to conceptualise than the role of interpretation. Some of these roles can also be mastered by one-off training that delivers skills and knowledge such as map-reading, first aid, vehicle/ boat operation and the like.

Interpretive guiding aims to reveal meanings and relationships of objects, places and events. *Credit*: Dan Nicholls (New South Wales National Parks and Wildlife Service Indigenous Ranger program, Australia)

In both the tour guiding and the interpretation literature there has been, and continues to be, much discussion centred on defining what the words interpretation and interpretive guiding actually mean (Pereira, 2005; Weiler & Ham, 2001). Those authors who do embrace the term cite Tilden (1977) and Ham (1992) to distinguish interpretation from education, noting that interpretation aims to reveal meanings and relationships rather than simply communicate factual information. More recent definitions of interpretation include 'a mission-based communication process that forges emotional and intellectual connections between the interests of the audience and the meanings inherent in the resource' (Interpretation Canada website). However, definitions that imply that meaning or significance is 'inherent' in an object, event or place and that a tour guide's job is simply to communicate that meaning have been criticised (Reisinger & Steiner, 2006). The US National Association for Interpretation's website states that 'interpretation enriches our lives through engaging emotions, enhancing experiences and deepening understanding of people, places, events and objects from past and present'. Finally, recent academic literature defines interpretation as 'engagement with visitors in ways that provoke them to think about and connect with natural and cultural heritage, including places, sites, people, artefacts, and natural and historical events' (Weiler & Kim, 2011: 115) and that 'fosters a sense of care and stewardship among visitors' (Skanavis & Giannoulis, 2010: 50). This more inclusive definition (introduced in Chapter 1), which allows for multiple meanings and acknowledges that guides aim to promote thinking rather than imposing a particular point of view or set of facts on the visitor, frames this chapter's discussion of interpretation.

All of these definitions describe interpretation as an approach to communication that goes beyond the provision of information or commentary and also goes beyond entertaining or amusing visitors. Most agree that good interpretation is *outcome focused*: its purpose is to enhance visitors' enjoyment and engagement with, their awareness and understanding of, their sense of connection with and their appreciation for people, places, cultures and environments, and sometimes to foster sustainable or pro-conservation attitudes and behaviours (Skibins et al., 2012). The word interpretation is used to describe an *approach to communication* that is practiced by national parks, museums, zoos, botanic gardens, galleries, indigenous and historic sites, science centres, state forests, urban parks and reserves. Interpretation's roots are in national parks and museum/heritage settings (Pond, 1993), and thus it has been embraced most easily by those working for public sector and not-for-profit organisations, but it is used increasingly by those guiding commercial nature-based and heritage tours, as well as by tourism attractions, resorts and other types of tourism businesses, governments, destinations, events and conservation organisations – indeed any organisation or entity that wants to use communication delivered by tour guides to achieve specific outcomes. 'Interpretive guiding' is used to refer to tour guiding that (i) seeks to achieve one or more outcomes and (ii) does this by applying interpretation principles to tour guiding (Pastorelli, 2003).

Good interpretive guiding enhances visitors' enjoyment and engagement to promote appreciation and a sense of connection. *Credit*: Mark Lees (New South Wales, National Parks and Wildlife Service, Australia, ochre painting)

A Chronological Perspective on Interpretive Tour Guiding

Some of the earliest mentions of interpretation in the context of tour guiding were by anthropologists and sociologists such as Almagor (1985), Bowman (1992) and of course Cohen (1985), who used the word to refer to the mediatory role of the guide. Almagor was highly critical of the lack of interpretation by the guide in his case study, which he attributed to the guide's lack of detailed understanding of the site and the environment being visited, particularly in comparison to the tour clients, and the cultural and socio-demographic distance between the guide and the tour clients. Bowman was also critical of the interpretation he observed as delivered by primarily Israeli guides to Christian tourists on 'Holy Land tours', describing it as an image-making tool that at times misrepresented the destination and the sites visited (see Chapter 1 for more on the sociopolitical role of the guide).

At the same time, however, a different and more positive perspective on interpretation was being introduced to the tourism and tour guiding literature, initially by Pond (1993) in her seminal text *The Professional Guide*. Pond makes the astute observation that the public sector environment in which interpretation developed, shaped its focus and perhaps constrained its early transition to the profit-making orientation of commercial tourism. For example, interpretation in the context of national parks and other public sector agencies had long subscribed to meeting three objectives: (1) to assist visitors in developing a keener awareness, appreciation and understanding of the area they are visiting; (2) to accomplish management goals by encouraging thoughtful use and reasonable behaviour that minimise impact; and (3) to promote public understanding of agency goals and objectives (Pond, 1993). It is not surprising that commercial tourism operators might find it difficult to identify with or embrace the latter two objectives in particular. Instead, tentative steps towards incorporating interpretive knowledge, skills and techniques into guided tours were taken by the tourism industry, primarily with the intention of value-adding to the tour product, thereby enhancing visitor satisfaction, customer loyalty and positive word-of-mouth advertising (Ham & Weiler, 2006; Van Dijk & Weiler, 2009).

At the time that Pond's (1993) book was published, interpretation was still invisible and the term rarely appeared in the tourism literature, with some researchers undertaking and publishing research on tour guiding practice without ever referring to interpretation (e.g. Arnould & Price, 1993). However, interpretation gained a more solid footing in the early 1990s with the growth of environmentally responsible nature-based tourism (Weiler & Davis, 1993), the forerunner of ecotourism and sustainable tourism. In that decade, interpretation continued to be poorly understood and was often undervalued by the tourism industry, perhaps because of the poor fit between its public sector origins and objectives and the needs of the private sector as already described. For example, Gardner and McArthur (1994) reported that a Tasmanian-based study found that visitors placed a higher value on interpretation than did operators. On the other hand, guides surveyed in Gurung et al.'s (1996) study of the Nepalese tour industry identified interpretation as a highly important role, second only to visitor safety, and also as a role that visitors perceived as being underperformed by guides.

As noted in Chapter 2, the relative importance of interpretation in the many roles that guides are expected to undertake has been sustained in some 20 years of research and scholarship. In a review of 12 studies on expectations, perceptions and performance of tour guiding roles over a 22-year period, Black and Weiler (2005) found interpretation to be the only role that was identified in all 12 studies. This does not necessarily indicate that interpretation is the most important role, but it does suggest that it is an ever-present one.

The notion of interpretive guiding achieving outcomes of importance to visitors and tourism operators began to emerge in the literature in the mid 1990s. In the first instance, the use of interpretation by guides was seen to be a key mechanism to enhancing the visitor experience, visitor satisfaction, positive word-of-mouth advertising and meaning-making and, as such, began to be promulgated as an indispensable part of guided tour products (Ballantyne & Uzzell, 1999; Mossberg, 1995; Weiler & Ham, 2001). As noted in Chapter 2, tourists/visitors, when asked, consistently rated the guides' interpretive and communication skills as equally or more important than the guides' knowledge and their other skills and attributes, particularly in facilitating a quality, nature-based experience (Haig & McIntyre, 2002; Ham & Weiler, 2003; Weiler, 1999).

Despite the acknowledged importance of interpretive guiding in delivering satisfying experiences (Chang, 2006; Geva & Goldman, 1991; Ham & Weiler, 2007; Mossberg, 1995), very few studies have set out to examine the relationship between interpretive guiding and visitor satisfaction. Wang et al. (2000: 183) applied the critical incident technique (CIT) in examining group package tours and found that 'interpretation' on coach tours and 'interpreting of the scenic-spot' were among the critical features leading to satisfaction with package tour services.

Chang (2006) studied package tours in Taiwan and noted that the service attitude of the tour leader was sufficient to satisfy tour participants but interpretation skills could improve visitors' levels of satisfaction. In Australia, Weiler and Yu (2007) investigated the performance of Chinese-speaking local tour guides and found that the mediation of understanding via interpretive guiding contributed to generating memorable experiences. These studies suggest that interpretation may be more important than other guiding roles in fostering visitor satisfaction and quality experiences and impacting other desirable outcomes. Research examining interpretive guiding's impact on outcomes relating to sustainability is the focus of Chapter 4, and the influence of tour guides' performance on visitor satisfaction is the focus of Chapter 5.

Some scrutiny of interpretation as a role used by guides has occurred in developing countries, mainly in Latin America (Brazil, Costa Rica, the Galapagos Islands, Panama and Peru) but also in Madagascar and Nepal. This has been mainly in the context of ecotour guiding (Black & Weiler, 2013). Case studies that explicitly examine the contribution of interpretation to ecotourism have also been undertaken in Antarctica, Australia, England, Greece, New Zealand and Japan, and the role of interpretation is alluded to in many other studies. Based on surveys with tourists/visitors, guides and sometimes other stakeholders, these studies almost always conclude that interpretation is a key element of effective ecotour guiding. The underutilisation or poor quality of interpretation delivered by ecotour guides is often noted (Gurung et al., 1996; Pereira & Mykletun, 2012; Randall & Rollins, 2009; Weiler, 1999; Weiler & Ham, 2001), with several studies highlighting the inadequacy or absence of interpretation training in particular contexts (Black et al., 2001; Christie & Mason, 2003; McGrath, 2007; Periera, 2005; Skanavis & Giannoulis, 2010; Thomas, 1994; Weiler, 1999).

Thus, the topic of interpretation has been of sustained interest to tour guiding scholars and researchers. It is only in the last few years, however, that some have turned their attention to discussing and providing theoretical arguments for the links between the practice of interpretation and its desired outcomes (Ham, 2009; Hu & Wall, 2012; Weiler & Kim, 2011). Ham (2009: 50) observes that the most cited phrase in the interpretation literature, a nine-word sentence written by an anonymous US National Park Service ranger in an obscure administrative manual a half century ago, has some theoretical basis: 'Through interpretation, understanding; through understanding, appreciation; through appreciation, protection'.

In other words, by provoking visitors to think and feel, a guide can help visitors to understand. By helping visitors to understand, a guide has a better chance of impacting a visitor's appreciation and valuing of an object (e.g. wildlife, wildlife habitat, threats to wildlife). Finally, a guide can harness this appreciation to promote action that can help protect cultural and natural phenomena, resources, environments and destinations.

By provoking visitors to think and feel, a guide can impact a visitor's appreciation and valuing of a site. *Credit*: Betty Weiler (National Park Guide, Mt St Helens, USA)

Uzzell (1998), however, notes that while a linear progression from understanding to attitude to behaviour change has intuitive appeal and some theoretical support, the presence of extraneous factors such as the individual's social/cultural context cannot be ignored. There is also little empirical evidence of this occurring in a tour guiding context, particularly with respect to how communication/interpretation can be leveraged to deliver the desired outcomes of interpretive guiding. Nonetheless, it is useful to outline the principles of interpretation that are seen to be relevant to tour guiding (addressed in the next section of this chapter) and to review research that has examined the application of interpretation principles in a tour guiding context.

The Application of Principles of Interpretation to Tour Guiding

As noted, interpretive guiding is distinguishable by being outcome focused and by its application of interpretation principles. This section of the chapter provides a brief synopsis of the latter, based on the interpretation literature. It then turns to the tour guiding literature to examine where the interpretive practices of tour guides have been applied. Particular attention is paid to studies where the practices of tour guides have been critically examined through the lens of selected principles of interpretation. It is only very recently that the applicability of interpretation principles to all tour guiding contexts has been questioned, particularly in a non-Western context. The last part of this section presents findings relating to the Chinese market, where the need for adaptation of tour content and guiding techniques has become evident.

Any discussion of the principles of interpretation must begin with Freeman Tilden. In his 1957 book, *Interpreting Our Heritage*, Tilden defined six principles of interpretation, some of which have proven difficult to create concrete specifications for in practice (e.g. provocation, to reveal meanings and relationships). Nonetheless, for the past 50 years, Tilden's principles have remained highly relevant to interpreters, even as interpretation has developed a body of theory, drawing on communication, museum and heritage studies and, more fundamentally, cognitive and behaviour psychology, to better understand and explain its effectiveness (Ham & Weiler, 2003). Since Tilden, at least a dozen other authors, some of whom have authored multiple textbooks and training manuals, have tried to capture the key 'best practice' principles of interpretation (Skibins *et al.*, 2012). In their meta-analysis of research that has sought to produce evidence of the efficacy of these principles in achieving desired outcomes, Skibins *et al.* (2012) identified 18 sources, mainly written for American audiences and nearly all for interpretation of nature and heritage in natural settings, particularly in national parks. Davidson and Black (2007) outline eight key interpretation sources that present best practice principles applicable to interpretation and tour guiding, some of which overlap with Skibins *et al.*'s but others of which were written for practicing guides outside the United States and some of which were written specifically for tour guides. Some of the principles identified by these two sets of authors are essentially the same, many are different and a few are not particularly applicable to face-to-face interpretation. Between them, there are some 30 interpretation best practices potentially applicable to tour guiding in Western contexts generally. It is not possible to discuss all of these in this book. Some of the principles are targeted at fostering change or reinforcing key values, attitudes and behaviours associated with conservation and are thus incorporated in the discussion of tour guiding sustainability in Chapter 4. Some that are particularly relevant to enhancing the experience of visitors on guided tours include: (i) interpretation via a diversity of *enjoyable* communication approaches, activities and experiences; (ii) interpretation designed to promote the use of two or more *senses*; (iii) interpretation designed to facilitate individual and group *involvement*, contact or participation; (iv) communicating the *relevance* of an object, artefact, landscape or site to visitors; (v) communicating by way of *theme* development/thematic interpretation; (vi) communicating *accurate* fact-based information that facilitates *understanding* and *provokes thinking and meaning-making*; and (vii) interpretation that makes people *feel empathy or emotion* (see Table 3.1).

The specific verbal, non-verbal and even trait items in the communication competency scales discussed at the beginning of this chapter are clearly applications of many of these principles and are evident in the detail of the various sources cited by Davidson and Black (2007) and Skibins *et al.* (2012). Examples include making comparisons to things that visitors already know

Table 3.1 Principles of interpretation applied to tour guiding

Interpretation principle	Examples of studies and meta-analyses that have examined and/or confirmed this principle in a tour guiding context
(i) Interpretation via a diversity of *enjoyable* communication approaches, activities and experiences	Ham and Weiler (2003); Davidson and Black (2007); Peake (2007); Skibins *et al.* (2012); Dioko *et al.* (2013)
(ii) Interpretation designed to promote the use of two or more *senses*	Davidson and Black (2007); Skibins *et al.* (2012)
(iii) Interpretation designed to facilitate individual and group *involvement*, contact or participation	Davidson and Black (2007); Peake (2007); Io and Hallo (2012); Skibins *et al.* (2012)
(iv) Communicating the *relevance* of an object, artefact, landscape or site to visitors (including communicating in a culturally relevant way)	Ham and Weiler (2003) Davidson and Black (2007); Peake (2007); Hongying and Hui (2009); Skibins *et al.* (2012); Xu *et al.* (2012); Dioko *et al.* (2013)
(v) Communicating by way of *theme* or message development/thematic interpretation	Weiler and Crabtree (1998); Davidson and Black (2007); Peake (2007); Hongying and Hui (2009); Skibins *et al.* (2012)
(vi) Communicating *accurate* fact-based information that both facilitates *understanding* and *provokes thinking and meaning-making*	Pond (1993); Ham and Weiler (2003)
(vii) Interpretation that makes people *feel empathy or emotion*	Davidson and Black (2007)

or care about, using examples that make unfamiliar things more familiar, linking intangible concepts and ideas to tangible and universal concepts, engaging visitors in role play, games, sensory activities and questioning techniques, invoking a conversational tone and non-technical language, making use of humour, analogies, personification and storytelling, using non-verbal communication techniques such as smiling, friendly body language and eye contact, and using visual aids and props.

The growing body of training literature targeted at tour guides (see Chapter 6) also includes training texts, workbooks and video packages that, while not reviewed for this chapter, discuss specific 'best practice' interpretation techniques in detail (e.g. Ballantyne et al., 2000; Pastorelli, 2003). Generally, these training resources focus on the use of interpretation to enhance the visitor experience, although the application of interpretation principles in order to achieve other outcomes such as understanding, attitudes and behaviour change is sometimes flagged. Ham (1992) is perhaps best known for advocating the use of theme development in order to achieve the latter outcomes; that is, interpretation content needs to be selected and delivered to convey a take-home message or theme if it is to impact understanding, attitudes and behavioural intentions and behaviour.

Finally, it should be noted that some authors have suggested that there is only one 'correct' interpretation of a place or object and that guides compromise the visitor experience by seeking to control and communicate this, thus mediating the ways that people engage with a site or place (Reisinger & Steiner, 2006). Others have argued that, while the importance of *accuracy and authenticity* in interpretation is acknowledged, messages may need to be adjusted to accommodate for the diversity of visitors who join guided tours (Ballantyne & Uzzell, 1999). Giving visitors the freedom to make their own 'interpretation' and their own meaning from the experience has also gained prominence both within interpretation and within tourism scholarship generally (Reisinger & Steiner, 2006). For example, as illustrated in Chapter 1, guides need to be sensitive to visitors with particular political, cultural or religious backgrounds so that the messages they take home are meaningful to them. While this is, in effect, the principle of relevance espoused by Ham (1992) and others as cited by Davidson and Black (2007) and Skibins et al. (2012), its implications for the practice of interpretive guiding has become particularly evident with the growth of new tourism markets such as visitors from new non-Western markets such as China (discussed later in this chapter).

To reiterate, what makes guiding 'interpretive' is not only that it is purposeful or outcome focused, but that it also utilises the principles of interpretation to achieve these outcomes. Moscardo (1996; Moscardo & Woods, 1998) was one of the first to engage theoretically and empirically with the applicability of the principles of interpretation to enhancing visitor experiences in a commercial tourism context. There has been a sustained call for applying the principles of interpretation to tourism and tour guiding (Davidson & Black, 2007; Peake, 2007; Pereira, 2005; Weiler, 1999) and a few studies have reviewed policy, training and management frameworks to illustrate where they fall short of facilitating 'best practice' interpretation (Giannoulis et al., 2006; Weiler & Ham, 2001; Yamada, 2011).

One avenue of enquiry has been research assessing the perceived *importance* of interpretation by various stakeholders (tourists/visitors, guides themselves, tourism operators and others), usually relative to other tour guide roles, beginning in the 1990s (Gardner & McArthur, 1994; Gurung et al., 1996; Weiler, 1999) and continuing into the new millennium (Ballantyne & Hughes, 2001; Haig & McIntyre, 2002; Ham & Weiler, 2003; Howard et al., 2001; Randall & Rollins, 2009). The results of these studies were presented in Chapter 2. Still others have focused on the perceived *performance* of guides as interpreters in particular (Beaumont, 2001; Peake, 2007; Randall & Rollins, 2009; Weiler, 1999; Weiler & Crabtree, 1999). Not surprisingly, the results have been mixed both with respect to importance (interpretation often, but not always, being perceived as relatively high in importance) and performance (interpretation often perceived as falling short of the expectations of visitors, assessors and others, see Chapter 2).

However, much of the tour guiding literature has been uncritical in its consideration of the application of specific interpretation principles and the relative efficacy of these principles in achieving desired outcomes in a tour guiding context. Only a handful of studies have sought to empirically investigate the guide's competency and/or the visitor's satisfaction with the guide's performance of specific interpretation principles. Weiler and Crabtree (1998), for example, used expert structured observation of guiding performance and feedback from visitors on a number of ecotour experiences in Australia to conclude that guides performed strongly on most evaluative criteria dealing with site knowledge, tour management and interpersonal communication skills, but poorly on indicators pertaining to the application of interpretation principles, especially the delivery of *thematic interpretation* (e.g. evidence of a theme, sequencing, introduction and conclusion).

Ham and Weiler (2003) found that guides were perceived by their clients (*n*=297) and the researchers as successfully applying the principles of *enjoyment* and *relevance* on their cruise-based tours to the Galapagos and Alaska. Guides who presented information in an enjoyable way, provided *understanding* of local features and phenomena and made the information relevant were viewed by visitors as delivering high-quality experiences.

In their qualitative study with cave guides and managers based in Australia and New Zealand, Davidson and Black (2007) elicited effective interpretation practices based on the cave guides and managers' 200 years of collective experience guiding groups in a range of cave environments. They confirmed a number of principles associated with successful guided cave interpretation, including *enjoyment, relevance, theme development, involvement* and *emotion*.

Peake (2007) used interviews, self-completed questionnaires and researcher observation to assess the percentage of guides on whale-watching boats who used specific techniques known to be associated with the principles of interpretive guiding. She found that the tour guiding was *involving* (e.g. by use of a hydrophone), *relevant* (e.g. by delivering content that visitors could understand) and *enjoyable* (e.g. through the use of stories), but, like Weiler and Crabtree (1999), the guides fell short of delivering messages/themes.

Io and Hallo (2012) used a self-completed questionnaire to compare the impact of two different styles of interpretive guiding (on-site versus sightseeing guides in Macao). Both types of guides applied techniques associated with the principles of interpretation (e.g. use of humour, eye contact, facial animation, gestures, anecdotes); however, on-site guides used *involvement* (i.e. asked questions) far more than sightseeing guides. The researchers found that a more interactive guiding style resulted in cognitive, affective and behavioural (intention) outcomes that were significantly higher for the 49 tourists guided by an on-site guide than by the 105 tourists guided by sightseeing guides.

In an important study, Skibins *et al.* (2012) conducted a meta-analysis of 70 peer-reviewed articles published between 1996 and 2009 that reported on studies attempting to link the application of one or more interpretation principles to outcomes. Of these, 57% of the studies examined face-to-face interpretation, although not all of these were necessarily by way of guided tours. Most of the studies were undertaken in the United States (60%) or Australia (30%), and 95% were undertaken in Western contexts. Methodologically, they included quantitative (76%), qualitative (11%) and mixed methods (13%). Notwithstanding some of these limitations in scope, some of the interpretation principles listed earlier that were prominent in these studies in fostering positive outcomes included *multisensory engagement*, *theme development* and visitor *involvement*. In terms of outcomes, these and other principles collectively were particularly effective at impacting visitor knowledge, awareness and satisfaction.

With the exception of Skibins *et al.* (2012) and the few studies reviewed in this section, the academic literature has been largely silent on the relative merits of particular interpretive techniques in achieving broader outcomes. As most of the studies in Skibins *et al.*'s meta-analysis focus on non-guided rather than face-to-face interpretation, there is still very little that can be concluded with respect to interpretive guiding, other than that the selection and application of interpretive techniques need to be driven by the context (tourist/visitor markets, destinations, tours and settings) in which guides are operating, as well as variability among the guides themselves.

As already flagged, a few authors have also been critical about the way interpretation has been conceptualised in the context of tour guiding, arguing that it inhibits rather than fosters understanding (Reisinger & Steiner, 2006). This, however, reflects some of the challenges raised earlier about the difficulty of evaluating the application of individual interpretive principles and techniques in a particular context with a particular market. The next section of the chapter looks at the findings of research examining interpretation in the context of guiding Chinese visitors, soon to be the world's largest tourist market.

The application of interpretation principles to guiding Chinese diaspora visitors

So far, this chapter has focused on interpretive tour guiding mainly in a Western context and, to some extent, the specific interpretive guiding principles and practices that contribute to desirable outcomes. A brief review of tour guiding and interpretation research conducted in Taiwan, Hong Kong, Macao and China and on Chinese guides in Australia raises some questions about the generalisability of the findings of tour guiding research generally, and interpretation in particular, to non-Western markets.

In perhaps the earliest examination of interpretive guiding by Chinese-speaking guides, Chang (2006) undertook a qualitative study involving in-depth interviews with 19 tour managers, participant observation of a Taiwanese guided tour and semi-structured telephone interviews with tour group participants. Interpretive skills were found to be key to tour group participants' satisfaction with and perceived value-adding to the tour.

Hongying and Hui (2009) drew on their firsthand experience and an observational study of 20 guided tours and interviews with a number of guides to criticise the performance of the guides and to challenge the application of Western principles of interpretation. However, the principles they present are basically adaptations or extensions of existing ones. For example, the need to 'relate to the audience's expectations and needs' and to 'refer to both historical facts and modern everyday life' (Hongying & Hui, 2009: 234–235) are different ways of saying that interpretation needs to be relevant. They also argue for guided tours to be structured and delivered around a theme, a principle that of course is already strongly conveyed in much of the interpretation literature.

More recent research has confronted the issues of the relevance of interpretation principles developed in Western countries to the tour content, themes and communication of Chinese guides. In this respect, Xu et al. (2012) offer a perspective on what constitutes quality interpretive guiding to Chinese visitors. Their case study of a World Heritage Site in China drew on multiple data sources and methods that included interviews with six managers and guides, observations of three tour groups and 16 individual visitors, and informal interviews with visitors. They present a more positive interpretation of what Hongying and Hui (2009) describe as the weaknesses of Chinese tour guiding. For example, Hongying and Hui are critical of the focus on cultural heritage (at the expense of nature) and the use of legends (which they acknowledge are fun but at the expense of scientific accuracy). In contrast, Xu *et al.* see these as strengths, noting that Chinese-speaking guides are more successful than non-guided interpretation at engaging and satisfying Chinese visitors. They point to the use of culturally relevant techniques such as telling stories (legends) and reciting poetry, as well as aesthetic and poetic (as opposed to more scientific) language as important adaptations of Western principles of interpretation in order for interpretive guiding to be relevant and effective in a Chinese cultural context. This is consistent with Dioko *et al.*'s (2013) study of the discourse of Chinese tour guides discussed earlier in this chapter, who concluded that Chinese guides make extensive and effective use of proverbs, metaphors, analogies, similes and humour to convey key messages to visitors, sometimes in ways that are quite culturally distinctive (particularly in their use of proverbs).

In summary, neither Hongying and Hui's (2009), Xu *et al.*'s (2012) nor Dioko *et al.*'s (2013) findings and recommendations provide a basis for discarding the principles of interpretation developed in Western contexts, but they do highlight the need for using cultural context as a lens to carefully consider the relevance and need for the adaptation of particular interpretive techniques in order to positively contribute to visitor satisfaction and experience.

Guiding Tours Through Drama, Storytelling and Narrative

Guides achieve greater outcomes when they engage their group in games, sensory activities, questioning techniques and other forms of interaction. *Credit*: Graeme Burgan, Phillip Island Nature Park, Australia

The newly emerging research area of the guide as performer, storyteller and narrator is conceptually very close to that of interpretation, having its roots (like interpretation) in communication theory, yet interestingly, research on the use of these interpretive media appears to have developed without an awareness of or reference to the interpretation literature. This section provides a synopsis of some of the findings emerging from recent research efforts in tour guiding performance, storytelling and narration.

The use of dramaturgical skills and storytelling by guides has been the focus of a number of researchers, particularly from Europe. One of the earliest papers to refer to guiding as a dramatic performance was Fine and Speer's (1985) ethnographic study of guides at a historic house in Texas. Utilising MacCannell's (1976) five stages of 'sight sacralisation' (Fine & Speer, 1985: 75), they found that the performances of historic house tour guides align almost perfectly with MacCannell's performance stages. The interpretive performance techniques used by the guides included metaphors of value and worth, superlative adjectives, role play, costume, language and speech, stories, meaning of objects and dramatic performance.

Two papers on dramatic performance were featured in a special issue on Guided Tours and Tourism of the *Scandinavian Journal of Hospitality and Tourism* in 2012. Overend's (2012) work is set in the context of the illusion/authenticity debate and explores the active construction of sites enacted by performances of the guided tour. He suggests that sites are not just 'read' or 'visited' by tourists but they are also 'written' and 'performed', and sees guided tours as part of a performative relational process that creates sites. Performance in this sense is not simply a dramatic metaphor but builds on Goffman's (1990: 32) understanding of 'all the activity of an individual which occurs during a period marked by his continuous presence before a particular set of observers'. Overend suggests that sites are constantly changing, contending that the performance of sites through guided tours has the potential to significantly affect how a site is interpreted and is subsequently constituted.

Jonasson and Scherle (2012) also explore the performative aspects of guiding, adopting a cross-disciplinary approach to understanding guided tours. Like other researchers, they highlight the guide's role as intercultural mediator (Cole, 1997; Macdonald, 2006; McGrath, 2007; Scherle & Nonnenmann, 2008; Weiler & Yu, 2007), but see this as a performative as well as a communicative function. Operating as 'cosmopolitans' with a foot in more than one culture (Scherle & Kung, 2010; Scherle & Nonnenmann, 2008), guides deliver new world views to tourists not only through verbal and non-verbal communication but also through performances, stories, interpretation and other forms of mediation. Jonasson and Scherle (2012) and Scherle and Kung (2010) present competencies that guides need in order to be intercultural mediators (see also Chapter 2) and to deliver these cosmopolitan performances (discussed in the final section of this chapter).

All guiding environments are to some extent 'sites for the elicitation of narrative themes' (Arnould *et al.*, 1998: 109). Tour guiding is often characterised as the telling of stories and 'narratives', defined by de la Barre (2013: 6) as 'storied ways of knowing'. As Arnould *et al.* (1998) illustrate, narratives are not necessarily scripted, so that guides can vary in how they draw on historical and environmental traditions to make use of, reinforce or instil new ways of knowing. Narratives are the focus of Bryon's (2012) study of Flanders (Belgium) heritage guides and de la Barre's (2013) study of Yukon (Canada) wilderness and cultural guides. Both are qualitative, inductive, exploratory studies that use methods such as analysis of textual documents, participant observation and interviews to capture the narratives and the storytelling techniques of the guides. Bryon demonstrates that the images presented by guides through their stories depend on whether they are official guides, alternative guides, entrepreneurial guides or relational guides, each of which tends to target different markets. Official guides (guides who have completed a two-year training programme and who possess government certificates) are more likely to confine their commentary to historical facts and to avoid criticising the country's heritage and culture, and are least likely to present themes, personal narratives and stories. In contrast, the narration of alternative guides (volunteer guides working for non-profit organisations) tends to be more layered, incorporating modern perspectives and personal life stories. Entrepreneurial guides (who are often non-locals pursuing guiding as a profit-making venture) are entertainers and select their content and delivery with this in mind rather than with any desire to make a point. Finally, relational guides (typically independent guides who target niche international markets) incorporate a strong local flavour and personal content in their narratives, thus their tours vary the most from one individual guide to the next and they are the most likely to include negative commentary. Bryon identifies two common characteristics of storytelling by guides: (i) the need for engagement, enthusiasm and passion – all of which are highly consistent with the interpretive role of the guide; and (ii) the centrality of history as the narrative. He suggests that as storytelling narratives become more widespread there is evidence of the increasing use of experimental techniques.

Similar to Bryon (2012), the narratives in de la Barre's (2013) study tend to align with different types of guides. She categorises these as the masculinist (stories that emphasise the self-sufficiency, individualism and freedom of life in the Yukon), the new sublime (conveying a sense of authenticity, pureness and originality) and narratives of loss (the Yukon as a place of change, disconnection and displacement). The storytelling and guiding techniques tend to differ for each, for example masculinist narratives tend to focus on physical/built infrastructure stories of people, the new sublime narratives try to incorporate informal encounters and unscripted accounts and the narratives of loss focus on information on historical, cultural or environmental issues.

Certainly there are other studies that have touched on the stories and narratives that make up tour guiding discourse (e.g. Dahles, 2002; Gelbman & Maoz, 2012; Giovannetti, 2009; Mitchell, 1996; Modlin et al., 2011; Salazar, 2006), how these are acquired and in some cases adapted by guides, how governments and other stakeholders influence the narratives (see Chapter 1), and the roles that individual guides play in visitors' understandings (and misunderstandings), engagement with and experiences of host populations, cultures and environments (see Chapter 2).

Defining and Measuring the Intercultural Communication Competence of Tour Guides

This final section of the chapter examines the communication of tour guides with individuals and groups who have a different cultural background to their own. This poses particular challenges and therefore the application of knowledge, skills and traits that may not necessarily be required in monocultural contexts. Intercultural competence is required, defined by Scherle and Nonnenmann (2008: 126) as 'the skills and abilities that an individual needs in order to interact appropriately and efficiently with persons from a different culture'.

In this role, the guide must often accommodate, straddle and even live between two or more cultures and develop the confidence, understanding and communication skills to move between them, becoming what Scherle and Nonnenmann (2008: 120) and Scherle and Kung (2010: 6) label as 'cosmopolitans'. Data from two European-based studies that collectively included interviews with 243 tour guides and 60 individuals representing tour operators and travel agencies, as well as some data from tourists, were used by both sets of authors to capture the communication techniques used by tour guides in intercultural contexts. Meged (2010), in her case, also looked at the intercultural communication strategies of European guides by way of participant observation of 17 guided tours, video-taping 11 tours and interviewing several guides conducting guided tours of Copenhagen in four different European languages. Others have undertaken similar types of research with different cultural groups such as Chinese tour guides (Huang, 2004; Yu, 2003). Yu (2003) investigated intercultural competence from the perspective of Australian-based operators, guides and tourists with the help of a 16-item scale and found that some skills, as highlighted in the following paragraphs, were more important than others. In contrast, Huang (2004), in her study of Chinese tour guides who lead groups of English-speaking tourists, took a qualitative approach, drawing on interviews with 19 Chinese-speaking guides, participant observation and document analysis.

Research on intercultural communication in the context of guided tours points to a number of communication competencies required of the guide (see Table 3.2). Examples from published studies help to illustrate some of these communication competencies. Many guides make use of well-known interpretive techniques such as making links by comparing objects or behaviours of the host culture to the culture of the visitor (Meged, 2010). Research on indigenous guides by Howard *et al.* (2001) found that they were proficient at using these types of techniques, including metaphors and analogies, to bridge any perceived cultural divide between Australian tourists and the indigenous culture being interpreted. Meged (2010) observed guides finding culturally fixed points (topics on which both the visited and the visiting culture either agree or can find common ground), such as referring to the age at which young people leave home, as a point of departure for a range of guiding narratives about Danish culture and lifestyles. Guides also make use of communication to break down barriers of understanding and attitudes between tour group members and between

Table 3.2 A summary of findings of studies on intercultural communication competence of tour guides

Communication competency	Examples of studies that have examined and/or confirmed guides demonstrating this competency
Language competence: fluency in the language of the visitor	Yu (2003); Huang (2004); Scherle and Kung (2010)
Cultural competence: knowledge of and the ability to explain or interpret the culture, including the use of interpretive techniques such as metaphors and analogies to compare objects or behaviours of the host culture to the culture of the visitor	Howard *et al.* (2001); Yu (2003); Huang (2004); Meged (2010); Scherle and Kung (2010)
Appreciation for what is culturally appropriate to communicate: including verbal and non-verbal communication as well as appropriate dress codes	Huang (2004); Gunnarsson (2010); Scherle and Kung (2010)
Social–interpersonal competence: a sense of respect for both cultures, including the use of communication to break down barriers of understanding and attitudes and to minimise culture shock	Yu (2003); Huang (2004); Scherle and Nonnenmann (2008); Scherle and Kung (2010)
Expression and demonstration of cultural pride: the guide self-identifying with the host culture and acting as an ambassador for the host culture	Yu (2003); Meged (2010)
Engaging in two-way communication: allowing the visitor to contribute to his or her own construction of the visited culture	Meged (2010)

host residents with differing cultures, for example 'Our guide continually drew our attention to little peculiarities in the guests' relationship with each other' (Scherle & Kung, 2010: 16) and 'Our tour guide tried to reduce the tension that even we could feel between the Afrikaner guides and the coloured bus drivers' (Scherle & Kung, 2010: 17). Many guides are conscious of their role in protecting the visitor, sometimes by actively 'choreographing the interaction between tourists, local people and local guides' (Scherle & Nonnenmann, 2008: 132). Elaboration and examples of guides engaging the visitor in co-creating his or her own experience (Meged, 2010) are provided in the concluding chapter of this book.

In her study of Chinese tour guides' intercultural competencies, Yu (2003) found that the intercultural competency of the guide was a good predictor of the level of satisfaction reported by visitors, and that they tended to rate the intercultural communication competence/performance of their guides somewhat lower than the guides rated themselves. It is thus concerning that Yu (2003), Huang (2004) and Scherle and Nonnenmann (2008) all found that the provision of training for intercultural communication was inadequate and provided recommendations for its improvement.

Implications for Research

As already noted, tour guiding research has provided relatively little evidence linking the principles of interpretation to delivering the desired outcomes of interpretive guiding. More research is needed to better understand the application of best practice communication and interpretation principles to tour guiding and the outcomes for visitors and others. While more of this kind of research is clearly necessary, it is difficult to do. For example, how does a researcher isolate and measure the use, let alone the effectiveness, of any particular interpretive technique or principle? In the case of Io and Hallo (2012), the researchers used the communication competency scale developed by Ryan and Dewar (1995) discussed at the beginning of this chapter. Others have developed assessment tools more broadly informed by the principles of good interpretation (see the discussion on the EcoGuide Program in Chapter 7). A number of issues need to be considered, however, in judging a guide's use and application of interpretation as effective. For example, does a single joke constitute the application of humour? How does one judge if the use of humour is appropriate to the target market and the tour? Does the use of humour by tour guides then entitle them to be judged as applying the principle of enjoyment to their tours, or do they need to demonstrate the use of multiple techniques that apply this principle? Similarly, if a guide uses an analogy or an example (see for example Dioko et al.'s [2013] study discussed early in this chapter), is their tour applying the principle of relevance? Or does a guide's interpretation need to be assessed in relation to how often, how consistently and how appropriately each technique is used? Taken to another level, how well or how often does a particular guide need to use a particular interpretive principle such as relevance, involvement or accuracy to be judged as an effective interpretive guide?

What is also unclear is whether, how and to what extent specific applications of interpretive guiding principles and practices contribute to specific outcomes. For example, does a guide's use of interpretive guiding techniques such as storytelling mainly lead to visitor satisfaction, or can it also serve as a tool for impacting a visitor's on-site actions and post-visit attitudes and behaviours? How does the use of relevance – that is, connecting with what visitors already know and care about a destination or a site – impact visitor satisfaction, understanding and valuing of the site? Does a tour need to be thematic in order to foster post-visit attitudes and behaviours? Is the use of any particular combination of interpretive techniques or principles particularly effective in impacting what visitors think, feel and do? These relationships between the practice of interpretation and its desired outcomes are promulgated in the literature but are rarely demonstrated in research.

At a broader level, is the use of any one of these interpretation principles better than another? Can this be assessed on the basis of observing one guided tour by the guide? Are all of these techniques appropriate to all markets? Better target market research is needed in order to deliver an interpretive experience that meets the expectations and preferences of visitors from different cultures and the applicability of interpretation principles to tour guiding in both non-Western and non-English-speaking contexts. There is also scope for research to examine the need for interpretive guiding to respond to changing consumer demand, as well as to cross-national and cross-cultural differences and changes in organisational and industry culture, employment and human resources practices and, following Yamada's (2011) example, government policy and practice.

Implications for Tour Guiding Practice

Given the challenge and complexity of the environments and contexts in which guides work, their communication can fall short of the expectations of stakeholders – tourism operators, host communities, the destinations and those who manage natural and heritage environments that depend on tourism – as well as visitors themselves. Maintaining and improving the practice of interpretive guiding and intercultural communication to meet these expectations is a complex and multifaceted challenge for tour guides and the industry. The communication competence, interpretation and intercultural communication literatures have helped flesh out what theories and principles underpin effective communication in the context of a guided tour, but the acquisition and application of communication and interpretation knowledge and skills by individual guides are another matter.

Kohl *et al.* (2001) make a particularly compelling case for revisiting the content and delivery of interpretive training in developing countries:

> The guide must be a critical thinker able to observe a site, boil down its contents, extract the essence, render it into interpretive form for a particular audience, and then communicate it. When the norm is memorization, students tend only to describe the barrel rather than reaching deep into the barrel and extracting the meaning. (Kohl *et al.*, 2001: 23)

Interpretation as a subset of tour guide education and training is discussed in Chapter 6.

With the diversity and dynamic nature of tourist markets now seeking the services of a tour guide, good interpretation and intercultural communication arguably require ongoing learning and professional development, role-modelling, mentoring/coaching and on-the-job assessment/feedback. Guides need to refresh their guiding practices so that they continue to add value to the experiences of the markets they currently serve, particularly as competition for attention is increasing from alternative non-guided media such as mobile phone applications. Guides also need to adapt their practices to new markets including those with different cultural backgrounds and those with special needs. Quality assurance schemes, particularly those that provide incentives and rewards for excellence, need to continue to reward the quality of the interpretation delivered by the guides (see Chapter 7).

Chapter Summary

This chapter has examined research, theory and practice relating to the guide as communicator, interpreter, storyteller and intercultural communicator. The following is a summary of some of the key findings in this body of literature.

Communication competency of tour guides can be measured across at least three dimensions: non-verbal communication, verbal communication and the guide's traits. There may be dozens of individual competencies that make up these dimensions, and visitors and guides can perceive the relative importance and performance of each of these differently. According to the relational model of communication competence, a visitor will judge a guide's overall communication competency based on the guide's knowledge, skill and motivation.

Visitors and stakeholders view interpretation as one of the key defining roles of a quality tour guide and a distinguishing feature of a quality guided tour. Being a good interpreter is more complex and more difficult to master than other roles required of and performed by guides. Thus, interpretive guiding practice often falls short of the expectations of visitors and other stakeholders.

A considerable body of literature has sought to progress the practice of interpretive guiding, mainly through the application of interpretation principles towards achieving predetermined outcomes aimed at benefiting visitors, other stakeholders, destinations and environments. Interpretive principles that have been found to deliver satisfaction and enhance visitor experiences include: (i) interpretation via a diversity of *enjoyable* communication approaches, activities and experiences; (ii) interpretation designed to promote the use of two or more *senses*; (iii) interpretation designed to facilitate individual and group *involvement*, contact or participation; (iv) communicating the *relevance* of an object, artefact, landscape or site to visitors; (v) communicating by way of *theme* development/thematic interpretation; (vi) communicating *accurate*, fact-based information that facilitates *understanding and provokes thinking and meaning-making*; and (vii) interpretation that makes people *feel empathy or emotion*.

Many interpretive media are used by guides, but the use of drama, storytelling and narratives is particularly pervasive in tour guiding. However, individual guides vary widely in how they use these techniques as tools to enhance their communication. These and other specific interpretive guiding techniques may also need to be customised to particular markets such as visitors from non-Western cultures.

In addition to being interpreters, guides must be effective intercultural communicators. To do so, guides require competence in languages; the ability to explain or interpret culture; an appreciation for cultural difference and for what is, and is not, appropriate to communicate; interest and a willingness to find common ground; social–interpersonal competence such as respect; and enough pride to act as an ambassador for their culture.

Many aspects of a guide's communication, particularly the application of interpretive guiding principles and practices, contribute not only to enhancing the visitor experience but also to outcomes that foster environmental, social, cultural and economic sustainability. The contribution of tour guiding to sustainability is the focus of Chapter 4.

Key references

(1) LeClerc, D. and Martin, J.N. (2004) Tour guide communication competence: French, German and American tourists' perceptions. *International Journal of Intercultural Relations* 28, 181–200.

(2) Weiler, B. and Ham, S.H. (2001) Tour guides and interpretation. In D. Weaver (ed.) *Encyclopedia of Ecotourism* (pp. 549–563). Wallingford: CABI Publishing.

(3) Io, M. and Hallo, L. (2012) A comparative study of tour guides' interpretation: The case of Macao. *Tourism Analysis* 17, 153–165.

(4) Dioko, L.A.N., Harrill, R. and Cardon, P.W. (2013) The wit and wisdom of Chinese tour guides: A critical tourism perspective. *Journal of China Tourism Research* 9 (1), 27–49.
(5) Bryon, J. (2012) Tour guides as storytellers – From selling to sharing. *Scandinavian Journal of Hospitality and Tourism* 12 (1), 27–43.
(6) de la Barre, S. (2013) Wilderness and cultural tour guides, place identity and sustainable tourism in remote areas. *Journal of Sustainable Tourism* 21 (6), 825–844.

4 The Contributions of Tour Guiding to Sustainability

Over the past few decades, considerable effort on the part of educators, researchers and practicing guides has been devoted to making tour guiding more enjoyable and memorable for visitors. As a result, a great deal has been learned about how guides can better attract and maintain the attention of visitors/tourists and how they can connect with, entertain, involve, provoke and inspire visitors, particularly through the use of interpretation (see Chapter 3). This has improved tour guides' capacity to enrich the visitor experience (Pastorelli, 2003), leading to more positive word-of-mouth advertising and other demonstrations of satisfaction and loyalty. But at the end of the day, is this enough to sustain and grow the demand for guided activities and to attract and keep good guides in the field? Perhaps more importantly, how can and does tour guiding help sustain the businesses, communities, cultures and environments that rely on tourism for their survival?

The purpose of this chapter is to present theory, research and practice relating to the tour guide's contribution to sustainability. The four pillars of sustainability – environmental, economic, social and cultural – inform the identification of three key dimensions in which guides can help contribute to sustainability outcomes. These are the enhancement of understanding and valuing of host destinations and resources, the management and monitoring of the on-site cultural and environmental behaviour of visitors and the development or reinforcement of positive post-visit attitudes and behaviours. The research evidence of guides contributing to each of these outcome dimensions is then outlined, followed by some of the inputs or antecedents that may help enable these outcomes.

Defining Sustainability in the Context of Tourism and Tour Guiding

Sustainability is a somewhat contested term. More than two decades of thinking about sustainability, sustainable development (SD) and sustainable tourism (ST) have led to a wide range of definitions but also a more sophisticated understanding of each of these concepts. Early definitions of *sustainable tourism* described it as tourism that is developed and maintained in a manner and at such a scale that it remains economically viable over an indefinite period and does not undermine the physical and human environment that sustains and nurtures it (Bramwell & Lane, 1993; Hardy et al., 2002). The World Tourism Organisation (WTO, 2013) defines ST as 'tourism that takes full account of its current and future economic, social and environmental impacts, addressing the needs of visitors, the industry, the environment and host communities'.

In keeping with this definition, an examination of tour guiding's contribution to ST must incorporate not only ecological and economic outcomes, but social and cultural dimensions as well (Hu & Wall, 2012; Hughes, 1995; Weaver, 2006). These outcomes (see column 1 of Table 4.1) can range from enhanced understanding and appreciation of the natural and cultural environment, to reduced negative cultural and environmental impacts, to increased social and community benefits, to greater respect for local culture and to improved economic prosperity. Whether at the site, business, community or destination level, quantitative indicators of sustainability that are easy to understand and economically and technically feasible to measure are the most useful (Vereczi, 2007). However, establishing such indicators for the range of desired outcomes (presented in column 1 of Table 4.1) can be difficult.

Despite the rhetoric and literally decades of dialogue, theorising and research about ST generally, how to measure it and how to make travel and the tourism industry more sustainable, the contributions of tour guiding to ST are rarely given more than lip service. One explanation for this may be that many aspects of sustainability, such as the improved economic, environmental and social outcomes listed in column 1 of Table 4.1, are viewed as being controlled by other stakeholders and largely beyond the influence of tour guides. Thus, isolating the contributions of tour guides (column 2 of Table 4.1) to these sustainability outcomes can be problematic. For example, *protected area managers* and *local and regional government authorities*, not guides, usually control visitor access and activity via licensing, regulations and law enforcement, and can restrict when, where and how tours operate. *Other government agencies* legislate, regulate and restrict (such as through pricing) the use of renewable and non-renewable resources by the tourism industry. These laws, policies and practices often have a more direct, observable or measurable impact on ST than tour guiding practices. At some destinations, *indigenous people* have a say in physical access and in the economic, social and cultural bounds within which a tour may operate. For example, they can limit or prohibit access to restricted sites, require the engagement of local guides or suppliers, specify the conditions under which indigenous stories and photo taking may occur and require payment for other services and privileges extended to visitors by local communities (Howard et al., 2001). Similar controls also operate in non-indigenous 'restricted access' sites such as guided tours of cathedrals and battlefield sites

Table 4.1 Potential areas of contribution of tour guiding to sustainability

A selection of sustainability outcomes	How tour guiding can contribute to meeting sustainability outcomes
Improved understanding of natural and cultural values	Enhancing visitors' understanding and valuing of communities, cultures and environments
Increased economic prosperity of local businesses and communities	Influencing visitors' behaviour en route and at destinations
Increased social benefits to/ engagement of local communities	Influencing visitors' behaviour en route and at destinations
Reduced production and responsible disposal of waste	Influencing and monitoring visitors' behaviour en route and at destinations
Reduced use of water and energy	Influencing and monitoring visitors' behaviour en route and at destinations
Protected/improved quality of environmental conditions (e.g. water, soil, air quality)	Influencing and monitoring visitors' behaviour en route and at destinations
Fostering visitors' post-visit attitudes and behaviours
Protected/improved biodiversity conservation of the destination	Enhancing visitors' understanding and valuing of communities, cultures and environments
Influencing and monitoring visitors' behaviour en route and at destinations
Fostering visitors' post-visit attitudes and behaviours
Greater respect for/enhancement of culture, heritage and/or traditions	Enhancing visitors' understanding and valuing of communities, cultures and environments
Influencing and monitoring visitors' behaviour en route and at destinations
Fostering visitors' post-visit attitudes and behaviours

Source: Adapted from Choi and Sirakaya (2006), Moore *et al.* (2009), Tonge *et al.* (2005) and WTTC (1996).

which, in addition to fostering sustainability, can be beneficial for the visitor experience. Finally, *tourism operators* can contribute in important ways to sustainability (or unsustainability), for example in the decisions they make, often driven by economic imperatives, about the mode of transport, group size, accommodation and the use of local suppliers, leaving limited options for what an individual guide can do. The guiding profession, let alone an individual guide, may thus feel relatively powerless to make a difference in contributing to the sustainability of a particular activity, tour, business, community, industry or environment:

> Travel agents, hoteliers, tour [operators] and vendors constrain tourists' movements, behaviours and even thoughts ... All these service providers contribute to customers' satisfaction or dissatisfaction [and to sustainability], whereas tour guides often face the brunt [of dissatisfaction]. (Prakash *et al.*, 2011: 66)

Notwithstanding these limitations, in the context of any guided tour whether nature- or culture-focused, on land or water, at a wildlife park or museum or on a multi-day tour, it is the tour guide more than anyone else who has the greatest opportunity for face-to-face contact with the tourist/visitor and thus both the delivery of sustainability messages and the monitoring and influencing of visitor behaviour. Thus, as early as 1992 (Jacobson & Robles, 1992), scholars were espousing the importance of tour guides in ST. Since then, Weiler and Davis (1993), Thomas (1994), Cole (1997), Haig and McIntyre (2002), Weiler and Ham (2002), Ham and Weiler (2003), Kayes (2005), Ormsby and Mannle (2006), Boren *et al.* (2007), Henning (2008), Randall and Rollins (2009), Huang and Weiler (2010), Skanavis and Giannoulis (2010), Jensen (2010), Weiler and Kim (2011), Hu and Wall (2012), de la Barre (2013), Pereira and Mykletun (2012), Poudel and Nyaupane (2013) and no doubt others, have described tour guides as key to achieving the goals of ecotourism, ST and/or SD. Indeed, Kohl (2007: 342) argues that an ecotour guide can be considered successful only if he or she is able to 'channel visitors' actions in order to meet the higher programmatic objectives of ecotourism such as returns to conservation, local empowerment, fairer distribution of wealth and turning a profit'. Until very recently, however, such specific and actual contributions of tour guides have rarely been conceptualised, let alone assessed or measured.

Vereczi (2007) suggested that indicators of sustainable outcomes by guides might include visitors' evaluations and measures of satisfaction of their tours. Such a conservative and narrow conceptualisation of the links between tour guiding and sustainability is, unfortunately, all too common. Even as recently as 2012, case studies such as de la Barre (2013) report mainly on the guide's contribution to achieving marketing outcomes (diversity and selectivity) and economic/business outcomes (local business ownership, appropriate planning, development and regulatory mechanisms) with less attention to other environmental, social and cultural sustainability outcomes.

The Dimensions of Tour Guiding's Contribution to Sustainability

In developing countries and economically depressed regions, the employment of local guides is a sustainability outcome in and of itself. *Credit*: Brian Alston (Inca guides, Peru)

Of course, the employment of local guides is a sustainability outcome in and of itself, especially in an economically depressed region or a developing country. These guides' income, job security and the achievement of their personal ambitions all potentially enhance the economic sustainability of a tourism destination or region, and thus the natural and cultural resources upon which the industry depends. This chapter seeks to broaden the conceptualisation of the potential and actual contributions of tour guiding practice. As suggested in column 2 of Table 4.1, these contributions may be captured under three dimensions:

- Dimension 1: *Enhancing* visitors' *understanding and valuing* of sites, communities, cultures and environments.
- Dimension 2: *Influencing and monitoring* visitors' *behaviours*, en route, on-site and at destinations.
- Dimension 3: *Fostering* visitors' *post-visit*, pro-environmental and pro-heritage conservation *attitudes and behaviours*.

Some may argue that these dimensions are neither exhaustive nor mutually exclusive; however, they provide a useful framework within which to present evidence from published empirical research of the contributions of tour guiding to ST. The next section of the chapter presents the findings of research within each of these dimensions and illustrates the achievement of each dimension through the use of (a) *interpretive guiding*, (b) *communication of messages*, (c) *role-modelling*, (d) *enforcement* and (e) *persuasive communication*. This is followed by a discussion of the inputs or antecedents to ST outcomes; that is, what specific guiding approaches or techniques associated with interpretive guiding, delivering sustainable messages, role-modelling, enforcing and persuasively communicating might contribute to or explain the effectiveness of tour guides in fostering ST outcomes. Theoretical explanations for why and how tour guiding can achieve these elements of ST are discussed elsewhere (Weiler & Kim, 2011).

Evidence of Sustainability Outcomes from Tour Guiding

While the rhetoric of tour guiding's contribution to sustainability is pervasive in the literature since at least Jacobson and Robles (1992), demonstration of guides achieving such outcomes, whether through observation or other methods, is less evident. Beginning with Moscardo (1998), a considerable number of studies have claimed, and in some cases sought, to demonstrate the impacts of interpretation and, more recently, tour guiding on constructs such as visitors' knowledge, understanding, beliefs, attitudes, feelings, behavioural intentions and behaviours. Indeed, a number of bibliographies (National Association for Interpretation, 2003; Wells *et al.*, 1995), critical reviews (Ham & Weiler, 2006; Marion & Reid, 2007; Munro *et al.*, 2008) and even meta-analyses (Skibins *et al.*, 2012; Zeppel, 2008; Zeppel & Muloin, 2008) have been undertaken on the outcomes of interpretation. Largely due to logistical and measurement challenges, most of these have focused on non-guided or self-directed interpretation, but a growing number are focusing on the relationship between face-to-face interpretation/tour guiding and sustainability (Ballantyne *et al.*, 2009; Zeppel & Muloin, 2008). Many of these studies suffer from flaws in research design, most notably that they report high levels of tour participants' pro-conservation understanding, attitude and behaviour on-site or post-visit as a result of interpretation and tour guiding, without controlling for the presence of these variables pre-tour. As Beaumont (1991: 317) noted more than two decades ago, participants on such tours may already have attitudes and behaviours that are pro-sustainability, and thus tour guides and others may simply be 'preaching to the converted'. Moreover, Skibins *et al.* (2012), in a useful meta-analysis of interpretive research, note that in most cases evidence of causal relationships between specific interpretive techniques and/or interpretive media and sustainability outcomes is absent. Nonetheless, a body of empirical research is now starting to emerge, building a picture of tour guiding's contributions to sustainability.

Dimension 1: Enhancing understanding and valuing

Regarding Dimension 1, it should be noted that there are many published studies reporting knowledge and attitudinal 'benefits', 'change' and 'impacts' as a result of interpretation and guiding activities. These tend to measure knowledge gain or general attitudes, often with spurious links to ST outcomes (Ballantyne et al., 2009; Zeppel & Muloin, 2008). As noted in Chapter 3, Skibins et al.'s (2012) meta-analysis of 70 published studies linking interpretation principles and outcomes found many 'pairings' between the application of interpretation principles and knowledge, attitude and behavioural outcomes. Almost none of these included pre- and post-measures of these variables. Notwithstanding that there is some evidence of links between understanding, attitude and behaviour as discussed in Chapter 3 (Ham, 2009; Tilden, 1977), there is no guarantee that factual knowledge gained as a result of an interpretive talk or guided activity will impact on a visitor's understanding and valuing of the site and its resources, let alone impact his or her on-site or off-site behavioural intentions and actions in ways that promote sustainability.

In addition, until recently there has been a lack of measurement tools that go beyond visitor enjoyment, satisfaction and factual recall to capture visitors' understanding and valuing of nature and culture. Recent success in the development and testing of self-reported measures by Weiler and Ham (2010) has led to the availability of an instrument for measuring and comparing ST outcomes across sites and experiences. Their validated, multi-item, self-report instrument can be used to assess the impact of interpretive guiding on elaboration (i.e. provoking the visitor to think – a five-item scale), connection (i.e. empathy for the people or place – a four-item scale) and caring (i.e. a positive attitude towards nature or heritage preservation – a three-item scale), which collectively measure the understanding and valuing of nature and heritage. For example, a study of 288 visitors to an Australian zoo sought to assess the extent to which interpretive guiding made them think (elaborate), helped them connect (empathise) and made them care (nature appreciation) (Weiler & Smith, 2009). All respondents were visitors to a relatively new, state-of-the-art lion exhibit who were exposed to messages delivered by experienced and trained interpretive staff about the difficulties faced by lions that live outside reserves, particularly when they come in contact with humans. Each visitor was exposed to interpretation delivered via up to three different media (a static display, a zookeeper talk, interaction with a volunteer guide, an encounter with a guide engaged in role-play and a behind-the-scenes tour with a zookeeper/guide), all aimed at helping visitors to understand the lions, their habitat and the threats to their survival, and to connect with and value the species and its environment (Dimension 1), and thus associated with ST outcomes. Mean ratings on all three scales were consistently higher for visitors exposed to greater numbers of interpretive media, with the combination of non-guided and guided interpretation resulting in higher levels of sustainable outcomes than non-guided interpretation alone (Weiler & Smith, 2009).

Another study using parallel self-reported measures of 285 Chinese visitors who were guided around an Australian heritage site for up to two hours by a bilingual, bicultural interpretive guide found somewhat lower but still positive mean ratings on elaboration, connection and attitude towards heritage preservation (Van Dijk & Weiler, 2009).

Interpretive guides can impact on visitors' understanding of and connection with heritage, and on their attitude toward heritage conservation. *Credit*: Sovereign Hill Museum Association (Chinese tour guide, Sovereign Hill Outdoor Museum, Ballarat Australia)

All of this suggests that (a) interpretive guiding can and does impact visitors, at least based on self-reporting, in ways that are theoretically associated with ST outcomes. However, the measures described here relate to the outcomes *as perceived by visitors*, and do not assess the extent to which tour guiding *actually impacts* a visitor's understanding of a site's natural and cultural values and thus contributes to sustainability. More direct and observable measures of understanding, beyond the overly simplistic 'factual recall' that has dominated earlier interpretation research, and measures of visitors' valuing of nature and heritage, are needed in order to assess the actual impact of interpretive guiding.

In a study that involved observation and interviews with 32 local guides from five different regions in rural Madagascar, Jensen (2010) reported that local guides who had strong local ties and social mediation skills were able to enhance understanding and social interaction and thereby moderate the negative effects on communities that can come from stereotyping. In addition, positive effects such as self-esteem building among community members were observed as a result of 'visitors' interest in their traditions and lifestyles framed within a socially relaxed atmosphere where community members were happy to share their thoughts and knowledge with their guests' (Jensen, 2010: 627). Jensen further argued that as a result of being employed as guides, interviewees gained the trust of the village chief and local residents, which in turn made the guides more motivated and empowered to practice ST themselves. Ormsby and Mannle (2006) and Kohl (2007) also similarly note the contribution of tour guides to social capital and capacity building, outcomes that are highlighted in the tourism literature as being closely associated with sustainability (Weiler & Ham, 2002). Pereira and Mykletun (2012: 81) comment on the potential role of guides in 'engendering an appreciation for local products' and assisting local artisans to produce goods that meet visitors' expectations. Similarly, Jensen (2010: 628) also sees greater potential for guides as contributors to sustainability, posing the question: 'Can local guides develop their middleman/honest broker roles further into some form of managerial role within a sustainable development strategy?'

Another recent study by Henning (2008) looked in particular at the degree to which tour guides communicate about local and regional sustainability issues and the practices of land managers, tourism operators and governments generally. This qualitative study in Banff National Park (Canada) included participant observation of the same guided hike on six separate occasions along with interviews with several of the participants, park staff and other stakeholders. The commercial guide conducting the walk was found to be highly successful at communicating the park agency's sustainability practices, such as habitat preservation and restorative efforts (including past mistakes), and the environmental consequences for the park and the wider environment. The environmental messages of the guide were well received by tourists who described the content of the tour with 'awe, respect and gratitude at the work being done' (Henning, 2008: 190). Those interviewed could articulate specific conservation messages and actions, and some outlined how these connected with and translated into action in their home countries.

Similarly, in a particularly comprehensive and innovative study of Masoala National Park in Madagascar that included 135 semi-structured interviews and several months of participant observation, Ormsby and Mannle (2006) were able to document impacts on understanding and valuing by both visitors and local residents:

> Guides provide a valuable service by explaining the park's goals to visitors and community residents ... The guides also ... influence park perceptions through their presentation of park information to visitors and to communities through which visitors pass when trekking in the park. By explaining to local residents [that] tourists are coming 'to see nature' and the potential [environmental] benefits from visitors [via a weekly hour-long radio program], guides also play an integral role in ecotourism success through encouraging conservation ...The guides also play an essential role in making connections with people in the villages and directing tourists' money to the peripheral areas of the park. (Ormsby & Mannle, 2006: 279–280)

Finally, Poudel and Nyaupane (2013) undertook to compare the attitudes and self-reported behaviours of 230 visitors on guided and non-guided tours in the Annapurna area of Nepal. While they used only post-visit measures, they did attempt to use rigorous methods including a 20-item ST attitude scale (Choi & Sirakaya, 2006) and a 20-item ST behaviour scale that they developed themselves. Interestingly, while the attitudes and behaviours of visitors on guided tours were significantly different to those on non-guided tours on the majority of the items on both scales, visitors on non-guided tours actually scored more positively on some of the items, particularly the behavioural items. Of course, visitors were not randomly assigned to guided versus non-guided tours, thus this result may simply reflect pre-existing differences between these two groups of visitors.

Dimension 2: Influencing and monitoring behaviour

With respect to Dimension 2, the (b) communication messages and (c) role-modelling of a guide in relation to influencing appropriate on-site behaviour are perhaps easier to identify and inventory than the guide's impact on a visitor's understanding. For example, during the time in which a visitor is under the influence and eye of the guide, messages and actions that can lead to negative impacts (e.g. trampling vegetation, picking flowers, collecting shells, feeding wild animals, harassing wildlife, taking photos of locals, buying products made from threatened species) can be heard and observed, as can messages and actions that lead to positive impacts (e.g. appropriate disposal of waste, picking up litter, keeping pets on a leash or out of natural areas, respecting local culture and traditions and buying products made by locals).

In a very early study in this vein, Cole (1997) reported that anthropologists acting as tour guides at one of two island case study regions in Indonesia were able not only to outline appropriate behaviour in relation to a small host village but also explain the reasons for the 'do's' and 'don'ts'. By comparing tourist behaviour and resident responses in the two case studies, the researcher concluded that a high level of compliance by the tourists and a low level of negative (as well as unexpected positive) sociocultural impacts were due to the presence and actions of the guides. Jensen's (2010: 624–625) study cited earlier of local guides in Madagascar also found that guides played an important role in educating tourists about the villages' traditions, norms, taboos and appropriate behaviours, and that the guides' presence 'may have had a reassuring effect on the villagers'.

In a recent study of nature-based guides working on cruise ships along the Kimberley coastline in North Western Australia, Scherrer *et al.* (2011) used visitor observations of their guides along with stakeholder interviews to examine the potential impacts of tour guides, tours and visitors on environmental and cultural sites, visitor safety and the visitor experience. They found that the tour guide's group management skills and level of knowledge strongly influenced the visitor's behaviour and potential impacts on the environmental and cultural sites and visitor satisfaction. They suggest that the tour guide plays a key role in operational and visitor management procedures to improve visitor management practices, but because tour guiding is only one of several functions of a crew member on these cruise ships, his or her performance can sometimes fall short of both visitor and management expectations.

Nature-based guides communicate messages about appropriate behaviour and monitor on-site behaviour and its impacts on wildlife and habitats. *Credit*: Kaye Walker (Clipper Cruise Line Tours)

Similarly, research by Armstrong and Weiler (2002), in cooperation with Parks Victoria in Australia, found that guides who are employed by licensed tour operators in national parks could be doing much more in the way of delivering messages relating to sustainability outcomes. Participant observation and audio recording of guide commentary on 20 guided tours found that 17 of the guides delivered 107 messages related to Parks Victoria's goals. In relation to the length of the tours (many were full-day tours) and the amount of commentary, this is a very small number, with only a handful of messages conveying minimal impact messages. Kayes' (2005) study of guides in Bocas del Toro, an island destination in Panama, replicated Armstrong and Weiler's methods and found that most reef-based guides delivered little information and virtually no environmental messages.

Randall and Rollins' (2009) study of kayak tour guides in a marine national park in Canada found that visitors perceived guides to be performing poorly in communicating environmentally and culturally responsible behaviour in comparison to what they expected. Finally, in their study of 36 tour guides in the Brazilian Amazon, Pereira and Mykletun (2012) found little evidence of guides communicating environmentally responsible messages or acting as cultural brokers. Indeed, they observed guides role-modelling inappropriate behaviours to tourists.

These studies rely on assessing what the guide says or does, or in some cases visitors' perceptions of these, rather than assessing the *actual* on-site behavioural responses of visitors. Littlefair (2003: 38) argued that monitoring actual change in visitor behaviour is the ultimate goal of ST as it identifies 'what people do, rather than what they say they do'. In recent years, a number of studies have evaluated communication interventions designed specifically to foster responsible on-site behaviour. These have tended to focus on the use of self-directed interpretation such as signs (Brown *et al.*, 2010; Curtis *et al.*, 2010; Hughes *et al.*, 2009), although there has been some success in researching the influence on visitors' on-site behaviours as a result of face-to-face or guided interpretation (Ballantyne *et al.*, 2009; Howard *et al.*, 2001; Littlefair & Buckley, 2008; Marion & Reid, 2007; O'Neill *et al.*, 2004; Widner & Roggenbuck, 2000).

Some of these involve (d) *enforcing ST practices* via monitoring and regulating problem on-site behaviour and its impacts (also Dimension 2) (Littlefair, 2003; Moscardo, 1998; Roggenbuck, 1992). It is acknowledged that visitors tend to perceive a tour guide as an authority figure, and thus behave in a more responsible way when the tour guide is present (Littlefair, 2003). Indeed, several studies have shown the successful impacts of tour guiding in reducing the level of non-compliant behaviour as well as illegal on-site behaviours that were unintentional (e.g. off-trail hiking, wildlife feeding and littering) (Howard *et al.*, 2001; Littlefair, 2003; Orams & Hill,

1998; Scherrer *et al.*, 2011; for further reviews, see Marion & Reid, 2007 and Skibins *et al.*, 2012). While many of these studies have relied on visitors' self-reports of how guiding impacted their behavioural intention or actual behaviour, a few have actually observed on-site behaviour such as reducing damaging behaviour on coral reefs by divers (Medio *et al.*, 1997), reducing removal of petrified wood (Widner & Roggenbuck, 2000), reducing noise, reducing off-track walking and increasing pro-environmental behaviour such as picking up other people's litter (Littlefair & Buckley, 2008).

A more complex research issue is to go from measuring visitors' on-site behaviours to assessing the *impacts* or consequences of visitors' on-site actions or non-actions on sustainability, since the impacts can be cumulative and long term. Boren *et al.* (2007), however, through observation and comparisons with a control group who were not guided, were able to conclude that the presence of a guide both during land-based seal-viewing and swim-with-seal programmes had a significant impact on reducing both the non-compliant behaviour of the tourist and avoidance behaviours of seals.

Dimension 3: Fostering post-visit attitudes and behaviours

The post-visit take-up of environmentally and culturally sustainable behaviours such as on future walks or tours, let alone pro-environmental and pro-heritage conservation behaviours in other contexts, is largely unknown. While there have been a number of studies (see, for example, reviews by Zeppel & Muloin, 2008) that have suggested that tourists/ visitors who are exposed to environmental messages report higher levels of pro-conservation behaviour, as already noted these may simply be a case of more environmentally conscious visitors self-selecting these kinds of tours and experiences. Indeed, both Armstrong and Weiler (2002) and Kayes (2005) found that, on guided tours where pro-environmental attitudinal and behavioural messages were largely absent, tourists expressed disappointment in the lack of environmental messages given by the guides. As Kayes (2005) comments:

> ... tourists really are interested in receiving more detailed information. By offering more detailed explanations of observed wildlife, guides will be able to offer longer more in-depth tours ... Higher satisfaction with the guides and the tour means tourists will return to the same guide the next day to learn more about somewhere else. Guides will receive great economic benefits from repeat customers, and may be able to charge more for higher-quality tours. It's a win-win situation. (Kayes, 2005: 24)

Only a limited amount of systematic research has examined the impact of the (e) *persuasive communication* of tour guides on visitors' post-visit attitudes and behaviour (Dimension 3), for example in support of wildlife conservation. A theme-driven communication campaign developed for Lindblad Expeditions passengers in the Galapagos Islands (Powell & Ham, 2008) resulted in significant increases in passenger donations to the Galapagos Conservation Fund (GCF). This campaign consisted primarily of persuasive messages that were developed and delivered to passengers via onboard interpretive panels, tour guide commentaries at various islands, evening debriefings and pre-visit information sent to passengers prior to their departure. The campaign was found to have increased stated behavioural intentions to donate money to support Galapagos conservation (as compared to pre-campaign donation levels), both at the end of the tour and post-visit (Powell & Ham, 2008). Such results do suggest that persuasive communication via tour guides and other interpretive media can indeed contribute in positive ways to the post-visit behaviour of visitors and thus potentially to ST.

Through strong messaging, role-modelling and persuasive communication, guides may be able to impact what visitors think, feel and do after their return home. *Credit*: Brian Alston (Uganda mountain gorilla guide)

As compared to the use of a communication campaign to which visitors were exposed for a full week, other studies report much lower levels of post-visit behaviour change. Stamation *et al.* (2007) found that six to eight months following a whale-watching tour, there was no overall change in the uptake of environmental behaviour among tour participants. In Smith *et al.*'s (2008) study, focusing on post-zoo visit behaviour, only a small number of visitors who said they intended to undertake a pro-conservation behaviour following a targeted communication campaign actually had done so in the three months after their visit. Changes that require effort such as volunteering are particularly unlikely (Zeppel & Muloin, 2008).

Inputs or Antecedents: How Tour Guiding Contributes to Sustainability

As noted at the outset of this chapter, there are many who like to claim that quality tour guiding is key to sustainability outcomes, but such a causal relationship is not easy to demonstrate. Studies cited in the foregoing section certainly provide illustrations of tour guiding practice – interpretive guiding, communicating/role-modelling/enforcing responsible behaviour and persuasive communication – leading to sustainability outcomes. Unfortunately, these studies tend not to explain *why* some guides and some tours achieve higher levels of ST outcomes than others, and the precise variables and antecedents to ST outcomes are unclear. For example, Littlefair and Buckley (2008) note that while their research was innovative in observing actual on-site behaviour and the environmental damage that resulted from it, theirs and the other studies cited here have not investigated theory-based interventions, and thus have fallen short of explaining these ST outcomes. Nor has research ascertained the extent and pathways by which tour guiding improves the economic viability and competitiveness of a business, local community or destination, or the social and cultural benefits to local communities and regions.

What is needed is an examination of what constitutes quality tour guiding in relation to various ST outcomes. The interpretation literature is rich with the principles or fundamentals of good interpretation, as discussed in Chapter 3. However, because of the challenges of isolating individual tour guiding techniques and practices (Skibins *et al.*, 2012), the degree to which a guide's delivery of 'good' interpretation actually enhances a visitor's experience, let alone contributes to sustainability, is much harder to demonstrate. How can one judge Guide A's tour to be more enjoyable than Guide B, for example, or more relevant and, even if this can be done, can a researcher then conclude that a sustainable outcome such as improved understanding, a positive attitude towards conservation or a commitment to undertake pro-environmental behaviour is attributable to any one or a combination of techniques used by Guide A and not by Guide B?

Thus, research is needed that isolates the tour guiding variables that potentially influence ST outcomes. For example, a combination of verbal appeals and role-modelling may help resolve problems of overuse, user conflict and depreciative behaviour (Littlefair, 2003; Marion & Reid, 2007). The impacts of an interpretive message on behavioural change may also be improved by controlling the timing of the message delivery and using repetition and reinforcement (Marion & Reid, 2007). Skibins *et al.* (2012) bring together a considerable number of relevant published studies to date, to present a meta-analysis of the effects of guided and non-guided interpretation 'best practices' on sustainability outcomes. Their findings suggest, for example, that actively engaging visitors using messages that focus on local resources and places, and conveying actions as being easy and beneficial for visitors to do were all associated with a positive influence on both self-reported intention to change behaviour and either self-reported or observed behaviour. However, the studies on which their meta-analysis is based cover a wide range of interpretive media and techniques, with only a small number of studies based on verbal communication by a guide or interpreter.

While a researcher can use the results of such studies to select a particular aspect of a guide's content or a specific guiding technique on which to focus, and hypothesise that it causes a particular ST outcome, ways need to be found to test such hypotheses without compromising the visitor experience. As Weiler and Kim (2011) note, a major challenge relates to the ethics of asking a tourism operator to intentionally deliver what may be inferior tour guiding to some visitors in order to assess its impacts.

Thus, even though (as outlined in the previous section) some progress has been made in measuring sustainability outcomes in the context of guided tours, such as understanding, appreciation, appropriate on-site behaviour, post-visit pro-environmental attitudes and conservation behaviours, there is still a dearth of research evidence that these outcomes are a result of specific tour guiding practices. Hu and Wall (2012: 84) bravely put forward five principles for interpretive guiding 'by which tour guides can contribute to the sustainable development of destination areas'. However, these are based on observations of industry practice and what the academic literature suggests is potentially good practice. Research demonstrating that these principles and practices do in fact foster sustainability is needed before they can be advocated as a foundation for the practice of tour guiding in relation to sustainability. Moreover, few tour guides have even a basic understanding or awareness of how to evaluate their own practice in a way that might facilitate improvement in relation to sustainability (or other) outcomes, and thus what guides do continues to be based on trial and error, intuition and anecdotal evidence as to what is working and what is not. Skibins *et al.* (2012) have made a considerable contribution in this regard, advancing understanding of how interpretation principles achieve a range of outcomes, including sustainability outcomes as outlined in this chapter. The jury is still out with respect to how and to what extent other tour guiding practices such as role-modelling, minimal impact guiding, monitoring visitor behaviour and group management practices contribute to sustainable outcomes.

Implications for Research

This chapter has brought together a range of empirical research on tour guiding's contributions to sustainability that had previously been reported only in a piecemeal fashion. In doing so, notable research gaps have been uncovered relating to guides' contributions to sustainability, especially with respect to sociocultural and economic sustainability. For example, there seems to be no research linking what guides say and do on their tours and visitors' post-visit attitudes and behaviours towards heritage and culture. There is a growing body of research on the links between a guide's environmental messages and role-modelling and visitors' pro-environmental attitudes and behaviour. Overall, however, more objective, verifiable evidence is needed in order to assess and explain the contributions of tour guiding to sustainability outcomes.

Weiler and Kim (2011) further the effort of progressing this area of research by articulating a research agenda for tour guiding and sustainability, including presenting a number of theories that can be and have been used to explain and strengthen the sustainable outcomes of tour guiding. They present a framework as a basis for future research directions that includes relevant theories, research designs and approaches. One avenue for further research noted by Weiler and Kim (2011) is the examination of communication impacts and outcomes across different target markets and cultures. There is considerable potential for misunderstanding tour guiding communication with respect to appropriate environmental and cultural behaviour, regardless of whether this is communicated verbally or non-verbally and whether or not it is in the native language of the visitor. Moreover, the diversity of visitors' ethnic and cultural backgrounds in many tour guiding contexts makes it difficult to control mediating variables and identify the direct impacts of tour guiding on visitor behaviour. In particular, there is a need for research that examines how sustainable tour guiding might vary for developing versus developed countries and for differing host populations, cultures and destinations.

The extent and pathways by which interpretive guiding improves the economic viability and competitiveness of a business, local community or destination and the social and cultural benefits to local communities and regions have not been investigated. Indeed the antecedents of, and pathways by which, guiding contributes to any aspect of sustainability – that is, why and how guiding does and does not foster specific sustainable outcomes – have been virtually ignored in research on tour guiding.

Finally, longitudinal research, or at least a longer time frame in which to measure cause and effect, is needed, as some of the impacts that are most important to sustainability may require an incubation period. Of course, as the period of time increases, the potential for extraneous variables such as exposure to additional communication from external sources grows, confounding the findings of any one individual study.

Implications for Tour Guiding Practice

The lack of evidence of links between tour guiding and sustainability outcomes reinforces the stereotype and resulting complacency with which much of the industry regards tour guides and guiding. It is in the interests of guides to try to collect such evidence and build up a picture of these relationships. However, few guides and operators have a sufficient understanding of research to assess the outcomes of their operations. Tour guides may also lack sufficient knowledge and training about sustainability and their potential role as agents of sustainability.

Sustainability needs to be embedded in tour guide training, recruitment and remuneration practices, and other employment benefits in order to attract and retain guides who can contribute to the outcomes discussed in this chapter (see Chapter 6). Outside of the ecotourism sector, such efforts are generally lacking.

Huang and Weiler (2010), in an isolated investigation of how quality assurance processes in tour guiding can foster sustainability, note the strengths and limitations of China's regulatory and licensing system for tour guiding. The country is progressive in implementing compulsory training, examinations, licensing and registration for practicing tour guides, all of which lay the groundwork for enforcing minimum tour guiding standards across the industry (see Chapter 7). China also has an award system for excellence in guiding. However, the emphasis in all of these initiatives tends to be on knowledge, skills and practices that are relatively easily measured, observed and enforced. As a result, sustainability outcomes such as the delivery of environmentally and socially responsible messages and the monitoring and mediating of visitor behaviour tend to be neglected.

Even in the ecotourism sector, examples of quality assurance schemes that attempt to both promote minimum tour guiding standards in relation to sustainability (such as Australia's EcoGuide Program) and reward excellence (such as Australia's National EcoGuide Award) are the exception rather than the rule (see Chapter 7). The place in which the links between tour guiding and sustainability outcomes is perhaps most evident is in the training of nature and ecotour guides. Black and Weiler (2005), Yamada (2011), Pereira and Mykletun (2012) and others have argued for ecotour guide training content to emphasise knowledge and skills relating to environmental and cultural sustainability, including the delivery of content aimed at influencing visitor attitudes and behaviour. Similarly, Dioko and Unakul (2005) argue that training local people to be ecotour guides is one avenue for local communities to gain economic, conservation and social benefits from ecotourism. Based on previous models for ecotour tour guide training, Skanavis and Giannoulis (2009) propose a training model for ecotour guides in Greece to address SD issues.

That said, there are few examples in the literature of existing training initiatives that focus explicitly and successfully on the development of knowledge and skills associated with all three dimensions discussed in this chapter. Kohl's (2007) theoretically informed programme for training ecotour guides in Central and South America is perhaps the best example of training with a focus on sustainability outcomes, including guides' contribution to improving the environmental, cultural and social conditions of a destination. The approach involves a deep engagement with capacity building, a focus on local priorities and values and an ongoing (rather than one-off) time commitment to training. By helping guides better understand conservation, conservation issues and their role in these, understanding and appreciation are leveraged to promote visitor actions that are both conservation related (e.g. donations of money and time) and business related (e.g. word-of-mouth advertising, making sustainable purchases).

Chapter Summary

This chapter has examined the guide's contribution to sustainability in relation to the four pillars of economic, social, cultural and environmental sustainability. The following is a summary of some of the key findings in this body of literature.

Viewing tour guiding through the lens of sustainability is of benefit to destinations and all stakeholders, including visitors themselves. More travellers are now looking for experiences that are not only enjoyable and memorable but are meaningful; that is, experiences that make a difference in their own lives and that help sustain the host environments and communities they visit. In addition to meeting the expectations of such visitors, tour guides can contribute to sustainability by enhancing visitors' understanding and valuing of sites, communities, cultures and environments, and by positively influencing their en route and on-site behaviour.

There is less evidence that tour guides can foster visitors' post-visit, pro-environmental and pro-conservation attitudes and behaviours. There is very little evidence that tour guides influence the social and cultural sustainability of destinations, although employing local guides has been found to be effective in some cases in enhancing positive economic, social and cultural impacts.

The strongest evidence between tour guiding and sustainability has been in the context of nature-based and ecotour guiding, and therefore the links between tour guiding and environmental sustainability have been more firmly established than the links between tour guiding and the other three pillars of sustainability. Finally, the antecedents of, and pathways by which, particular tour guiding practices contribute to the sustainability of sites, businesses, communities and destinations have been theorised but have yet to be demonstrated. There is enthusiasm for, but little evidence of, using training and quality assurance schemes to enhance the links between tour guiding and sustainability.

Harnessing the potential power of tour guiding for sustainability outcomes requires continued efforts to explain and improve how and why tour guides are able to influence visitors' thoughts, feelings and actions. The fact that the jury is very much still 'out' with respect to exactly how and to what extent tour guides and guiding contribute to sustainability is not beneficial for either tour guiding or for tourism generally. Individual guides are robbed of a sense of importance and meaning in what they do, which may well work against their valuing of themselves, their work and their commitment to guiding as a career. In addition, initiatives to embed sustainability outcomes into tour guiding practice, quality assurance and training, particularly outside of the ecotourism sector, appear to be thin on the ground. Much more attention needs to be given to both research and industry practice, particularly beyond the nature-based and ecotourism contexts, before the contribution of tour guiding to sustainability can be elevated from rhetoric to reality.

Up to this point the contributions of tour guiding to visitor satisfaction, including the guide's communication, interpretation, role-modelling and delivery of sustainability messages, have been implied but not specifically reported. Research on the influence of a tour guide's performance on visitor satisfaction, while touched on in this and earlier chapters, is the focus of Chapter 5.

Key references

(1) Weiler, B. and Kim, A.K. (2011) Tour guides as agents of sustainability: Rhetoric, reality and implications for research. *Tourism Recreation Research* 36 (2), 113–125.
(2) Henning, G.K. (2008) The guided hike in Banff National Park. A hermeneutical performance. *Journal of Sustainable Tourism* 16 (2), 182–196.
(3) Jensen, O. (2010) Social mediation in remote developing world tourism locations – the significance of social ties between local guides and host communities in sustainable tourism development. *Journal of Sustainable Tourism* 18 (5), 615–633.
(4) Powell, R.B. and Ham, S.H. (2008) Can ecotourism interpretation really lead to pro-conservation knowledge, attitudes and behaviour? Evidence from the Galapagos Islands. *Journal of Sustainable Tourism* 16 (4), 467–489.

(5) Pereira, E.M. and Mykletun, R.J. (2012) Guides as contributors to sustainable tourism? A case study from the Amazon. *Scandinavian Journal of Hospitality and Tourism* 12 (1), 74–94.

(6) Ormsby, A. and Mannle, K. (2006) Ecotourism benefits and the role of local guides at Masoala National Park, Madagascar. *Journal of Sustainable Tourism* 14 (3), 271–287.

5 Visitor Expectations of and Satisfaction with Tour Guides and Guiding Services

There is a growing body of literature on the influence of tour guide performance on visitor/tourist satisfaction (visitor satisfaction). This is in response to government agencies and the tourism industry increasingly recognising the pivotal role of tour guides (Ap & Wong, 2001; Bowie & Chang, 2005, 2006; Huang *et al.*, 2010; Mak *et al.*, 2011), as well as their performance, potentially affecting visitor satisfaction, benefitting tourism operators and being critical to the image of the destination they represent (Aloudat, 2010; Ap & Wong, 2001; Huang *et al.*, 2010; Mak *et al.*, 2011). In contrast to other types of tourism and hospitality services, it is the intense and extended nature of the client contact that differentiates tour guiding from these other services.

Early studies exploring the relationship between tour guide performance and visitor satisfaction emanated mainly from European researchers in the context of package tours to Europe and the United States, while the more recent literature in this area has come from researchers based in Chinese-speaking countries, mainly involving Chinese-speaking guides and tour groups. While both sets of studies provide useful data, in most cases their generalisability to other cultural and guiding contexts is largely unknown. However, at least in the contexts in which the studies have been carried out, the research provides strong evidence that the tour guide's performance has a positive effect on satisfaction and, to a lesser extent, the likelihood of repeat visits. The influence of trained guides and more experienced guides on higher levels of visitor satisfaction in particular has important implications for the tourism industry.

Research shows that tour guide performance has a positive effect on visitor satisfaction. *Credit*: Betty Weiler (Okanagan Vineyard, Canada)

The purpose of this chapter is to present an overview of the research on the influence of tour guide performance on visitor satisfaction as perceived by visitors (including tourists), guides and operators. This chapter begins with a brief overview of the key concepts of satisfaction, service quality and service performance, and how researchers have measured the influence of tour guide performance on visitor satisfaction. This is followed by two sections that focus on early and more recent studies that explore the influence of tour guide performance on visitor satisfaction, service quality and service performance. Sub-themes that are discussed include the influence of tour guide performance on other visitor behaviours, such as shopping, and in the context of specialised nature-based tours.

Service Quality, Service Performance and Satisfaction and Their Application to Tourism

The concepts of service quality and customer satisfaction have been widely researched in fields such as consumer behaviour and marketing, as well as tourism and tour guiding (Baker & Crompton, 2000; Huang *et al.*, 2010). This section provides a brief overview of these concepts as they have been applied to the broader tourism and marketing literature. One of the most popular and widely applied theories on service quality is the SERVQUAL model (Parasuraman *et al.*, 1985, 1988) that conceptualises service quality as a construct with five dimensions (tangibles, reliability, responsiveness, assurance and empathy). This model implies the multiple-attribute nature of service quality that has been applied in both service quality and satisfaction studies in tourism and hospitality with the majority of the dimensions focusing on service personnel performance. According to Parasuraman *et al.* (1988), *service quality* is conceptualised as the gap between customer expectation and perception of performance of a multitude of service attributes. *Service performance* is a similar concept to service quality and is often used as a good proxy for service quality. *Customer satisfaction* is also regarded as the result of the comparison of service performance with expectation (Barsky, 1992). This gap between expectation and perception, conceptualised as the expectancy disconfirmation mode, derives from the general consumer behaviour and satisfaction literature and has been widely applied in tourist satisfaction studies (Oliver, 1980). The model proposes that the difference between expectation and perception determines the level of satisfaction (Barsky, 1992; Oliver, 1980). However, this model has been criticised by some in the literature as an unreliable measure of satisfaction (Johns *et al.*, 2004). The attribution model has also been frequently applied in studies of tourist satisfaction in a range of settings, especially destination services (e.g. Hsu, 2000). For example, Hsu (2003) found that the main determinants of tourist satisfaction among mature motor coach travellers were a flexible schedule, the tour guide, price and value.

Despite the similarities between the two concepts of service quality and satisfaction, some researchers make a distinction between them (Parasuraman *et al.*, 1994). In the more recent literature, the concept of service quality is generally accepted as one, but not the only, determinant of satisfaction (Heung *et al.*, 2002). In other studies on service industries (Heung *et al.*, 2002), it is widely accepted that service quality dimensions affect satisfaction, yet this is a relatively underexplored area of research in tour guiding.

Customer satisfaction is a concept that is often associated with service quality both conceptually and methodologically and is considered to be one of the key constructs in visitor behaviour studies and many other associated studies (Bowen & Clarke, 2002). Although there are many definitions of customer satisfaction, it can be regarded as having both emotional and cognitive components. More recently, Bowen and Clarke (2002) and Chang (2006: 98) note that satisfaction 'is a psychological concept and an attitude based on the needs and desires for goods and services, which change constantly at multiple levels during service encounters'. The cognitive–affective model represents an integrated approach that acknowledges both cognitive and affective inputs that appear to explain the tourist satisfaction process and has been applied by a number of researchers (Bosque & Martin, 2008; Huang *et al.*, in press). The three-factor satisfaction model (Füller & Matzler, 2008) proposes that satisfiers, dissatisfiers and hybrid factors contribute differently to overall satisfaction. Dissatisfiers are minimum requirements that lead to dissatisfaction if not fulfilled but do not lead to visitor satisfaction if fulfilled, such as keeping to the itinerary. Satisfiers are unexpected and surprise the client (such as firsthand contact with local people), increasing satisfaction; however, they do not lead to dissatisfaction if not delivered. Hybrid factors lead to satisfaction if performance is high and dissatisfaction if performance is low, and are usually connected to the client's explicit needs and desires.

The broad service quality, performance and satisfaction literature indicates that researchers have tended to use both attribute-based and global satisfaction concepts. The former approach allows an in-depth understanding of satisfaction in relation to key service attributes and dimensions. In contrast, researchers generally use a global concept of satisfaction when they are studying relationships between satisfaction and dependent variables.

The next section looks in detail at a range of studies that have sought to explore the relationship between tour guide performance and visitor satisfaction.

An Overview of Research on Tour Guide Performance and Visitor Satisfaction

Temporally, geographically and methodologically, the tour guiding performance literature to date can be broadly divided into two categories. Early studies that explored the relationship between visitor satisfaction and guide performance were carried out between 1980 and the late 1990s by European researchers, mainly with international package tours using a global measure of visitor satisfaction with the tour guide's performance. In contrast, the second group of studies was undertaken between 2001 and 2012 by Chinese researchers with Chinese-speaking tour groups and tour guides using quantitative methodologies and established frameworks to measure satisfaction on a number of dimensions. These include: satisfaction with the *tour guiding service*, referring to visitors' evaluations of various services (e.g. commentary, interpretation) provided by the tour guides at a destination and what could be termed tour guide performance; satisfaction with *tour services*, referring to visitors' evaluations of various non-guided service components (e.g. itinerary, transportation, hotel and meal arrangements, accommodation) provided by ground tourism operators at a destination; and satisfaction with the *overall tour experience*, referring to visitors' evaluations of their personal experiences on their visit to the destination (Huang *et al.*, 2010). Other Chinese-based studies have explored specific tour guide attributes or factors that influence satisfaction such as interpretive skills and intercultural communication skills (see Chapter 3).

Researchers in this field have used a range of methodological paradigms and data collection methods to study the relationship between tour guide performance and visitor satisfaction. The majority of studies used a quantitative approach, while some adopted a qualitative approach and several applied a mixed methods approach. The majority of studies have collected data from tour group participants with a few exceptions where the perceptions of other tour guiding stakeholders have been sought (Aloudat, 2010; Chang, 2006; Chang & Chiu, 2008). Methods used to collect data have included self-administered questionnaire surveys, focus groups, interviews, participant observation, internet discussions and pre- and post-tour surveys. Participant observation has been used in many studies (Bowie & Chang, 2005; Chang, 2006; Mossberg, 1995). For example, Bowen (2001) used researcher participant observation of a long-haul tour, while Arnould and Price (1993) found that participant observation data enriched the interpretation of their qualitative results of white-water rafting guides' performance. Many studies have used tour group self-completed questionnaires, such as Geva and Goldman (1991), Mossberg (1995) and Huang et al. (in press), while a few studies have applied pre- and post-tour trip self-administered questionnaires to tourists, such as Hughes (1991) who studied a boat cruise to Palm Island in North Queensland, Australia.

Visitor Satisfaction with Guided Versus Non-guided Experiences

Studies that compare visitor satisfaction between a guided versus a non-guided visitor experience have received limited attention, probably because they are generally difficult to operationalise in the field both ethically and practically, yet they offer many insights. One of the few examples is a study by Morgan and Dong (2008) that measured passenger satisfaction by comparing the expectations and outcomes of interpretive programmes on two Amtrak trains in the US Midwest. Using a quasi-experimental design with a control group and a 'treatment' group, they compared visitors who were exposed to an interpreter/guided experience with those who were not. The majority of the group that had a guide felt very satisfied with the experience and expressed a high degree of satisfaction with the presentation, including interpreter characteristics, message quality and programme benefits.

While not comparing a guided versus a non-guided experience as such, an early study by Moscardo and Woods (1998) surveyed and observed visitors at Skyrail in the World Heritage rainforest of North Queensland, Australia, to determine how satisfied they were with the guided interpretation compared to the non-personal interpretation such as signs. Using a pre- and post-visit questionnaire survey and observation of the attracting power of the interpretive component of the visitor experience, they found that the interactions with the guides were highly rated by visitors and they made a significant contribution to visitors' overall satisfaction with their Skyrail visit.

Satisfaction is enhanced by getting the group involved in activities and encouraging interaction within the group. *Credit*: Sovereign Hill Museum Association (Chinese tour guide, Sovereign Hill Outdoor Museum, Ballarat Australia)

The impact of specific interpretive components of a tour guide's performance on satisfaction has been the subject of relatively few studies, which is surprising given the importance placed on the interpreter role in the study of guide roles (see Chapter 2). Interpretation by tour guides has been found to positively influence visitor satisfaction and behavioural intention in a number of different tourism settings (Ham & Weiler, 2003, 2007; Huang *et al.*, 2010; Skibins *et al.*, 2012), though this is largely based on self-assessment by visitors and rarely tested by, for example, comparing satisfaction levels of groups exposed to high-quality interpretation versus little or no interpretation, let alone different styles of interpretation by guides (Skibins et al., 2012). The importance of best practice interpretation on visitor satisfaction and other visitor outcomes was demonstrated in a recent paper by Skibins et al. (2012), who carried out a meta-analysis of studies investigating the influence of interpretive best practices on six visitor outcomes including visitor satisfaction. A meta-analysis is viewed as a method that overcomes the contextual limitations of individual studies. Of all the studies, 57% described first-person (guided) interpretive activities and 10% of all the studies sought to evaluate the effect of the interpretive programme on visitor satisfaction. Of the 11 times that satisfaction was evaluated at the programmatic level, 57 pairings with particular best practices were generated. Of those pairings, 88% were correlated with positive outcomes.

The Influence of Tour Guide Performance on Visitor Satisfaction: Early Studies

While the focus of Schmidt's (1979) sociological study of US city guides and Almagor's (1985) anthropological study of Tswana guides in the Okavango Delta was not specifically on the relationship between tour guide performance and visitor satisfaction, they represent some of the earliest studies that highlight the important role of the guide in visitor satisfaction. Lopez's (1980) study was the first to explicitly explore the relationship between tour guide performance, specifically the guide's leadership style, and tourist satisfaction. She established that travellers were more satisfied with their tour leader early in the tour when he or she adopted an authoritarian leadership style that provided a more structured environment with effective communication and emotional security. In contrast, the travellers preferred a more democratic leadership style later in the tour that created a freer relationship between the tour leader and the group members, was more flexible and encouraged participation in more unscheduled group activities. Based on these findings, Lopez then sought to investigate the effect of tour leader training on travellers' satisfaction with tour quality. One group of leaders was given eight hours of human relations group training and Lopez found that the travellers with those leaders were more satisfied with the leader on both the initial and latter parts of the tour compared to the leaders who did not receive any training. However, as Lopez points out, there are many variables that may have contributed to these findings, such as group composition, member characteristics and expectations, tour length and group cohesiveness.

It should also be noted that in both her studies (Lopez, 1980, 1981), the tour leaders were high school teachers of Spanish and the tour participants were high school students, indicating that her results may have limited generalisation to other guided tours involving professional, full-time tour guides.

In 1988, Whipple and Thach illustrated that the quality of the tour guide was the most important attribute of tour satisfaction and interest in another tour, the latter finding contrasting with the work of Geva and Goldman (1991) that followed three years later looking at 15 guided tours from Israel to Europe and the United States. Whipple and Thach found that while visitors rated the guide's performance as highly important in determining their satisfaction with their tour, this did not automatically translate into benefits for the tour company in terms of corporate image or repeat purchase intentions. Despite this finding, their study reveals that the guide's 'conduct' (relations with tour participants) and the guide's 'expertise' were the two most highly rated attributes of 15 tour attributes in terms of their importance to tour satisfaction.

A few years later, Mossberg (1995) carried out a study of Scandinavian charter tours to look at the importance of the tour leader's performance during the tour. He used a multi-attribute model with eight variables including reliability, the ability to handle complaints, willingness to take part at any time, ease of reach, being informative about manners and customs, being knowledgeable about sights, as well as pleasantness and helpfulness. He established that the tour leader is important to the tourists' perceptions and satisfaction of the whole tour and this depends on the tour leader's performance and characteristics, such as his or her work experience, skills and knowledge. In contrast to Lopez's (1980) findings, the tour leader's performance was a key factor in differentiating a tourism operator from its competitors, as his or her performance influenced the company's image, customer loyalty and word-of-mouth communication. This latter finding is supported in a recent study on emotional labour in guiding by Torland (2011a), where she noted that the emotional performance of guides can impact visitors' experiences and satisfaction and benefit the tourism operator, such as delivering increased profits, repeat visits and improved image, though she does not measure these in her study. In summary, researchers have found that the performance of tour guides/leaders can be important to visitors' perceptions and satisfaction with their tour experience, but that other situational variables such as time, place and reasons for joining a tour can also have an influence.

Tours and tour guiding are often culturally and context specific, limiting what can be generalised about tour guiding expectations and satisfaction to other tour guiding contexts. *Credit*: Rosemary Black (Cambodia tour guide)

The Influence of Tour Guide Performance on Visitor Satisfaction: Recent Studies

As already noted, more recent studies on the relationship between tour guide performance and visitor satisfaction have tended to originate from researchers located in China, Taiwan and Hong Kong, with studies focusing on package-based tours of Chinese-speaking tourists led by Chinese-speaking tour guides. These studies explore satisfaction with tour guide performance from a number of perspectives: satisfaction with the *tour guiding service*, satisfaction with the *tour services* provided by ground tourism operators at a destination, and satisfaction with the overall *tour experience* at a destination as well as specific tour guide attributes.

One of the earliest studies was Wong's (2001) investigation of international tourists' perceived satisfaction with the quality and service provided by local guides in Hong Kong. His study is important as it is one of the few studies that correlates tourist satisfaction responses with the demographic profiles of the respondents. Overall, the perceived satisfaction with the guides was 4.12 (on a five-point scale). The explanation of this rating aligns with the two-factor model of satisfaction: that some attributes lead to satisfaction while others create dissatisfaction, thus they were categorised by Wong (2001) into: *satisfying dimensions*: professional skills, customer relationship/empathy and communication; and *unsatisfying dimensions:* shopping/tipping, poor guide conduct, bad communication and poor customer relations. According to Wong (2001), the *satisfying dimensions* supported the previous literature on guide roles, key skills and service attributes found in other studies (for example Cohen, 1985; Geva & Goldman, 1991; Mossberg, 1995). He correlated and found a statistically significant relationship between the mean satisfaction level with the guide's service and performance and the demographic variables of age, educational level, annual household income levels, country of residence and purpose of visit, but not with gender. Of particular interest was the finding that tourists from Western countries were generally more satisfied with their Chinese guides than were tourists from mainland China. This is supported by the work of Huang *et al.* (2010) discussed later in the chapter. This finding raises the question of whether these culturally different markets have different expectations or if the guides and operators behave and interact differently with the two different markets.

Chan and Baum (2004) also sought to explore tour guide role performance and assess its impact on satisfaction. In their study tourists in Hong Kong were asked to assess their overall satisfaction with the tour guide's performance. Tour guide performance was conceptualised as three complementary, interactive behavioural dimensions including instrumental role behaviour, expressive role behaviour and customer-oriented role behaviour. Analysing their findings using role theory, the researchers found that instrumental role behaviour exerted the greatest influence on satisfaction. Specific forms of role behaviour that were important to the respondents were clear communication, getting them involved in activities and concern for customers' well-being. Their results confirmed those of previous researchers that tour guide performance is significantly correlated to visitor satisfaction (Hsu, 2000; Mossberg, 1995; Price *et al.*, 1995). The instrument they developed was both valid and reliable and could be used by future researchers and tourism operators to more fully understand tour guide performance.

A number of the more recent studies on tour guide performance have applied specific frameworks or models. For example, Zhang and Chow (2004) used the importance-performance analysis (IPA) model to assess the performance of Hong Kong's tour guides as perceived by mainland Chinese outbound visitors. The study did not seek to measure client satisfaction. The service quality attributes that ranked of high importance were punctuality, knowledge of the destination and ability to solve problems. Sense of humour, introducing visitors to reliable shops and informing visitors about the destination's customs were perceived as the least important attributes. The guides' performance was perceived as satisfactory in the aspects of punctuality, informing visitors of safety regulations, briefing them on their daily itinerary and politeness. Guides received low ratings for introducing visitors to reliable shops, informing visitors about local customs and their ability to solve problems, suggesting that these guides need additional training in these areas.

In contrast to many of the above studies that have adopted a quantitative approach, Bowie and Chang (2005) used a qualitative approach to identify variables related to tourist satisfaction during a guided package tour, including the role of the tour leader and the service performance by suppliers. Using participant observation during a mixed-nationality tour of Scandinavian destinations, they identified external and internal factors that put pressure on the tour leader. External factors were issues such as delayed flights, bad weather, lost luggage, illness and language obstacles. Internal factors primarily involved the tour leader's professional skills such as his or her character, personal experience and knowledge. Their study found that an inexperienced tour leader can potentially jeopardise tourists' satisfaction because of a lack of core knowledge and an inability to interpret and explain the destination's culture and customs, a result that supports Mossberg (1995). Bowie and Chang (2005) found that:

> ... customer satisfaction ... is the combination of, on the one hand, the service performance of the tour leader and the tour operator and, on the other, the customers' anticipation and perceptions of the vacation, their expectations prior to the tour, their attitudes and behaviour (past travel experience) and their perceptions of equity and unforeseeable events during service encounters. (Bowie & Chang, 2005: 317)

These findings align with the expectancy–disconfirmation theory outlined earlier in the chapter. Bowie and Chang (2005) suggest that satisfaction will be developed through confidence in the tour product and the leadership of the tour leader. The latter finding supports other studies that suggest that leadership is an important variable (Lopez, 1980; Pond, 1993). However, this study has some limitations as they conducted participant observation of only one tour group that could also have been influenced by the researchers' subjectivity. Another more recent qualitative study (Aloudat, 2010) using grounded theory that sought tour guides' views found that the guides consider that their performance is key to visitor satisfaction as well as to promoting their tourism operators and country to future visitors. These Jordanian guides thought that to be effective guides they needed product knowledge, language and communication skills, a sense of humour, empathy, moral responsibility and to be good listeners.

While most studies to date have used tourist or visitor surveys to assess tour guide performance, Chang (2006) used semi-structured interviews with managers of Taiwanese travel agencies and participant observation of one 10-day Taiwanese guided package tour in Italy, with follow-up, selected semi-structured telephone interviews with tour participants. In the context of a long-haul escorted group, he investigated the elements of a tour leader's service that affect satisfaction. Like many of the other studies, he also found that the tour leader played the most important role in determining the success of the tour. More specifically, the service attitude of the tour leader, such as interactions with tour participants, is sufficient to satisfy the tour participants; however, presentation skills will enhance their level of satisfaction. He also established that the performance of the tour leader was a key factor in influencing the return of customers – a finding that supports the work of Whipple and Thach (1988) and Mossberg (1995). As with other studies of Chinese-speaking tour guides (e.g. Chang & Chiu, 2008), Chang found that the tour guides' attitudes to tips negatively affected their performance. Like Bowie and Chang (2005), this study used participant observation of one tour and therefore the results may have limited generalisation.

In contrast to the many studies on Chinese-speaking tour guides based in Chinese-speaking countries, Weiler and Yu (2007) explored the cultural brokering or mediating of guides and its contribution to the visitor experience among Chinese-speaking tour guides based in Australia. They considered the three cultural mediation dimensions of access, understanding and encounters in servicing inbound Chinese visitors and found that the mediation of understanding – that is, the guide's brokering of a cognitive/affective dimension of the experience – contributed most to generating a memorable and satisfying visitor experience. They found that, consistent with the three-factor model described earlier in the chapter, some aspects of a tour guide's performance are particularly influential as satisfiers, for example when a guide provides a deep understanding of culture and lifestyle.

One of the few studies to measure tour guide performance as perceived by two culturally different respondent groups is the work of Huang *et al.* (2010). They investigated tour guide performance and its relationship with satisfaction in the context of package tours in Shanghai with foreign English-speaking tourists and Chinese tourists. The relationship between tour guide performance and tourist satisfaction was explored at three levels: satisfaction with tour guiding service, with services provided by ground tourism operators at a destination and with overall tour experience at a destination.

Their findings revealed that Chinese tourists consistently rated the performance of their Chinese-speaking guides lower than the foreign tourists did, a finding that supports Wong (2001). The authors theorise that this difference could be attributed to the cultural differences between the two groups, suggesting that Chinese people tend to view things from a broad perspective in contrast to Westerners who view things in a more analytical way. However, they also acknowledged that it could also be that the English-speaking guides actually performed better than the Chinese-speaking guides did. This may be because the Chinese guides are only required to achieve high school education and the English-speaking guides are required to obtain an undergraduate level of education.

In the case of the Chinese tourists, two factors explained 65% of the total variance in satisfaction: *intrapersonal servability* and *interpersonal servability*. *Intrapersonal servability* represents the guides' personal and innate readiness and capability to serve tourists, including their knowledge, empathy for tourists, passion for work, service attitude and health conditions. *Interpersonal servability* represents how the guides present themselves to others and their capability of working and communicating effectively with other tourism workers and tourists. In the case of the foreign, English-speaking tourist sample, four factors explained 68% of the total variance of the satisfaction items: professional competence, interpersonal skills and organisation, empathy and problem solving. According to the authors (Huang *et al.*, 2010), the factors identified for both groups were similar in intent. Tour guide performance largely determined tourist satisfaction: in the case of the Chinese sample 57% and with the English-speaking tourists 70%. Their findings are consistent with those of Chan's (2004) and Hsu's (2000), although Chan (2004) found that satisfaction with the tour guide determined satisfaction with tour experience, whereas Huang *et al.* (2010) found that there was no direct relationship between the two levels of satisfaction. Huang *et al.* also found that the path coefficient from satisfaction with tour services to satisfaction with tour experience for the English-speaking sample was much higher than the Chinese sample, suggesting that foreign tourists depend more on tourism operators' services when they are in a foreign country.

With both the Chinese and foreign tourist samples, Huang *et al.* (2010) established that tour guide performance had a significant positive effect on satisfaction with the guiding service, and that their satisfaction with the guiding service affected their satisfaction with tour services, and hence affected their satisfaction with the overall tour experience. However, a surprising result was that the effect of satisfaction with the guiding service on satisfaction with the overall tour experience was insignificant for the Chinese tourists. In the case of the foreign tourists, they found that satisfaction with the tourism operators' services had a very strong effect on satisfaction with the overall tour experience.

While these Chinese-based studies are providing very interesting and useful results, there are some limitations to these studies (Chang, 2012; Huang *et al.*, 2010) as they are based on the performance evaluation of specific city-based and/or Chinese-speaking tour guides and generally involve Chinese package tourists in specific cultural contexts and therefore may not be generalisable across other parts of China or other countries or destinations. However, opportunities exist to extend this work to larger studies with more participants and to different cultures and nationalities.

The Influence of Tour Guide Performance on Specific Visitor Behaviours

While the majority of recent studies have explored the influence of service attributes of tour guides on visitor satisfaction, some studies have also considered the effect of tour guide performance on specific visitor behaviours such as shopping. A number of studies (Chang, 2012; Chang & Chiu, 2008; Zhang & Chow, 2004) have sought to investigate the effect of tour guide performance on tourist shopping behaviour and its relationship to satisfaction. Zhang and Chow (2004) for example found that tourists did not perceive the Chinese guides to be honest or trustworthy in terms of introducing them to shops. Chang (2012) proposed a research framework that related tour guide performance to tourist shopping behaviour in which the roles of perceived *credibility trust*, perceived *benevolence trust*, tourist satisfaction and flow experience are examined in the model. A questionnaire was used with tourists from mainland China visiting Taiwan on package tours and the results supported previous research findings that tour guide performance significantly affects satisfaction (Huang *et al.*, 2010). In contrast to Hsu (2000), although guides performed reasonably well in most areas, areas for improvement were identified including punctuality, friendliness and knowledge of the destination. Chang also found that if tourists are satisfied with a tour guide's performance they are more likely to engage in shopping behaviour. This supports previous research that, in the context of tourist shopping, the performance of the tour guide is one of the key factors stimulating purchase intention (Tosun *et al.*, 2007). Specifically, shopping activity increases if the tourists are satisfied with the tour guide's performance and in response to their perceived trust in their guide. However, Chang found that it was only credibility trust and not benevolence trust that had a significant effect on the relationship between tour guide performance and satisfaction.

Tour guides' behaviour in relation to tipping, that is, actively prompting tourists to tip their guide, is also an issue raised in a number of tour guiding studies (Ap & Wong, 2001; Chang & Chui, 2008) and in some cases in how this behaviour impacts guide performance and visitor satisfaction with Chinese-speaking guides (Chang, 2006). Chang and Chiu's (2008) study specifically examined the factors that influence tour participants to tip the tour leader when participating in a guided package tour. From the literature on tipping, they suggest that tipping is related to a number of factors: social norms/customs, selfish economic considerations, perceived equity, guide service performance and company tipping policies. The tour leaders reported that the tourists' desire for good service was the key determinant for tipping, followed by the travel agencies' tipping policy, but there were mixed views among the tour leaders as to whether their service performance affected the tip amounts. Chang and Chiu (2008) suggest that this weak relationship may be due to pressure from travel agencies on customers to tip, avoiding psychological distress and maintaining equitable relationships with service providers and the feeling of empathy and compassion with service providers. In this study, tour leaders considered that building good relationships with the tour participants was one of the most important factors influencing the tip amount. A previous paper by Chang (2006) confirmed that the amount of tip given by tourists was mainly influenced by the tour leader's service performance.

Two recent and interesting studies have focused on the tour leader as the public face of tourism operators and thus the role they play as recipients of tourist complaints (service failure) and the complainants' level of satisfaction with the tour leader's actions with respect to service recovery. Raikkonen and Monto (2010) used an online survey with 456 individuals who had filed a written complaint about their tour with one Finnish tour company in one specific season. The majority of the complaints were in relation to the accommodation on the tour, with only 3% of the complaints caused by the services of the tour leader. However, in seeking a solution from the tour leader, 45% of respondents were not satisfied with the tour leader's response with respect to service recovery. Most complainants were satisfied that their tour leader encouraged them to inform them about service failure, they were polite, that they were approachable and that their apology was sincere. Tourists tended to be less satisfied with the tour leader's ability or willingness to provide an explanation for the service failure. The tourists who were dissatisfied with the tour leader's response to the service failure were statistically significantly more likely to be dissatisfied with their vacation overall than those who were satisfied with the tour leader's response to service failure.

The same authors (Monto & Raikkonen, 2010) undertook a second study that gathered complaint data from a different set of customers, in this case 84 complaints regarding a visit to Thailand, of which 56 were critical incidents related to tour leaders. Of the 84 complaints, only 17 primary complaints related to the service of the tour leader; however, they were the secondary cause of dissatisfaction for an additional 25 complaints. Nearly all of the complaints about the tour leaders related to communication issues: a perceived lack of information or help, provision of information, help being too slow, insufficient personal interaction and the tour leader's impatient or unfriendly behaviour. It is interesting to note that many of the complainants' satisfaction and dissatisfaction with the tour leader related to his or her communication competence (see Chapter 3).

Tour Guide Performance and Visitor Satisfaction in Nature-based Tourism

While most of the studies previously described have evaluated tour guide performance and its relationship to visitor satisfaction in the context of international package tours, a limited number of studies have looked at the relationship between guide performance and satisfaction among specialist guides in contexts such as nature-based tourism, ecotourism and adventure tourism. The findings from these studies will assist the burgeoning ecotourism and nature-based tourism sectors, but, like many of the other studies described above, have limited generalisabilty to other guiding contexts.

The literature profiling nature-based tourists suggests that visitor satisfaction among this segment is based on expectations of high-quality interpretation by knowledgeable guides, minimal impact messages, a sense of authenticity and quality customer service (Orams, 1996). This probably reflects the emergence of green consumerism and values (Weaver, 2001) and the desire for environmentally responsible guided tour experiences (Dolnicar, 2006).

One of the first published studies in the context of nature-based guided tours was Hughes' (1991) work that explored the factors responsible for visitors' satisfaction with one-day guided boat tours of Palm Island in North Queensland, Australia. She found that the guide's performance had a considerable impact on visitors' satisfaction with the guided tours, and the degree to which visitors' expectations were met determined their level of satisfaction with the overall tour. Three important components of guiding emerged from this study: first, the ability of the guide to effectively interact with the group; second, providing commentary of interest; and third, ensuring the smooth running of the tour. Hughes' findings suggest that connecting with the group, providing meaningful commentary and a participatory approach are important elements of effective interpretation and influenced visitors' satisfaction. The study findings appear to align with the principles of tourist–environmental fit theory whereby satisfaction increases as the ability of a holiday to satisfy an individual's needs and motives is maximised. In the case of commercial river guides, Roggenbuck et al. (1992) found that interpretive guide training increased the level of interpretation given to clients and enhanced visitor satisfaction (see Chapter 6).

Effective group interaction, commentary and a participatory approach can contribute to the smooth running of a tour and enhance visitor satisfaction. *Credit*: Ellen Bradley (Tag-along tour, Australia)

The literature in this area also indicates that, as well as influencing visitor satisfaction, having high-quality guides has advantages for nature-based and adventure tourism operators. Some research suggests that guides may provide a competitive edge for a company (Nature and Ecotourism Accreditation Program, 2000; Tourism Tasmania, 2000; Weiler & Ham, 2001), although this depends on whether the company markets itself as having high-quality guides. These studies indicate that providing interpretation and tour guides is an effective way of adding value to the experience, and operators are recognising that interpretation is a way of differentiating their product in the market. In the context of adventure tourism, Arnould *et al.* (1998) investigated river guides' performance and its effect on visitor satisfaction during white-water river rafting trips in the United States. They conceptualised three facets of river guide performance as contributing to visitor satisfaction: overall performance, authentic understanding and the provision of extras. They argued that the guides' communicative and performative roles are important in influencing the behaviour of the tour group and, like the nature-based and ecotour guides, may give a company a competitive advantage.

Finally, Ham and Weiler (2003) examined the theoretical underpinnings of 'quality' in nature-based interpretive guiding in the context of two nature-based cruises, one in Alaska and the other in the Galapagos Islands. Passengers were first asked to identify what types of defining ideal qualities they associated with their guides' performance and then assess the performance of their shore-based guides. They found that passengers both define and assess high-quality guides as those who are passionate, insightful, enjoyable, relevant and easy to follow. These attributes resulted in passenger satisfaction. Attributes that passengers identified as dissatisfiers included ending the tour too soon, being disjointed, providing too little information, providing no new insights and being too simplistic. These findings corroborate Skibins et al.'s (2012) meta-analysis of the links between effective interpretation and satisfaction.

Drawing on the analysis presented in this chapter, Table 5.1 provides a summary of published research on visitor expectations and satisfaction in the context of international package tours, nature-based tours and Chinese-speaking groups. The summary includes the temporal and geographic foci, the main study methods used and the aspects of guide performance and other variables that were investigated in each of these contexts.

Implications for Research

The results of these studies highlight many opportunities and avenues for future research on the influence of tour guide performance on visitor satisfaction. With a few exceptions, not many studies have explored the difference in satisfaction between guided and non-guided experiences and, while these may be difficult to operationalise, more work is required in this area.

The recent Chinese studies have drawn on a range of existing models and frameworks that could be applied in other contexts. Opportunities exist to explore the relationship between affective determinants and visitor satisfaction to further our understanding of the relationship between satisfaction and tour guide performance, particularly in non-Chinese-speaking countries. An under-researched aspect of tour guide performance is interpretation, which is surprising given the importance placed on it in the study of guide roles (see Chapter 2). There is considerable scope for research on the performance of other guide roles with a range of visitor segments and tourism contexts and the consequences in relation to visitor outcomes and satisfaction.

Further work is needed to identify antecedents for visitor satisfaction such as service quality, perceived value, motivation, positive and negative emotions and other aspects of a guide's performance. Very few studies have attempted to correlate the demographic profile of visitors with satisfaction responses, which would be very useful information for a range of visitor stakeholders. More studies could be undertaken on the guides themselves, such as the service characteristics and leadership styles of tour guides from different cultural groups and nationalities and which style(s) fits best for different cultural groups. Future research could also look at visitor satisfaction and different variables such as guides' education and training, knowledge and expertise, and specific aspects of communication competence (see Chapter 3).

Table 5.1 A summary of studies on visitor expectations of and satisfaction with tour guides and guiding

Study focus (type of tours)	Dates of publication	Main geographic location of research/ researchers	Main methods used	Elements of performance found to have a positive influence on satisfaction	Other elements investigated in the research
International package tours	1980–1990s	Europe	• Participant observation • Tourist self-completed questionnaires • Pre-/post-surveys	• Leadership style • Guide–client relationship • Guide's expertise • Guide's professional skills • Guide's emotional performance • Guide's work experience • Guide's knowledge	• Demographic variables • Cultural differences of clients • Impact on tour company reputation/satisfaction/ credibility • Purpose of visit, country of residence, educational level • Effect of training
Nature-based tours	1991–2012	Australia United States	• Self-completed questionnaires	• Interpretation/commentary • Minimal impact messages • Authenticity • Customer service • Effective interaction/ participation • Passion	• Effect of training • Impact on tourist behaviour (e.g. towards the environment)

| Chinese-speaking tour groups | 2000–2012 | China | • Self-completed questionnaires
• Participant observation
• Telephone interviews | • Professional presentation skills
• Customer relationship/empathy/concern for customers
• Clear communication
• Service attitude
• Passion
• Cultural mediation skills
• Problem-solving skills
• Guide's experience
• Leadership
• Politeness
• Briefings
• Knowledge of safety
• Knowledge of destination | • Demographic variables
• Cultural differences
• External factors e.g. bad weather
• Impact on tour experience versus satisfaction
• Impact on satisfaction with tour versus satisfaction with operator
• Impact on tourist behaviour (e.g. shopping, tipping, complaining) |

While many of these studies are culturally specific, they raise a number of questions around whether culturally different markets have different expectations of guides or if the guides and operators behave and interact differently with different markets. More studies are required on tour guide performance across a range of different cultural and ethnic contexts, with different cultural tour groups and culturally different tour guides, including the intercultural communication competence of guides. In addition, as previously mentioned, the majority of the studies to date have been carried out with package tour groups so there are opportunities to study different types of visitors (e.g. free and independent travellers) compared to package tourists, as they may have different perceptions of tour guide performance.

Implications for Tour Guiding Practice

A significant number of studies have now demonstrated that tour guide performance has a positive influence on visitor satisfaction. The implications of these study findings are significant for the tourism industry and the role of the tour guide should be acknowledged and rewarded accordingly.

Tourism operators and managers must recognise that tour guide performance directly influences visitor satisfaction with guiding services and may indirectly determine visitor satisfaction with tourism operators' services and with the overall tour experience. Tourism operators should also be aware that visitor satisfaction is a complex phenomenon and that different contextual settings can result in different determinants of visitor satisfaction and predictive power. Providing continuing professional training to their tour guides will help maintain high guide performance (see Chapter 6). At a broader level, government agencies may need to establish a quality performance scheme for guides to assess and enhance their knowledge, attitudes and interpersonal skills (see Chapter 7).

Many of these studies have identified specific tour guide attributes, qualities and skills that contribute to visitor satisfaction and dissatisfaction. These findings can be used to develop the content of tour guide training programmes and continuing professional development (see Chapter 6). An important finding from a number of studies is that trained guides result in higher levels of visitor satisfaction, and this is one finding that tourism operators and governments should heed. These studies can be used to inform tour guide training in terms of identifying and understanding the different expectations and cultural backgrounds of different cultural visitor groups and tour guides' skills, knowledge and attitudes that are relevant and appropriate to different cultural groups (see Chapter 6). For example, interpretive training resulted in, and increased the level of, interpretation given to visitors and enhanced visitor satisfaction. The delivery of effective interpretation can be enhanced using a range of strategies such as training, encouraging and supporting the use of interpretation and through incentives such as awards and bonuses.

Another important result is that some studies have shown that the use of more experienced guides increases visitor satisfaction, which suggests that tourism operators would be wise to employ these types of guides as well as provide good working conditions and a career path to encourage and support long-term employees. Less-experienced guides seem to lack core knowledge and the ability to interpret and explain the destination's culture and customs.

Many of the study findings have important implications for tour guides, tourism operators and tourist destinations. In particular, the recent studies that have been undertaken in Chinese-speaking countries with Chinese guides are especially useful given the changing global inbound tourist markets with increasing numbers of mainland Chinese now travelling to non-Chinese-speaking countries. The ethical practices and behaviour of guides were factors that influenced visitors' level of satisfaction, for example some studies found that tourists did not perceive their guides were honest or trustworthy in terms of introducing them to shops. These practices can be addressed through a number of strategies implemented by the relevant tourism boards that could monitor both tourism operators and guides, such as advertising all shopping activities clearly in tour brochures and advertisements and enforcing fixed tipping practices. These types of practices could be reduced or eliminated if a reward system, in both financial and non-financial terms, was established for tour guides to raise the professional image and social status of guides in Chinese-speaking countries such as Hong Kong. Quality assurance mechanisms (see Chapter 7) such as guide licensing with associated training could also be introduced so that inbound tourism operators would have to employ licensed tour guides. A monitoring system could be established to measure and monitor both tourism operators and tour guides to ensure their qualifications and professionalism. These and other quality assurance mechanisms aimed at ensuring minimum guiding standards and raising the awareness of the benefits of guiding are addressed in Chapter 7.

Chapter Summary

This chapter examined the influence of tour guide performance on visitor satisfaction as perceived by visitors, guides and operators. The following is a summary of some of the key findings in this body of literature. The research on the influence of tour guide performance on visitor satisfaction generally falls into two sets of studies. The first were studies undertaken in the 15 years between 1980 and 1995 conducted by

English-speaking researchers and are all based on tours to Europe or the United States with Western tour participants. The second were studies carried out between 2001 and 2012 with the majority emanating from Chinese-speaking researchers and tour guides and mainly based on Chinese-speaking visitors.

Most of these studies view guide performance from the visitor perspective, although a few studies have drawn on the guides' perspectives and perceptions and in some cases, those of tourism stakeholders. Researchers in this field have used a range of methodological paradigms and data collection methods to measure the influence of guide performance on visitor satisfaction; however, most have adopted a quantitative approach and data collection methods. As many of the study authors themselves note, however, much research on tour guiding is culturally and context specific and relies on studying only one tour with the consequent limited generalisability of the results to other tour guide contexts. While these study results are clear it is important to acknowledge that there are many other situational variables such as time, group composition, member characteristics and expectations, tour length, group cohesiveness, cultural differences, place and reasons for joining a tour that influence visitor perceptions and satisfaction.

There is a growing body of literature on the influence of tour guide performance on visitor satisfaction and to date all the studies indicate that tour guide performance has a positive effect on visitor satisfaction and in some studies this correlation is statistically significant. More recent studies have also demonstrated that satisfaction with the guiding service positively affects satisfaction with tour services and overall tour experience, although the latter finding is not consistent across all studies (Huang et al., 2010). Some studies show that the guide's performance influences the future return of customers, differentiates a tourism operator from its competitors and that customer loyalty and word-of-mouth communication can be used as competitive tools (Chang, 2006; Mossberg, 1995; Whipple & Thach, 1988). The work of Ap and Wong (2001) and Mak et al. (2011) also suggests that the guide's performance is critical to the image of the destination they represent. The destination's economy can also benefit, as some studies indicate that if visitors are satisfied with their guide they are more likely to engage in shopping.

Many of these studies have identified specific tour guide attributes, qualities and skills that contribute to visitor satisfaction; however, these results should be regarded cautiously. The findings from these studies indicate that the attributes that are highly regarded by visitors and influence satisfaction are: clear communication and knowledge of the destination; interpersonal skills, getting the group involved in activities and interactions with tour participants; interpretation, presentation skills and commentary; and professionalism in terms of punctuality, sense of responsibility, politeness, concern for the clients, organisation, empathy and problem solving. In the case of nature-based tourists, the attributes that affect visitor satisfaction are in some cases different from the generalist guides discussed above and include communication, interpretation, knowledge, minimal impact messages, a sense of authenticity, quality customer service, emphasis on learning, interacting with the group, interesting commentary, organisation, group management, activity skills and assistance for visitors. Hughes' (1991) study suggests that interpretation appears to act as a stimulant for interaction between visitors, guides and the setting, and that the effective aspects of a tour, such as connecting with the group, providing meaningful commentary and a participatory approach, are all important elements of effective interpretation (see Chapter 3). These findings are supported by Skibins *et al*.'s (2012) work on the importance of best practice interpretation on visitor satisfaction.

Many of the studies reviewed for this chapter also indicate areas where guides tend not to perform well and how that affects visitor satisfaction. Examples include problem solving, dealing with emergencies, honesty and ethical practices, guiding language, fostering a sense of humour, destination knowledge, punctuality and friendliness. Again, these findings should be viewed with some caution as many of the studies are culturally and context specific; however, they do provide some general directions for tour guiding practice and avenues for further studies. Finally, the findings reported in this chapter point to the need for guide training and education, the focus of the next chapter.

Key references

(1) Arnould, E.J. and Price, L.L. (1993) River magic: Extraordinary experience and the extended service encounter. *Journal of Consumer Research* 20 (1), 24–45.
(2) Bowie, D. and Chang, J.C. (2005) Tourist satisfaction. A view from a mixed international guided package tour. *Journal of Vacation Marketing* 11 (4), 303–322.
(3) Chang, J.C. (2006) Customer satisfaction with tour leaders' performance: A study of Taiwan's package tours. *Asia Pacific Journal of Tourism Research* 11 (1), 97–116.
(4) Ham, S.H. and Weiler, B. (2003) Toward a theory of quality in cruise-based interpretive guiding. *Journal of Interpretation Research* 7(2), 29–49.
(5) Huang, S., Hsu, C.H.C. and Chan, A. (2010) Tour guide performance and tourist satisfaction: A study of the package tours in Shanghai. *Journal of Hospitality & Tourism Research* 34 (1), 3–33.
(6) Morgan, M. and Dong, X.D. (2008) Measuring passenger satisfaction of interpretive programming on two Amtrak trains in the Midwest: Testing the expectancy disconfirmation theory. *Journal of Interpretation Research* 13 (2), 43–58.

6 Improving Tour Guide Performance Through Training and Education

As early as the 1960s (Smith, 1961), many authors have noted the lack of and need for adequate guide training and education to improve tour guide performance, raise guiding standards and advance professionalism (Ap & Wong, 2001; Brockelman & Dearden, 1990; Christie & Mason, 2003; de Kadt, 1979; Hughes, 1994; Mason & Christie, 2003; Pond, 1993; Weiler & Davis, 1993; Weiler *et al.*, 1997). More recently, changes in the tourism industry have put increasing emphasis on having trained guides: firstly, the tourism industry is evolving from a service-based economy to an experience-based economy; secondly, visitors are now well informed, more interested and have high expectations of their guides; and finally, tour guides are now required to have not only the ability to convey factual information but other skills such as interpretation and intercultural skills, the ability to contextualise information and the transmission of emotion.

The desire for and benefits of tour guide training and education occur at the individual, operator and industry levels. *Credit*: Betty Weiler (Tonga tour guide training)

As discussed in Chapter 2, tour guides are expected to perform a number of diverse roles (Black *et al.*, 2001; Black & Weiler, 2005; Cohen, 1985; Weiler & Ham, 2001), and many researchers have argued that training and education are critical to acquiring knowledge and skills, such as communication, interpretation and intercultural communication, to perform a diversity of roles such as interpretation and mediation between the local community and visitors (de Kadt, 1979; Gurung *et al.*, 1996). Roles such as ensuring the safety, comfort and health of visitors are also generally underpinned by training as discussed in Chapter 2. A range of mechanisms can be used to achieve quality assurance outcomes, such as raising an awareness and appreciation of the positive impacts of guiding, enforcing minimum standards and recognising and rewarding advanced levels of performance.

This chapter examines training, education and professional development as tools for quality assurance and explores the strengths and weaknesses of different tour guide training approaches in both developed and developing countries. Other quality assurance mechanisms such as professional certification and licensing are discussed in Chapter 7. This chapter begins with a discussion of the need for guide training, including the barriers to accessing training and the consequences of inadequate training. This is followed by a discussion of the advantages and disadvantages of guide training and education as a quality assurance mechanism, with descriptions and explorations of tour guide training approaches in both developed and developing countries. More specific aspects of guide training and education are then discussed, including training and sustainability, the content of training programmes and the development of training materials. The chapter concludes with a review of studies that have focused on the evaluation of tour guide training.

Lack of, and Barriers to, Training and the Consequences of Inadequate Training

Many guides in the past – as well as today – do not have any formal education or training and learn through experience on the job. According to Carmody (2013), some tour companies inadvertently fail to train their guides adequately and guides are often just given a book or manual to read or they accompany another guide for a few hours before guiding on their own (Eberts *et al.*, 1997). Carmody also found that there is little transfer of knowledge and skills between staff on how to best deliver information and environmental messages (Metry, 2000).

In some instances, tour guides' lack of training may reflect their lack of awareness of or access to information on training and training resources because of their remote work location or not being a member of a tour guide association. A report by Social Change Media (1995) found that Australian ecotourism operators and ecotour guides (Social Change Media, 1995) lacked the knowledge to access information on ecotourism training and training resources. Other guides may also be excluded from programmes based on their ethnicity or nationality (Bowman, 1992; Sizer, 1999). In Machu Picchu, Peru, McGrath (2003) noted that local indigenous people do not currently participate in the tourism industry and are not supported to attend tour guide training programmes. In some cases, such as in Sri Lanka, even though guide training exists many informal guides are not trained (Crick, 1992).

Research has highlighted problems and issues associated with untrained guides (Ap & Wong, 2001; Mak et al., 2011; Pond, 1993) that can affect the guides themselves, the visitors, tourism operators and a country's tourism industry and image (see Table 6.1). Lack of training can result in unethical guiding practices, poor guide performance, negative publicity towards the guiding profession, damage to the destination's image (Ap & Wong, 2001; Mak et al., 2011) and the quality of visitors' experience and level of satisfaction (Department of Resources, Energy and Tourism [DRET], 2013; Ham & Weiler, 2003; Lopez, 1981; Roggenbuck et al., 1992). Guides themselves have identified how the lack of training can affect them, including low self-esteem, lack of recognition as a professional, lack of rewards and incentives, job burnout and poor quality service (Ap & Wong, 2001; Kong et al., 2009; Pond, 1993).

Unfortunately, in many cases, employers do not require trained guides (Pond, 1993; Weiler & Ham, 2001) and some guides argue that the meagre opportunities for income and advancement do not justify the time and cost required to invest in training. According to Pond (1993), many tourism operators fail to acknowledge the time that guides invest in self-education and training and do not compensate or support guide training. However, she suggests that this is slowly changing and some operators now have graduated pay scales and increased benefits for suitably trained guides.

Table 6.1 Consequences of poor or inadequate training highlighted in the tour guiding literature

	Consequences for		
	Visitors	Guides	Operators/industry
Poor guiding performance/service	✓		✓
Unethical guiding practices	✓		✓
Poor quality of visitor experience	✓		✓
Low visitor satisfaction	✓		✓
Low guide self-esteem		✓	
Lack of recognition, rewards and incentives		✓	
Job burnout		✓	✓
Negative publicity towards the guiding profession		✓	✓
Damage to the destination image			✓

Pond suggests that until there is a greater recognition and opportunity for guide training, the guiding industry will remain substandard, poor quality, unprofessional and unethical.

In Australia, for example (DRET, 2013), there are concerns about the supply and quality of untrained Mandarin-speaking tour guides servicing the Australian inbound tourism industry. Often, the guides are not trained and do not have the necessary product knowledge of Australia, reducing the quality of the Chinese visitors' experience. The government plans to address these issues through training and incentives to improve the supply and use of quality guides through non-legislative measures as has been done in New Zealand. In the latter country, guides must show evidence that they have met the criteria for approval, which includes guiding experience, English and Chinese language qualifications and completion of the specified training. One Australian regional tourism organisation, Tourism Tropical North Queensland, has already introduced a training initiative for Chinese-speaking tour guides working for that region's tourism operators. The training aims to provide Chinese-speaking guides with destination information to enable them to speak knowledgeably about the region while guiding Chinese tour groups (DRET, 2013).

The Desire for Training and the Advantages and Disadvantages of Training and Education as a Quality Assurance Mechanism

The tour guiding literature indicates that the desire for training is coming from a range of tourism stakeholders, including the guides themselves, professional tour guide associations, tourism operators, government agencies and the tourism industry (Ap & Wong, 2001; El-Sharkawy, 2007; Mak et al., 2011). Mak et al. (2011) interviewed tour guiding stakeholders about guides in Hong Kong and Macau. Their results indicate that training was seen as an important means of improving guiding standards and professionalism among guides in both countries. Stakeholders indicated that effective training needed to be adequate, appropriate and consistent, and should be a collaborative endeavour between industry and educational institutions.

A number of country-specific studies in Costa Rica (Jacobson & Robles, 1992), Nepal (Gurung et al., 1996), Hong Kong and Macau (Ap & Wong, 2001; Mak et al., 2011) and China (Kong et al., 2009) have demonstrated that guides themselves have expressed the desire for some or more training to improve their performance and knowledge, raise guiding standards and increase the recognition of their profession. In a comprehensive study of tour guides in Hong Kong, Ap and Wong (2001) found that guides wanted training to improve their standards of service and product knowledge.

El-Sharkawy (2007) found a similar situation among Egyptian tour guides who, despite being licenced, lack the relevant education and knowledge to perform effectively. He studied the effect that this had on their recognition as a professional tour guide by the relevant tourism authority. He found that while most Egyptian guides did their own research for their tours or learnt from other experienced guides, they lacked formal training and suggested that tour guiding courses should be delivered consistently across educational institutions.

According to Black and Weiler (2005), the advantages of training and education as quality assurance mechanisms are that they offer anyone the opportunity to take up employment as a guide, and that existing guides can upgrade their skills and knowledge. In addition, the provision of different levels of training can provide guides with the incentive to further their skills and knowledge and to achieve higher standards and improved rewards and recognition. This may result in many more guides continuing to improve their levels of qualifications, thereby improving the standards across the industry (Mak et al., 2011; Whinney, 1996). Training may also be a prerequisite to, or be required for, licensing or professional certification.

However, there are a number of disadvantages to training and education. First, the delivery of training may vary across a country and between educational institutions. Second, training may set minimum standards only. For example, a common criticism of competency-based training, compared to grading systems, is that since students are only assessed as competent/not yet competent there is no incentive to strive for excellence. Third, training opportunities may be less accessible to guides or students living in remote locations, such as ecotour guides. Lastly, prerequisites may be required to enter a training course that may limit access to those with the relevant qualifications or experience.

Tour Guide Training Models and Approaches

In the context of ecotour/nature guiding there is considerable literature on training and education in both developed and developing countries (Ballantyne & Hughes, 2001; Black, 2002; Carmody, 2013; Shephard & Royston-Airey, 2000). Christie and Mason (2003) argue that formal, standardised programmes emphasise skill acquisition and development, an approach they feel fails to consider the complex nature of ecotour guiding. They express some concern with competency-based training programmes, suggesting that they lack a philosophical and theoretical base and are unlikely to focus on developing a guide's critical analytical abilities. Similar to Kohl et al. (2001), they argue that ecotour guides require self-reflective skills and awareness, especially when working in cross-cultural situations. Drawing on adult education and theory, Christie and Mason argue that tour guide training should be 'transformative' and improve the knowledge, attitudes and behaviour of the guide, which may then be passed on to the visitor. Transformative learning is based on the model of competency-based training coupled with techniques that 'promote critical reflection' of the guide's own values and assumptions (Christie & Mason, 2003: 11). They suggest that guides need to have the skills to motivate visitors both emotionally and intellectually, and this can be achieved through a range of personal reflection techniques such as journal writing, sharing case studies and life histories, recording critical incidents and reflecting on results to improve future presentations. Mason and Christie (2003) suggest good training should include not only competencies but also soft skills such as cultural sensitivity, critical self-assessment, values and attitudes, and propose transformative learning as a more reflective approach that incorporates these elements. At a practical level, they propose that this training approach can achieve improved performance, clarify tour aims and objectives and inform guides' interpretation of a site.

The remainder of the literature on different approaches and models for tour guide training and education can usefully be split into two categories: training for guides in developed and developing countries, reflecting countries' different social and economic environments; and the level of tourism development. Collectively, the various training providers use a wide range of training approaches and philosophies, a summary of which are presented in Table 6.2.

Tour guide training approaches in developed countries

While most studies on tour guide training and education have been country-specific studies, such as those mentioned above, a recent international study of tour guide associations across 61 countries conducted by Orde (2011b) on behalf of the World Federation of Tourist Guides Association gives a global picture of guide training and education in mainly developed countries. The study found that 45 out of the 61 countries delivered tour guide training with considerable variability across countries. Orde's study revealed that training programmes come in many different shapes and forms and can be delivered by a wide range of organisations, a finding that supports Pond (1993). Training may target local, regional or national guides; be formal or informal; be competency based or on the job; have a range of different assessment methods; and can vary in length, the type of trainers and the type of organisation delivering the training. Orde's study found that training and education were delivered by a range of organisations, including community colleges, regional governments, private trainers and universities, ranging from five days to 2.5 years in length and with varying levels of practical and theoretical components. For example, in the United Kingdom the Guild of Registered Tourist Guides has

Table 6.2 A summary of tour guide training providers, approaches and philosophies highlighted in the literature

Training provider	Training approach	Training philosophies most evident
Higher education institution	Formal training programme	Curriculum standards based Content driven (e.g. modules) Training materials/delivery based Knowledge based Competency (skills) based Transformative
Employer/ in-house	Apprenticeship Formal training programme Informal on-the-job training Formal on-the-job training	Training materials/delivery based Knowledge based Content driven (e.g. modules)
Private training provider	Formal training programme Short courses	Curriculum standards based Content driven (e.g. modules) Training materials/delivery based Knowledge based Competency (skills) based
Non-government organisation	Formal training programme Short courses	Content driven (e.g. modules) Training materials/delivery based Knowledge based
Tour guide association	Formal training programme Short courses	Curriculum standards based Content driven (e.g. modules) Training materials/delivery based Knowledge based Competency (skills) based

an accredited training course of 18 months that results in gaining Blue Badge Guide accreditation. The courses cover background knowledge of the United Kingdom; in-depth, city-specific and regional knowledge; practical training and assessment; and preparation of a tour planning project. In contrast, in Spain, training is delivered by regional governments with 1500 hours of theory and 500 hours of practical components. In Australia, Weiler and Black (2003) found that there were 77 courses offering nature and heritage tour guiding and interpretation courses at Australian tertiary institutions that ranged in length, level, location and mode of delivery.

A number of different approaches and models for tour guide training and education have been described and promoted in developed countries. In Hong Kong, Ap and Wong (2001) argued that an apprenticeship system was an appropriate approach for tour guide training, while others have proposed and discussed more formal programmes (Arslanturk & Altunoz, 2012; Valsson, 2010) that are knowledge based and competency based (Haase, 1996; Hutchinson & Bramwell, 1996). For example, in Australia, Hutchison and Bramwell (1996) described the development of the Certificate III in Ecotourism Operations, a regionally focused, competency-based short course that develops skills and knowledge to transition staff including guides from tourism to ecotourism.

Carmody's (2013) study of Savannah Guides Ltd. (SGL), an organisation for (eco)tour guides interpreting and protecting the tropical savannahs of Northern Australia, supports and promotes the value of intensive professional development schools as a training model. The foundational elements of SGL schools are continuous learning, practical training, mentoring, certification and standards of professionalism. These schools benefit the guide and tour guiding industry, particularly in remote parts of Australia, and Carmody suggests this approach be adopted more widely across other regional destinations as a way of improving the quality of tour guiding and professionalism.

Two recent European tour guide training initiatives potentially herald a new era in tour guide training. The first is the development of a European standard for tour guide training, known as the *Tourist Services – Requirements for the provision of professional tourist guide training and qualification programmes (EN 15565)* (Council of Europe, 2007). This standard recognises the valuable role that guides play 'to promote the cultural and natural heritage whilst on the other hand to help ensure its sustainability by making visitors aware of its importance and vulnerability' (Council of Europe, 2007: 1). The standard supports the European Union's (EU) efforts to facilitate free movement of services within member states, as well as emphasising the importance of region/area-specific guides. The aim is to achieve a common high standard of qualification for tour guides across all European countries and provides minimum requirements for the provision of professional tour guide training and qualification programmes. The standard outlines details of the competencies, framework of training programmes (a total minimum of 600 hours training), generic and region/area-specific subjects, assessment, practical training and training providers.

The second initiative sponsored by the EU is the Innoguide Tourism project (Ministry of Enterprise and Labour, 2013: 1), which recognises that tour guides play an important role in the European integration process, in the projection of Europe abroad and a changing tourism industry: 'their role goes far beyond guiding and information provision: they are the human element that enables us to build bridges between different cultures visiting the region'. A joint initiative among eight countries, the project has three aims. First, to undertake a comparative study of existing tour guide training programmes using the European standard for tour guiding as a point of reference. Second, to develop three training modules with the corresponding trainer and guide manuals focusing on sustainability (a theme revisited later in this chapter as well as in Chapter 4), intercultural skills and the creation of experience. Third, to encourage mobility between teachers and students, involving training sessions for trainers to check on the quality and suitability of training materials across different countries. As the training materials will be available online, they will be accessible to any tour guide training organisation around the world. This is an exciting and innovative approach to tour guide training that has the capacity to raise guiding standards and individual guide performance globally.

Tour guide training approaches in developing countries

The growth in ecotourism and nature-based tourism in developing countries and the corresponding demand for guides, especially ecotour/ nature guides, has prompted a number of studies on guide training in developing countries (see Gurung *et al.*, 1996; Jacobson & Robles, 1992). According to Black *et al.* (2001), probably the first formal training of ecotour guides in a developing country was in the Galapagos Islands National Park. In 1971, legislation was introduced which specified that all visitors had to be accompanied by trained and licensed guides. This training is delivered by the national park service and the guides provide interpretation and ensure minimal impact behaviour among visitors (Britton & Clarke, 1987). As another example, in Nepal, both trekking guides and managers of trekking agencies endorsed the requirement for guide training. The guides said that they wanted training so that they could provide the expected services to visitors who were generally highly educated and knowledgeable, and they desired both a practical and theoretical understanding of the guiding profession (Gurung *et al.*, 1996).

Guides trained with skills and knowledge relevant to the group's activities can do much to enhance the visitor experience. *Credit*: Kaye Walker (Clipper Tours)

A number of models for training programmes that meet the specific needs of guides and destinations in developing countries have been described (Black & King, 2002; Calvo, 2010; Clark & Gonzalez, 1991; Gurung et al., 1996; Jacobson & Robles, 1992; McGrath, 2007; Paaby et al., 1991). In a systematic review of selected ecotour guide training approaches in developing countries, Black et al. (2001) found that guide training varied considerably in terms of providers, length of training and content. Most guide training was provided on a formal basis by training providers and non-government organisations (NGOs), while others delivered informal in-house training. The length of the training varied considerably from 7 to 140 days, depending on whether the trainers were operators (short training courses) or tertiary institutions (long training courses). Based on their review, the authors proposed that developing a guide training programme for developing countries requires research to determine training needs, programme aims, curriculum structure and content, selection of trainees and trainers and programme assessment and evaluation (Black et al., 2001).

Weiler and Ham's (2002) guide training work in Central and South America highlighted the importance of targeted training delivered in partnership with in-country counterparts. They suggest an ideal curriculum should incorporate: expansion and refinement of product knowledge, language training where required and interpretive guiding skills for managing and delivering high-quality experiences. In developing the content of their interpretive guiding course, they used competency-based training, particularly the occupational competency standards in Australia and Canada, to identify the standards deemed necessary for interpretive tour guiding. They emphasised the need for a culturally sensitive approach based on best practice guiding principles and that any programme be continually evaluated and support given to the trainer. Their experience in delivering these programmes resulted in a model approach with four key principles and recommendations for the design, delivery and evaluation of future training courses in developing countries. The four principles are:

(1) The initiative for training should come from the host country and ownership should remain with the host country.
(2) Training content and methods should be informed by the literature on what constitutes good and best practice guiding, the adult training literature, the trainers' prior experience, with appropriate customisation to meet local needs.
(3) Training efforts must be systematically evaluated, and lessons learned from these evaluations must be documented and disseminated widely and used to inform future training efforts.
(4) Training and supporting in-country trainers is essential for building sustainable human capacity and for ensuring that ecotourism benefits host economies. (Weiler & Ham, 2001: 64)

The initiative for training should come from the host country via the industry and the guides. *Credit*: Rosemary Black (Vanuatu tour guide training)

In some instances, existing training may need to be modified. For example, based on her work with indigenous guides working at Machu Picchu in Peru, McGrath (2007) recommended the redesign of an existing tour guide training programme to facilitate inspirational tour guiding and encourage quality assurance in both curriculum design and service delivery. Like Weiler and Ham (2002), she emphasises the necessity to include interpretive skills.

Ham and Weiler (2003) note that the initiative for training should ideally come from the guides and the community rather than being imposed by other stakeholders. In the case of developing countries, any training programme developed should be 'owned' by the local community. This can be achieved in a number of ways, including the way the programme is initiated and set up, how the training is delivered, through the selection of trainers and by ensuring the central involvement of stakeholders – especially the guide trainees and local representatives. Where the training is undertaken by both foreign and local trainers, there are opportunities for collaboration and two-way transference of knowledge and skills, and there may be a need for train-the-trainer and capacity-building programmes.

Designing and formulating appropriate and effective training programmes in developing countries requires consideration of a range of issues unique to these guiding contexts. The selection of trainees will depend on the sponsors of the programme and other factors, but how should trainees be selected? Should there be prerequisites for entering the programme, such as a minimum education and literacy level for trainees, and if so what should they be? Is there room for different types of guides with different educational levels, or is this likely to cause friction between the guides? These issues are particularly relevant in developing countries where education levels and language skills may be lower than in more developed countries. Weiler and Ham (1999) suggest that widely discrepant education levels among trainees can be managed, and even capitalised on, if trainers plan carefully. In developing countries, consideration should be given to which types of training providers are most appropriate to provide guide training, who should be the trainers and what should be their qualifications and experience. Ideally, over time, training should increasingly be delivered primarily by nationals of developing countries as in-country expertise is developed.

In formulating training programmes in developing countries, focus should be given to identifying and developing appropriate assessment methods. Many guides in these countries may have low literacy rates, in which case written assessment may be inappropriate. Some trainees may be located in remote locations which may also preclude some forms of assessment. Further work is required to establish if a combination of assessment methods should be used and, if so, which are the most appropriate. The trialling and evaluation of different assessment methods would be worthwhile.

Sustainability and Guide Training

As discussed in Chapter 4, the guide's contribution to meeting the goals of sustainability is a new and emerging theme in the tour guiding literature. The relationship between guide training and guides' contribution to sustainability has been discussed by a number of authors in reference to developing countries (Carmody, 2013; Goodwin, 2006; Kohl, 2007; Novelli & Hellwig, 2011; Weiler & Kim, 2011) and to a limited extent in developed countries (Carmody, 2013; Dioko & Unakul, 2005; Ministry of Enterprise and Labour, 2013). Black and Weiler (2005) suggest an emphasis on leadership roles and environmental knowledge and they and others (Skanavis & Giannoulis, 2009; Weiler & Ham, 2002) argue for ecotour guide training content to include environmental and cultural sustainability, including the delivery of content aimed at influencing visitor attitudes and behavior. Kohl (2007) promotes a holistic and systematic approach to ecotour guiding training that is context specific and explicitly connects guides to biodiversity conservation. He regards guides as an integral part of a whole ecotourism operation, not just the outputs of a training programme. His theoretically informed work on training ecotour guides in Central and South America concluded that guides should strive to achieve the environmental, cultural and social sustainability of a destination. Consistent with the work of Mason and Christie (2003; Christie & Mason, 2003), Kohl promotes the value of continuous learning, a shared vision between the guide and the organisation and site-specific information. He emphasises the necessity for trainers to understand the context of the guides' work, their motivation for learning and the ecotourism programme in which they work.

Having discussed some of the different models and approaches to guide training and education in both developed and developing countries, this chapter now turns to some of the broader issues around planning, developing and implementing guide training and education such as programme content, training materials and programme evaluation.

The Identification of Content and the Development of Materials for Tour Guide Training Programmes

As discussed above, there are a number of different existing and proposed tour guide training models and approaches. Some studies have sought to analyse and discuss the specific content of training programmes. Many suggest that training programme content should be based on guide roles and the abilities, skills and knowledge needed to perform these roles (Black & Weiler, 2005; Weiler & Ham, 2002) and others (Black & Ham, 2005; Black & Weiler, 2005; Weiler & Ham, 2001) have identified the key areas of knowledge and skills relevant to tour guides, such as the ability to meet visitors' needs and expectations; the ability to guide according to legal, ethical and safety requirements; general knowledge about the destination; the ability to deliver accurate and relevant commentary; sensitivity to cross-cultural needs and differences; the ability to deliver enjoyable yet educational messages; and the ability to manage a group.

The literature on tour guide training indicates the specific skills and knowledge that guides and other tourism stakeholders believe need to be included in training programmes. Some (Ballantyne & Hughes, 2001; Social Change Media, 1995) have argued for the inclusion of interpretation skills, specifically the interpretation of indigenous culture (Howard *et al.*, 2001); minimal impact practices (Ballantyne & Hughes, 2001); and in the developing country context, Prakash *et al.* (2011) found that Indian guides, particularly from the east of the country which has a less-developed tourism industry, expressed a desire for skills in interpretation, communication, presentation skills and knowledge of the tourism product.

While most studies focus on training content that assists in improving tour guides' performance, a few studies have called for training on issues affecting the health and safety of guides, such as sex education and self-care (Avcikurt *et al.*, 2011; Cabada *et al.*, 2007; Torland, 2011a, 2011b; Van Dijk *et al.*, 2011). These relatively new areas of research are explored further in Chapter 8.

In some cases, the views of guides themselves have been sought to determine and inform training programme content. Ballantyne and Hughes (2001), in an early phase of developing ecotour guide training materials, sought guides' perceptions of their roles and found that they considered their key roles to be informer and entertainer, and thus considered their main focus should be on the skills and knowledge for delivering the content of presentation and audience awareness, with less focus on using interpretation and minimal impact techniques.

In the case of ecotour guide training, a few studies have critically analysed the training content. Skanavis and Giannoulis (2010) in Greece, and Yamada (2011) in Japan, suggest that the training programmes studied inadequately cover interpretive skills. Some authors consider the tailoring of ecotour guide training content to meet the specific regional and site-specific context of ecotour guide work to be important (Christie & Mason, 2003; Hutchison & Bramwell, 1996; Yamada, 2011). This reflects the specific nature of ecotourism sites and destinations as well as interactions with host communities, with Christie and Mason (2003) stressing the need for culturally sensitive guides. In some instances, the views of other tourism stakeholders as well as potential trainee guides have been sought prior to the development and commencement of the training programme. For example, in Costa Rica, Jacobson and Robles (1992) sought the views of local resource managers and hoteliers, visitors and trainee guides on the feasibility and desired content of a proposed training programme. They found that the guides wanted information on wildlife and botany as well as foreign language training.

While there has been some discussion in the literature on specific elements of guide training programmes, such as programme content, there has been little discussion of the specific nature of the training materials themselves. Ballanytne and Hughes (2001) recognised that one of the issues of delivering tour guide training, particularly to ecotour, adventure and nature-based guides, is that they often live and work in remote areas and their training is often on the job. They sought to address these issues by developing flexible training materials comprising a video and associated workbook. Other flexible training materials include online courses such as the new European Innoguide Tourism project, DVDs, online videos and other study-at-home options. The materials were grounded on theory from the literature and on 'best practice' guiding and were informed by the results of pre-training questionnaires that investigated ecotour guides' perceptions of their roles, responsibilities and training needs. Ballanytne and Hughes concluded that developing guide training materials should be a collaborative process involving academics, researchers, trainers and guides to ensure that theory and research findings inform both training approaches and practice that realistically reflect guides' working conditions.

Evaluation of Tour Guide Training

The literature shows that there has been limited systematic evaluation of the effectiveness and impacts of tour guide training on guides, visitors and the tourism industry (Black et al., 2001; Welgemoed, 1993), yet this process can provide valuable information about the specific aspects of programmes that will allow for continued improvement programmes as well as identify the need for more or different guide training. In cases where training has been evaluated, guides reported that the training had been effective in improving their performance, knowledge and skills as well as providing an opportunity for self-evaluation, reflection and discussion.

In terms of programme evaluation, Weiler and Ham (1999) found that a combination of quantitative and qualitative methods provided a rich context for evaluating both trainees and the training. Most training evaluation has targeted guides immediately after completing the training programme, while a few studies have sought feedback from guides post-training after their return to work, either from the guides themselves (Ballantyne & Hughes, 2001; Jacobson & Robles, 1992) or from other relevant stakeholders (Jacobson & Robles, 1992; Weiler & Ham, 2002). Kohl (2007) suggests that when guides return to their workplace, supervisors need to be receptive and supportive of the newly trained guides who have gained new ideas and actions through their training. This long-term, follow-up evaluation is useful to determine if the training has been effective in improving guide performance; however, it is essential that baseline data are collected prior to the training to allow for a comparison of guide performance.

Weiler and Ham (2002) evaluated their training programmes in Central and South America using pre- and post-training questionnaires based on trainees' self-assessment of their own competencies, guides' reflective journals and observations by trainers. Follow-up assessment with trainees and institutional evaluation found that guides assessed themselves as more capable after the training than prior to the training in all areas of the course. In the case of Panama (Weiler & Ham, 2002), follow-up feedback revealed that English language training was a priority for the guides. The issue of whether language training should be integrated into tour guide training or delivered as a separate course is an ongoing debate in the literature and the industry (Jacobson & Robles, 1992; Weiler & Ham, 2002).

In Vanuatu, Black and King's (2002) evaluation of a tour guide training programme delivered on the outer islands of Vanuatu aimed to determine the effectiveness of the programme from the perspectives of the guides and trainers. The guides were generally satisfied with the training and considered that it had improved their guiding skills but expressed a strong desire for additional training in first aid, complaint handling and language training. An important component of this programme was the capacity-building aspect of mentoring a ni-Vanuatu (a person indigenous to Vanuatu) tour guide trainer as an effective use of foreign aid and a contribution to national self-reliance.

At the broader tour guiding organisational level, Carmody (2013) evaluated the SGL professional development schools and found that continual learning, practical training, mentoring, certification and standards of professionalism were facilitated by these training schools and contributed to the continued success of this tour guiding organisation. She found that the SGL schools benefit individual members and the organisation in three ways: increasing the guide's knowledge, learning about a specific site and embracing the SGL vision. The schools also benefitted the tourism industry more broadly, supporting and encouraging professionalism, safety, customer service and informed interpretation.

Ballantyne and Hughes' (2001) study of ecotour guide training is one of the few studies that carried out an evaluation immediately after training as well as one month later. Interestingly, they found that most of the guide feedback on the training related to the opportunity for self-evaluation and reflection provided by the training materials, in particular seeing guiding from the visitor's perspective. Being able to discuss ideas and issues with colleagues was also regarded as a valuable aspect of the training process that had a positive impact on their attitudes and motivation. One month after the training, they found that 67% of the guides considered that their guiding practice had improved, particularly in incorporating interpretive techniques.

Few studies have compared the performance of trained and untrained guides, although, as mentioned in Chapter 5, some findings indicate that trained tour guides result in higher levels of visitor satisfaction. An early but innovative and far-sighted study by Roggenbuck et al. (1992) on commercial guides demonstrated that those who underwent training delivered by the US National Park Service were better than untrained guides at eliciting desirable outcomes from their tours, including visitors' self-rated knowledge, levels of enjoyment and satisfaction with the amount of information included on the tour. This was a carefully designed experimental study that included control groups and statistical testing, although the measures of 'outcomes' of the training are somewhat dated compared to those discussed elsewhere in this book.

The influence of organisational culture on the training and learning abilities of guides (Carmody, 2013; Carmody et al., 2010; Lugosi & Bray, 2008) is an important area requiring further research. Based on a case study of a tour company, Lugosi and Bray (2008) suggested that the development of a participative learning culture within a tour guiding organisation creates a positive environment for guides. They identified two factors needed to enhance this culture: the provision of physical or virtual learning spaces and learning opportunities where guides can meet, discuss and share experiences; and formalised guidance and monitoring by more experienced guides to ensure best practice is shared among all the group members. These mechanisms facilitate a process of 'experiential learning, colleague-led development and organisational socialisation' (Lugosi & Bray, 2008: 478).

While much of the tour guiding education and training literature is descriptive, some recent studies have focused on model and theory building (Black & Ham, 2005; Black & Weiler, 2005) and critical analysis (Carmody, 2013; Carmody et al., 2010; Yamada, 2011); however, there are numerous opportunities for further research in training and education across a range of guiding contexts in developed and developing countries.

Implications for Research

One of the main research gaps and needs is the *lack of systematic evaluation and measurement* of training outcomes to determine the *efficacy of guide training and education*. Programme evaluation is needed to assist in developing new programmes and improving existing programmes. Studies are needed to undertake long-term evaluation of guides when they return to their workplace, to determine the impact of their training and how it has influenced their performance, visitor satisfaction (see Chapter 5) and long-term outcomes, particularly in relation to sustainability outcomes. In cases where the performance of trained and untrained guides has been compared, the research demonstrates that trained guides have a greater influence on visitors' knowledge, enjoyment and satisfaction with the tour than untrained guides do. A useful contribution to the literature would be to evaluate the performance of trained versus untrained guides in a range of contexts. Another avenue of fruitful research would be gaining improved insights into the development, delivery and post-delivery phases of training from a range of perspectives – guides, trainers, the tourism industry, government agencies, employers and visitors. Although not mentioned in the literature, research on the motivations and training of volunteer guides and relevant training approaches would also be a worthwhile area to explore.

Research is needed to evaluate which training models and approaches are most appropriate for different guiding groups. A number of factors, including the location and employment status of the guide, may influence the selection of a training approach. For example, some freelance guides may be located in remote areas, experience working long hours and cannot easily attend a formal, city-based course. In such cases, training needs may be best met through informal channels, such as on-the-job training and 'shadowing' of skilled and experienced role models.

Further work is required to determine where formal training is required and not required, which approaches are best suited to particular learning outcomes and where follow-up training may be needed, particularly among culturally and intellectually diverse groups of tour guides (Weiler & Ham, 2002). More research is required to determine the skills and knowledge needed to be a good tour guide, which of these are core and universal and which are specific to certain activities and/or contexts. This will assist in developing the content of training programmes and materials, and in assessing trainees and evaluating guides. The development and systematic testing of instructional training materials and curricula will also be important as momentum towards standardisation and other cost-saving training strategies grows. In the context of developing countries, research is needed to determine how and whether guest language training should or should not be integrated into training programmes. Finally, at a theoretical level more research is needed on testing and advancing the *conceptual training frameworks and models* that exist, such as those proposed by Weiler and Ham (2002) and Mason and Christie (2003).

Implications for Tour Guiding Practice

This review demonstrates that guides and other guiding stakeholders are expressing their desire for training, education and professional development opportunities to improve guides' performance and develop as professionals. In conjunction with this is the need for more training and education to eliminate unethical guiding practices, improve visitor experiences and enhance the reputation of tourism operators and visitor destinations. Ideally, any initiative for training should come from the industry and the guides rather than being imposed on them. Educational and training institutions, professional associations, employers and the tourism industry need to respond to this need and desire with appropriate, consistent and high-quality training opportunities. These opportunities need to be promoted to guides through a range of communication avenues so they are aware of and can take up these openings. There are many different training models and approaches from both developing and developed countries and particularly from Australia which has a strong focus on ecotour guide training. These training approaches and materials must be grounded in best practice guiding and sound pedagogy including tour guiding, educational theory and learning styles.

Training and education need to be consistent, certainly across a country but even across regions. The Innoguide Tourism project and the European standard for tour guiding will hopefully provide a good model for other regions across the world. Given the evidence that trained guides result in higher visitor satisfaction, tourism operators should be encouraged to employ trained guides and, once employed, they should support their guides with paid time and resources to undertake advanced training. Employers should reward further professional development through increased salaries. Establishing a good organisational culture can facilitate professional development and life-long learning among guides. If employers require and advertise for trained guides, then guides will be more likely to undertake training in preparation for entering the guiding workforce.

The diversity and complexity of guiding does not allow a 'one-size-fits-all' approach to training and education. Programmes need to be flexible and modified for different groups of tour guides in both developed and developing countries. Training and education need to reflect the complexity of guiding and acknowledge the diverse guiding contexts, and the cultural and learner differences among individual guides. While training and education programmes can offer generic guiding skills, they also need to deliver skills and knowledge to meet the complex roles of specialist guides, such as interpretation, intercultural communication and sustainability. As such, curriculum content needs to be flexible, learner centred and critically reflective. Finally, in developing these programmes and associated training materials, links need to be established between academics, researchers, trainers and guides to ensure that theory and research findings inform both training approaches and practices that are relevant to the field.

Chapter Summary

This chapter has examined training, education and professional development as tools for quality assurance and has explored the strengths and weaknesses of different approaches to training in both developed and developing countries. The following is a summary of some of the key findings in this body of literature.

Many authors acknowledge the multiple roles of the guide and note that the relevant skills and knowledge to perform these roles can be addressed through training and education (Black, 2002; Black & Weiler, 2005). The growth and evolution of tourism globally from a service-based economy to an experience-based economy, and the increasingly diverse range of roles expected of and played by tour guides, are acknowledged as factors that have raised the urgency for tour guides to gain qualifications and expertise through training, education and professional development. Criticisms of the lack and inconsistency of training in both developed and developing countries are pervasive in the literature, but most authors caution that the *initiative for training* ideally needs to come from the industry and the guides.

This review reveals that tour guide training and education is an effective *quality assurance mechanism,* in particular it can provide a vehicle for ensuring minimum standards and that levels of training and qualifications can serve as incentives for achieving higher standards; however, more evaluation needs to be undertaken in terms of the expected and actual training outcomes from a range of perspectives – the guide, employer and visitor.

The findings from these studies indicate that the benefits of tour guide training and education accrue at the individual, operator and industry levels. At an individual level, training can increase guides' knowledge of relevant topics, including the tourism product, and provide and enhance specific skills, as well as improve a guide's employment prospects, career opportunities, level of pay and conditions of work. Offering different levels of training from basic to advanced can encourage guides to advance their skills and knowledge, and develop more professional full-time guides. Training was also seen by guides as an opportunity for self-evaluation, reflection and discussion. From the employer's perspective, having trained guides may help guides embrace the organisation's vision, provide a commercial advantage in terms of marketing, repeat trips, superior service and, in the long term, increased profits (Kong *et al.,* 2009). At an industry-wide level, training can support and encourage professionalism, safety, customer service and informed interpretation, and can help lift standards and improve the quality of the tourism product and thus the competitive advantage of regions and destinations (Kong *et al.,* 2009).

Training programmes vary considerably in terms of elements such as programme content, length and assessment methods. *Standardisation* of training, such as a focus on core knowledge and skills, and assessment of competency together facilitate the portability of outcomes, but some scholars argue that this training approach fails to consider the complex nature of guiding and can compromise relevance to local/cultural contexts and customisation of training to individual learning styles and capacities (Mason & Christie, 2003). The work of some scholars (Kohl *et al.,* 2001; Mason & Christie, 2003) suggests that with the growth in diversity and the maturation of visitor markets and guides themselves, curriculum content needs to balance generic guiding skills and knowledge with the needs of individual learners and be more *flexible, co-created, experience focused* and *critically reflective.*

In both developing and developed countries, *competency-based approaches* to training have been criticised for *overemphasising hard skills* at the expense of the more complex elements of guiding such as interpretation and intercultural communication. The work of Weiler and Ham (2002) provides some useful principles for developing and delivering training programmes in developing countries. A new theme emerging in the training literature, particularly in developing countries, is the inclusion and integration of sustainability goals in guide training to deliver relevant environmental, communication and interpretive skills and knowledge. These skills allow guides to be environmental role models, make visitors aware of the importance of sustainability and help protect the destination. Finally, Lugosi and Bray (2008) suggest that professional development and life-long learning can be facilitated by good organisational culture, but this is challenging due to the lack of industry commitment to training, as well as the remote location of many guides. Research relating to the tour guiding industry's experience of and engagement with a number of other mechanisms that support and enhance quality tour guiding are discussed further in the next chapter.

Key references

(1) Black, R., Ham, S. and Weiler, B. (2001) Ecotour guide training in less developed countries: Some preliminary research findings. *Journal of Sustainable Tourism* 9 (2), 147–156.
(2) Carmody, J. (2013) Intensive tour guide training in regional Australia: An analysis of the Savannah Guides organisation and professional development schools. *Journal of Sustainable Tourism* 21 (5), 679–694.
(3) Kohl, J., Brown, C. and Humke, M. (2001) Overcoming hurdles: Teaching guides to interpret biodiversity conservation. *Legacy* 12 (4), 19–28.
(4) Lugosi, P. and Bray, J. (2008) Tour guiding, organisational culture and learning: Lessons from an entrepreneurial company. *International Journal of Tourism Research* 10 (5), 467–479.
(5) Mason, P.A. and Christie, M.F. (2003) Tour guides as critically reflective practitioners: A proposed training model. *Tourism Recreation Research* 28 (1), 23–33.
(6) Weiler, B. and Ham, S.H. (2002) Tour guide training: A model for sustainable capacity building in developing countries. *Journal of Sustainable Tourism* 10 (1), 52–69.

7 Conceptualising and Fostering Quality in Tour Guiding

Since Cohen (1985) highlighted the progression from the traditional guide to the professional guide and the increasing recognition of the pivotal role of the tour guide in the tourism experience, a number of authors have explored the issues of professionalism and quality assurance in tour guiding (Ap & Wong, 2001; Black, 2002; Black & Weiler, 2005; McGrath, 2007; Pond, 1993; Ponting, 2009; Quiroga, 1990; Welgemoed, 1991). Many of these authors have pointed to the importance of and the need for quality assurance or have described various quality assurance mechanisms, but few have examined the efficacy of these mechanisms or defined what professional tour guiding involves and how to achieve professionalism.

The purpose of this chapter is to examine the literature on the use of professional associations, professional certification, licensing, codes of practice and awards of excellence as mechanisms for quality assurance in tour guiding practice. The chapter begins with a discussion on tour guide professionalism and the process of professionalisation that sets the context for the chapter. Each of the five quality assurance mechanisms is then discussed in turn, highlighting their capacity to meet quality assurance outcomes and their respective advantages and disadvantages. The chapter concludes by summarising the findings and suggesting the merits of a combination of mechanisms to meet quality assurance outcomes and the needs of all tour guiding stakeholders.

Tour Guide Professionalism and Professionalisation

As early as the 1990s, Quiroga (1990: 189) described the image of tour guides as 'unflattering' and Welgemoed (1991) acknowledged the complex roles of the tour guide and the need for professional training. In discussing the evolution of guiding as a profession, Pond (1993) lamented that it was a slow and fraught process, suggesting that this was due to four factors: the seasonality of the work, supply and demand of guides, lack of professional standards and proper training for guides and traditional perceptions of guiding as a glamorous yet unrecognised profession. According to Ponting (2009), the tour guiding sector became subject to the process of professionalisation as guide training programmes emerged and regulations to the practice of guiding were introduced, both of which are an acknowledged stage in the professionalisation process (Pond, 1993).

Ponting's (2009) study is one of the few to explore the issues of professional guiding in any depth. She argues that in the context of the tour guiding industry, particularly in ecotour guiding, the terms 'profession', 'professionalisation' and 'professional' have been adopted as 'unproblematic, and are used arbitrarily and interchangeably in describing the occupation of tour guiding without clarification of what *professional* tour guiding involves' (Ponting, 2009: 8) (cf. Ap & Wong, 2001; Pond, 1993; Weiler & Ham, 2001). Ponting investigated the work of Australian ecotour guides, and the impact that professionalisation has on raising ecotour guides' levels of professionalism. She suggests that a useful definition of 'professional' is a person who is a specialist, a trained, qualified and licensed expert. She noted that some of the most distinctive characteristics of professions are autonomy of work, control of work and recognition of professional status through society. She argues that occupations that achieve professionalism go through a series of stages such as extended vocational training and experience and higher education, and are licensed in order to exert control over the occupation and in some cases to monopolize the market. Using the case study of the Australian ecotour guiding industry, Ponting demonstrates that professionalisation of tour guiding is occurring with the emergence of a full-time occupation, training and education, founding of professional associations, political action aimed at protecting these associations, adoption of codes of conduct, as well as the development of a professional ecotour guide certification programme. She argues that through these concepts, occupational groups attain professionalism, which enhances group standards, behaviours and values that establish hierarchies, membership requirements and informal rules. In her study, she found significant disparities between the perceptions of ecotour guides and key industry stakeholders in relation to professionalisation, with the former conceptualising a professional in their field in terms of his or her passion for nature and people. She recommended that professionalism could be achieved through collaborative professionalisation between ecotour guides and the ecotourism industry. Many of the above-mentioned indicative factors of professionalisation are also applicable to the tour guiding industry in general, particularly in developed countries such as the United States (Pond, 1993), the United Kingdom (Pond, 1993), Australia (Weiler *et al.*, 1997; Weiler & Ham, 2001), Serbia (Rabotic, 2011) and Hong Kong (Ap & Wong, 2001).

With the exception of Ponting (2009), the issues and challenges of professionalism and professionalisation in the tour guiding profession have received cursory mention in the literature, apart from some more in-depth studies by researchers in Hong Kong and Macau (Ap & Wong, 2001; Mak *et al.*, 2009, 2011) that demonstrate that professionalism of tour guides is a problem in these two countries. In the context of Hong Kong, Ap and Wong (2001) found that at that time there was no basic training course for new guides which led to variable levels of professionalism, often due to broader unhealthy industry practices, a lack of recognition and a poor image of the profession, while low levels of remuneration resulted in a heavy reliance on commissions and tips. Ten years later, Mak *et al.* (2009, 2011) noted that many of the same issues still existed in Hong Kong and Macau, although by then both countries had adopted some quality assurance measures, which are discussed later in this chapter. In a similar vein, a recent study of guides working in China (Kong *et al.*, 2009) found that they had poor career prospects and lacked training opportunities, resulting in job burnout and poor-quality service. In contrast, Huang and Weiler (2010) found that in China the government has put its tour guiding quality assurance system at the centre of its tourism policy practices, legally enforcing minimum guiding standards, although Kong *et al.* (2009) consider that tour guides in China are poorly prepared for the expanding tourism industry as the sector is dominated by young staff with vocational education, with limited career paths and poor training.

Training and membership in a professional association can improve the professionalism of guides. *Credit*: Wendy Hillman (Savannah Guides)

Many authors have drawn attention to the need for professional guides to ensure the long-term viability, competiveness and sustainability of the tourism industry (Ap & Wong, 2001; Huang & Weiler, 2010). Some of these authors (Ap & Wong, 2001; Black & Weiler, 2005; Weiler & Ham, 2001) have highlighted a range of measures for enhancing the service professionalism of tour guides such as formulating an effective monitoring and evaluation system, identifying a clear career path and training as well as specific mechanisms such as licensing and codes of conduct. Thus, the focus of this chapter is on quality assurance mechanisms that have the potential to support, facilitate and improve guides' performance of their roles as discussed in Chapter 2.

Tour Guide Quality Assurance Mechanisms

Over the past 20 years, the tourism industry has increasingly focused on quality and its role in providing a competitive edge, including in the tour guiding arena. Across the industry, there has been increasing interest in accreditation, professional certification, licensing and other means of measuring and increasing levels of professionalism (Harris & Jago, 2001; Issaverdis, 1998, 2001). Many of these quality assurance initiatives are used by other sectors of the tourism industry to improve professionalism and enhance visitor experiences (Harris & Jago, 2001; Honey & Rome, 2001; Issaverdis, 1998; Manidis Roberts Consultants, 1994). This trend, together with consumers becoming more discerning in their choice of tourism experiences, has resulted in a range of mechanisms being developed and implemented in an attempt to ensure high standards of tour guiding in all types of guided tour experiences (Black & Weiler, 2005). At the same time that expectations of quality from both tourism industry stakeholders and consumers have been increasing (Page & Dowling, 2002), the role of the guide has gained prominence as an important factor in facilitating a quality visitor experience (Page & Dowling, 2002; Weiler & Ham, 2001). In response, governments, the tourism industry, professional industry associations and guides themselves have been showing interest in and exploring strategies for supporting and enhancing the performance of tour guides (Australian Tourism Export Council and Tourism Queensland, 2001; Commonwealth of Australia, 1994; Ecotourism Australia, 2012).

As noted above, some studies of the tour guiding industry in certain countries such as Australia, Hong Kong and Macau (Ap & Wong, 2001; Australian Tourism Export Council and Tourism Queensland, 2001; Mak et al., 2009) have highlighted problems associated with current tour guiding practices. Other studies have demonstrated that some guides are performing poorly in some roles and not fullfilling their potential to deliver quality visitor experiences (Weiler & Crabtree, 1998). The tour guiding discourse is punctuated by calls for more theoretical bases, benchmarks, best practice principles and standards (Christie & Mason, 2003; Mason & Christie, 2003) and frequently mentions the need for professionalism, more comprehensive training programmes and greater monitoring and enforcement of standards (Christie & Mason, 2003; Dioko & Unakul, 2005; Mason & Christie, 2003).

Collectively, the results of these studies suggest the need to develop and implement quality assurance mechanisms in order to achieve some or all of the following outcomes:

(1)   awareness, appreciation and documentation of the importance, positive impacts and value-adding of tour guiding for all stakeholders including visitors and guides themselves;
(2)   a minimum standard of practice for all tour guiding roles required by all guides across the industry;
(3)   advanced levels of performance of roles that are recognisable and rewarded.

Black and Weiler (2005) examined the potential of a range of tour guiding quality assurance mechanisms to achieve a range of guiding roles, including codes of conduct, professional associations, awards of excellence, training, professional certification and licensing. Black and Weiler's framework has been used by a number of other researchers to analyse specific tour guide quality assurance mechanisms such as professional certification, as well as quality assurance mechanisms generally, in other countries including Japan (Yamada, 2011) and China (Huang & Weiler, 2010). Using the six mechanisms identified by Black and Weiler (2005), Yamada (2011), in a study of ecotour guiding in Japan, found that professional associations, awards of excellence and training had already been implemented, but professional certification, licensing and codes of conduct could be taken up in order to improve tour guiding standards in that country. She recommended the establishment of a professional certification programme and codes of conduct by a non-profit organisation, such as the Japan Ecotourism Society or the National Ecotour Centre, and compulsory licensing by the Ministry of the Environment. The findings of Yamada and other studies are discussed later in this chapter in relation to specific quality assurance mechanisms. Training and education are also important mechanisms to assist in raising guiding standards and individual performance; however, as these were discussed in the previous chapter, they are not covered in this chapter.

Mechanisms that have the Capacity to Improve Tour Guide Performance and Standards

Based on previous work (Black & Weiler, 2005), this chapter outlines the advantages and disadvantages of, and draws on, previous research to consider the potential of a number of quality assurance mechanisms to achieve three outcomes: (i) raising awareness and appreciation of the importance of guiding among stakeholders, (ii) helping achieve minimum guiding standards and (iii) rewarding advanced performance of guiding roles. Most of the literature on quality assurance describes the various quality assurance mechanisms but fails to assess the efficacy of these mechanisms in meeting these three quality assurance outcomes.

The five mechanisms reviewed are:

- professional associations;
- professional certification;
- licensing;
- codes of conduct;
- awards of excellence.

Professional associations

Previous work (Black & Weiler, 2005) suggests that professional associations may have the capacity to help facilitate guides to perform their various roles and meet a minimum guiding standard (Pond, 1993; Weiler & Ham, 2001). Associations have the ability to provide professional support and a number of other benefits that can assist in raising guiding standards (Finlayson, 2000; Harris & Jago, 2001; Sheldon, 1989); however, the provision of benefits and opportunities varies across professional associations and there is no evidence to demonstrate their effectiveness and is therefore an area for further research. Pond (1993) suggests that, at a broad level, tour guide associations can play an important role in uniting the guiding industry and elevating its image.

Professional associations can provide a wide range of services for guides including improving the profile of guides, individual certification and awards for excellence. (See Appendix)

Professional associations can provide a wide range of services to their members and are often instrumental in introducing or supporting other mechanisms discussed in this chapter, such as codes of conduct, awards of excellence schemes, training and certification programmes. Through these mechanisms, either individually or in combination, a professional association may contribute to meeting minimum standards and/or improving professional standards and performance. However, tour guiding associations are often involved in many other activities, such as maintaining contact and meeting the needs of a diverse group that may include tour guides, tour managers, tourism operators and educators, and their limited resources may restrict their involvement in performance enhancement schemes. In a study of tourist guide associations worldwide, Orde (2011a) found that all of the 35 responding associations were run by an elected and voluntary committee of guides. For example, the Guiding Organisation of Australia (GOA, 2012) is the peak industry body for Australian tour guides. Established in 2003, it represents all state and territory tour guide associations across the country, yet it only represents a small percentage of all Australian tour guides. With limited resources and relying on the goodwill of volunteers, it demonstrates the challenges for professional tour guide associations (Orde, 2011a).

The training opportunities that were discussed in Chapter 6 can be provided by a professional association to assist guides in effectively and successfully performing a range of roles and may be effectively delivered in collaboration with other professional associations. A professional association may also have a code of ethics or conduct, which each member must endorse on joining the association, although these are generally not enforced. As will be discussed later in this chapter, codes of conduct aimed at individual guides may help improve guides' awareness of their various roles and professional and ethical behaviour. Associations may also play an important role in representing the profession and providing expert advice and input to training organisations and government agencies responsible for specifying tour guide competency standards, which can in turn influence the content and structure of training programmes. An overview of selected international, national and regional tour guide associations is provided in the Appendix.

In summary, the literature suggests that professional associations have the potential to be one of the most comprehensive mechanisms in addressing the three quality assurance outcomes. Depending on the breadth of services that the association offers, it has the potential to achieve all three outcomes through strategies such as marketing and promotion, developing tour guide standards, delivering professional development and developing and promoting certification programmes. However, an association's influence can be limited by its small membership numbers, limited finances and paid support staff, its activities being largely non-enforceable and often depending on the enthusiasm and voluntary contributions of some members.

Professional certification

A review of the literature suggests that professional certification programmes, sometimes referred to as accreditation programmes, are a mechanism that is being increasingly used across a number of countries (Black & Ham, 2005; Huang & Weiler, 2010; Yamada, 2011). This mechanism is regarded as an effective tool to meet minimum guiding standards and performance, yet there is little evidence to demonstrate its effectiveness in meeting the three quality assurance outcomes, and is an area requiring further research. Professional certification is a tool used to formally recognise an individual's skills, knowledge and attitudes as defined by some standards (Altschuld, 1999; Morrison et al., 1992). Professional certification refers to an individual's performance, whereas accreditation generally refers to a product, process or institution (Issaverdis, 1998). Professional certification in the tourism industry is generally voluntary and is a process in which individuals are tested and evaluated to determine if they have the skills and knowledge required by their profession. The terms 'certification' and 'accreditation' are frequently used interchangeably and are applied differently across the world, often resulting in confusion among visitors and those working in the tourism industry (Black, 2002; Honey & Rome, 2001; Issaverdis, 1998).

Professional certification programmes for tour guides exist in many countries and cities around the world (Black, 2002; Black & Ham, 2005; Pond, 1993). In Australia, for example, there are three professional certification programmes: Savannah Guides Ltd. (SGL) for guides working in northern Australia, the Australian EcoGuide Program that certifies ecotour guides and the more recent Guides of Australia Accreditation Program that is open to all tour guides. A number of papers (Black, 2007; Black & Ham, 2005; Black & Weiler, 2002, 2005) have described various aspects of the EcoGuide Program, including Black's (2002) comprehensive study that critically analysed the development of the programme as a basis for building a best practice model for tour guide certification (Black & Ham, 2005). The proposed model has three components: a general process model for developing a tour guide certification programme, key process principles and key programme elements (Black & Ham, 2005).

Professional certification is an effective tool to meet minimum guiding standards and performance. *Credit*: Tom Augustine (Bryon Bay Eco Cruise and Kayaks, Australia)

Following Black's work (2002, 2007), a number of other studies have been published on quality assurance and certification in ecotour guiding in other countries (Calvo, 2010; Nasopoulou, 2011; Yamada, 2011). One study by Kayes (2005), based in the Bocas del Toro reef area of Panama, recommended the establishment of an ecotour guide certification programme to address some of the unsustainable practices of tour guides and the local community. Tour guide certification is also mentioned in the context of certification of tourism operators, for example in Costa Rica (Calvo, 2010). While tour guide licenses have been required there since the 1970s, more recently the Costa Rica Tourism Board has developed a Certification of Sustainable Tourism (CST) for all tourism operations, requiring certified operators to train their employees, including tour guides, in sustainable behaviours and community development activities. Mandatory tour guide certification and training has now been introduced and hiring certified guides is one of the requirements to obtain the CST.

Utilising Black's (2002; Black & Ham, 2005) tour guide certification model, Carmody (2013) critically examined SGL. Her study investigated whether the organisation's training, mentoring, accreditation and professionalism approach could be transferred to other locations across Australia. She found that the organisation met most of the characteristics identified by Christie and Mason (2003), Black and Weiler (2005) and Black and Ham (2005) as being essential for good guiding practice and could be applied to other regions.

China has a tour guide classification system that is similar to a professional certification programme. Criteria and assessment procedures are driven by the China National Tourism Administration (CNTA). The classification system has four levels from elementary to supreme. To progress through the levels, guides must complete written examinations that are content focused rather than skill driven. Interestingly, Huang and Weiler (2010) indicate that most guides are not motivated to seek progression through the classification levels and they suggest that this may be because the levels do not relate to remuneration and there is little incentive to upgrade their professional level. Huang and Weiler suggest that the current classification system is inadequate without an effective recognition/remuneration system in place.

In Greece, Nasopoulou (2011) described the Guides of National Parks and Recreation Areas, known as ecoguides, as a relatively new certified specialty for conducting guided tours in Greece's natural and protected areas. Despite the existence of these specialist guides, Nasopoulou (2011) noted that many agencies do not employ them and she recommended that a registry of professional ecoguides be created, and legislation be developed to support tour guide certification.

The requirements of a professional certification programme may vary depending on a number of factors, including the aims of the programme, forms of assessment and level(s) of certification. Most programmes are based on generic core competencies that in turn are based on an analysis of the roles that guides are required to perform. However, one of the challenges of developing a certification programme is the diversity of tour guides and the various roles that they are required to perform. Today, many guides work in specialised contexts and activities and are required to perform additional specialist roles apart from generalist guiding roles. For example, the requirements for certification for a specialist guide, such an adventure guide, would differ from those of a historic site guide or a zoo guide because they perform different specialist roles.

An advantage of certification for the individual tour guide is that it can provide a portable and nationally recognised industry 'qualification' (Crabtree & Black, 2000). At a wider industry level, certification establishes minimum standards which professionals must meet and maintain through recertification. Certification can also assist in identifying training gaps both for the individual and the employer, and assist the latter in selecting employees (Crabtree & Black, 2000). Recertification ensures that professionals remain current in the profession's body of knowledge and skills. Despite the potential that professional certification programmes offer, a number of studies (Mak et al., 2009, 2011) have shown that even when these programmes are implemented, problems still exist in relation to unethical and unhealthy tour guiding practices.

For example, in a study of tour guiding in Hong Kong, Ap and Wong (2001) investigated tour guiding practices, assessing the existing level of professional service standards and identifying issues and challenges facing the profession with a view to recommending strategies and mechanisms to address poor tour guiding practice and performance among Hong Kong tour guides. Their study recommended the establishment of a monitoring system to ensure high standards of service performance by the tour guides. In a more recent study of tour guiding issues and practices in Macau and Hong Kong, Mak et al. (2011) found that in Hong Kong they have adopted a Tourist Guide Accreditation System (Mak et al., 2011) where guides are required to hold a Tourist Guide Pass akin to a professional certification. This accreditation system requires the guides to hold a recognised tour guiding qualification/certificate, complete written and practical examinations held by the Travel Industry Council of Hong Kong (TIC) and hold a first aid certificate.

However, one of the weaknesses of the accreditation system in Hong Kong identified by the study participants was that the monitoring of guides in Hong Kong is undertaken by the TIC, comprised of representatives of local travel agencies who have a self-interest, which as a non-government organisation (NGO) lacks legal power. In contrast, their findings showed that the Macau tour guide licensing and monitoring systems were considered more effective because they have been enshrined in legislation and monitoring is undertaken by the Macau Government Tourist Office, a government body that is responsible for monitoring any illegal practices among the guiding profession. Mak et al.'s (2009) analysis of tour guiding in Macau found that many of the tour guiding issues actually originated from external factors that affected the tour guides directly, such as the unhealthy business practices of the Chinese outbound travel agencies and the exploitative measures by inbound tourism operators, rather than from the practices of the tour guides themselves.

An evaluation of the Australian EcoGuide Program (Black, 2007) four years after its implementation suggests that the experiences of this professional certification programme offer some lessons for other organisations planning to develop and introduce a tour guide certification programme. First, a programme must have sufficient staff and financial resources to support it. In addition to gaining funding to develop a programme, funding must be secured for programme implementation, particularly in the inital stages when funding may be limited. Second, all programme components including all necessary documentation and processes must be fully functional when the programme is launched. Third, the programme managers must promote and sell the tangible benefits of the programme to potential guides and tourism operators, a finding supported by Ponting (2009).

A number of studies (Black, 2002; Black & Ham, 2005) suggest that while certification programmes may help meet the three quality assurance outcomes, they are costly to establish and manage. This is supported by a survey of Australian tourism certification programmes (Harris &

Jago, 2001) that identified lack of funding, lack of industry support and inadequate levels of rigour associated with these types of programmes. In particular, the capacity of tourism industry associations to operate voluntary certification programmes that were self-funding was limited. They found that in the case of the now defunct Australian Guide Qualification Program, the inbound tour operators association responsible for managing the programme had not been able to meet its operational costs resulting in human resources being diverted from other areas of the association's work. In addition, many of the benefits promised to guides in the programme had not been provided (Ponting, 2009) due to lack of funding, a finding supported by Black's (2002) evaluation of the Australian EcoGuide Program.

A further disadvantage of certification is that it may exclude some guides who cannot enter the certification process because they do not meet the eligibility criteria or who cannot enter the programme for logistical, financial or other reasons. These barriers to entering the certification process reflect the realities of tour guiding, where guides are poorly paid, lack permanent employment and may be located in remote areas (Ap & Wong, 2001; Mak et al., 2011).

Depending on the structure of the certification programme, it has the capacity to achieve all three quality assurance outcomes through programme promotion and benefits, establishing minimum standards and rewarding advanced levels of role performance. However, these programmes are costly to establish and manage (Black, 2002; Black & Ham, 2005) and some guides may be excluded for the reasons outlined above.

Licensing

In contrast to professional certification, licensing is a mandatory, legal requirement for some professions to practice (Hoskins, 1986; Morrison et al., 1992; Pond, 1993). The intention of licensing is often to restrict a profession to those who are considered competent or to delimit the scope of practice for a particular profession (Hoskins, 1986), thereby protecting consumers. The desire to protect the public from incompetent practicing guides or other practitioners (Barnhart, 1997) can extend to enforcement by governments in the form of fines and jail sentences (Huang & Weiler, 2010; Mak et al., 2009).

Licenses for tour guiding are generally issued and required by government agencies (Issaverdis, 1998, 2001). In a study of countries that are members of the World Federation of Tourist Guides Associations, Orde (2011b) found that 29 out of 61 countries required tour guide licensing. Many countries around the world require a license to practice as a guide, including Singapore (Henderson, 2002), Serbia (Rabotic, 2011), Macau (Mak et al., 2009), Indonesia (Bras, 2000), China (Huang & Weiler, 2010), Israel and the United Kingdom (Guild of Registered Tourist Guides, 2001; Pond, 1993).

Some countries and cities require guides to complete a specified or recognised training course before they can be licensed to work as a tour guide (Bras, 2000; Wong *et al.*, 1999). For example, the UK Blue Badge licensing programme requires guides to complete an intensive training course, which varies in scope and length depending on the region. All guides must successfully complete the academic work and pass written and oral examinations to receive the Blue Badge. Guides that achieve this qualification are members of the Guild of Guide Lecturers and are officially licensed to conduct tours by the regional tourist boards (Pond, 1993). In Singapore, guides must apply and meet a set of criteria, attend an interview with tourism representatives and complete a prescribed training course.

The advantages of licensing are that it enforces, through law or regulation, a minimum standard that must be met by all tour guides, and provides an element of consumer protection (Henderson, 2002; Huang & Weiler, 2010). However, this mechanism may only require a minimum standard to be met and does not necessarily support advanced levels of role performance or provide an incentive for excellence (Issaverdis, 1998, 2001). It is also a blanket approach that generally applies to all tour guides and may be inappropriate for specialist guides. Other issues include how and who undertakes the monitoring and enforcement of the licensing process as discussed by Mak *et al.* (2009, 2011), and the stringency of the application and renewal procedures (Pond, 1993). The experience in Singapore (Henderson, 2002) suggests that since its introduction in the 1970s, tour guide licensing has been very successful in protecting visitors and ensuring a high standard of guiding. However, there are still problems of enforcement and some unlicensed guiding and, according to Henderson (2002), opportunities exist to improve the licensing approach, for example evaluating the effectiveness of training and guide performance and developing a code of conduct. The successful licensing approach adopted in Singapore may, however, reflect the particular situation in that country, which is a small land area with a political culture of government intervention and regulation.

In Macau, as previously mentioned (Mak *et al.*, 2009, 2011), despite the fact that they have licensing, there are still significant problems in retaining and recruiting qualified and trained guides and, more importantly, monitoring and controlling the service quality (Mak *et al.*, 2009, 2011). Mak *et al.* (2009, 2011) found that licensing was considered more effective than the professional certification programme in Hong Kong because it was enshrined in legislation and had effective and unbiased monitoring. Mak *et al.*'s (2009) pilot study of tour guiding issues in Macau found that a number of factors were responsible for unethical and unhealthy tour guiding practices, most of which were factors external to the guides themselves and were related to two key issues: the tourist-generating country and the host destination. For example, the former relates to the unhealthy business practices of travel agents in mainland China such as below-cost tour fares and below-cost reception fee practices. These cost-cutting measures shift the financial pressure onto the tour guides with inbound tourism operators, forcing the guides to set a shopping quota per visitor for the tour guides to meet. This forces tour guides to shift their focus to the role of 'salesperson'. Intense competition exists between Macau-based inbound tourism operators as a result of the below-cost tour fare practice in mainland China and this has resulted in a number of problems affecting the tour guiding profession such as diminishing guide fees, shopping quotas and prepayment of tour expenses by the tour guides themselves. These external factors are compounded by a number of human resources issues affecting the guides, including lack of recognition of the tour guide by the employer, low and unstable income, lack of commitment by tour guides, high turnover rate of guides and new immigrant tour guides from mainland China.

The work of Huang and Weiler (2010) indicates that in China tour guide licensing is separate from the qualification examination process, although the latter is closely related to licensing and serves as a preparation stage for it. To work as a tour guide in China, one must hold a license and apply to a provincial-level tourism administration. All tour guides are required to wear a license certificate that uses intelligence card (IC) technology. This licensing system allows the CNTA and local tourism administrations to enforce a demerit system for tour guide infringements, such as smoking or eating while interpreting, using regular on-the-spot inspections. According to Huang and Weiler, the use of IC technology and the demerit system represents a well-designed and centralised quality assurance approach by the government. However, the implementation of such a system comes at a cost, with considerable administrative costs, employment of inspectors and annual auditing of guides. While this licensing system is powerful in enforcing tour guide standards, it is criticised by Huang and Weiler for focusing on compliance regarding the legal, ethical and customer service roles of guides to the detriment of other key tour guiding roles.

In summary, the literature suggests that while licensing generally does not help achieve the quality assurance outcomes of raising awareness and appreciation of the importance and value of guiding, and rewarding advanced levels of role performance, licensing does set minimum guiding standards.

Codes of conduct

A commonly used mechanism that may contribute to meeting the first quality assurance outcome of raising awareness of the positive impacts and importance of guiding is the development and implementation of tour guide codes of conduct or codes of ethics (Font & Buckley, 2001; Issaverdis, 2001; Mason, 2007; Pond, 1993). Some authors argue that codes are only effective as awareness-raising tools rather than as a form of quality control (Font & Buckley, 2001; Issaverdis, 2001; Weaver, 2001; Weiler & Ham, 2001).

However, over the last 20 years there has been a proliferation of codes within the tourism and ecotourism industry (Font & Buckley, 2001; Issaverdis, 2001; Mason, 2007), with many aimed at the tourism operator and visitor rather than the guide (Mason, 2007). Codes are often criticised for being 'vague, voluntary and based on a system of self-regulation' (Weaver, 2001: 658); however, their advantages include the potential to apply fundamental principles across a sector, and their generally voluntary nature which provides moral suasion among members of professional organisations. In Indonesia, the *Rules of Conduct for Local Tourist Guides* (Bras, 2000: 128) were developed particularly to promote professional detachment and cross-cultural sensitivity among guides, and are implemented as part of both training and licensing.

General tour guide codes of conduct often address a range of guide roles such as safety, navigation and access (Guild of Registered Tourist Guides, 2001; Pond, 1993). In addition to these more generic roles, specialist guide codes also include reference to the roles of interpreter, motivator of conservation values, role model and cultural broker (Bras, 2000; Crabtree & Black, 2000; Savannah Guides, 2009; The Ecotourism Society, 1993). The main disadvantage of codes of conduct are that they are difficult to enforce (Mason, 2007), and they may not be disseminated widely or multilingually and therefore may not be fully understood due to cultural or other differences. Mason and Mowforth (1996), in their analysis of codes of conduct, identified the following additional issues and problems associated with such codes. First, there has been a lack of monitoring and evaluation of codes of conduct to determine their uptake, efficacy and effectiveness. Second, there may be a conflict between codes as a form of marketing and codes as a genuine attempt to improve the practice of tourism. Third, there is a plethora of different codes incorporating a variety of standards that may be confusing to recipients. The study by Mak *et al.* (2011) of tour guides in Hong Kong and Macau found that codes of conduct in both countries were considered to be 'workable'. In Hong Kong, the TIC and the Hong Kong Association of Registered Tour Coordinators both have respective codes of conduct, and in Macau the code of conduct has been stipulated by law in a regulation in the form of a 'professional norm'. As the latter is enshrined in law, a member who violates the code of conduct can be suspended or have his or her membership cancelled. However, despite the benefits of these codes of conduct, Mak *et al.* (2011) found that they are failing to prevent unethical and poor tour guiding practices in either country.

In China (Huang & Weiler, 2010) there is a national tour guide standard that comprises a formalised set of behaviours and performance standards that goes beyond a voluntary code of conduct as outlined by Black and Weiler (2005). It is highly prescriptive and widely adhered to; however, it is primarily focused on tour guiding procedures with respect to customer service and falls short of addressing some of the social, cultural and environmental responsibilities of a guide. According to Huang and Weiler (2010), the professional ethics of guides are very important to China's tourism authorities, partially in response to widespread media exposure of the unethical behaviour of some tour guides. Thus, researchers identify the potential of codes of conduct to help achieve the first quality assurance outcome of raising awareness of the importance and positive impacts of tour guiding, but suggest that they fail to address the other outcomes of minimum guiding standards and rewarding advanced role performance.

Individual awards of excellence

Awards of excellence programmes are the final mechanism for targeting the individual tour guide, yet only focus on the third quality assurance outcome: recognising and rewarding excellence in guiding. Like some other forms of quality assurance, awards can be at three levels: business/organisational, product and individual levels. With respect to environmental awards, the United Nations (United Nations Environment Programme Industry and Environment, 1995) regards awards as a way of both implementing environmental codes of conduct in the tourism industry and monitoring their effectiveness, and that as consumer demand for 'greener' tourism increases, '... awards often prove to be a valuable marketing tool, and method of public disclosure'. However, in his review of the literature on tourism awards, Toplis (2000) found that little research had been undertaken to evaluate the efficacy of the many tourism awards systems in achieving their stated aims.

Collectively, accreditation, professional certification, licensing and awards of excellence can both ensure a minimum level of performance and reward individual tour guiding excellence. (See Appendix)

Some of the advantages of award programmes are that they recognise and reward outstanding individuals, provide role models for the industry, promote excellence in guiding to the industry and the wider community, provide a benchmark for 'best practice' and give an incentive for other professionals to improve their skills and performance (Toplis, 2000). Depending on the assessment or evaluation method of the programme, such programmes can be a relatively cost-effective mechanism, as there are few associated administration tasks and these may be undertaken by association members. The disadvantage of awards is that they focus on rewarding an individual or a few people for excellence (Buckley, 2001), rather than achieving minimum guiding standards like professional certification and licensing, which may apply more generally to all guides. In addition, the application process for awards may be lengthy and time consuming, which may limit the number of applicants and exclude some guides.

A number of government and non-profit organisations around the world (e.g. the United States; the State of Sarawak, Malaysia; and Western Australia and the Northern Territory in Australia) have developed awards of excellence programmes aimed at individual guides. In Australia, for example, the Golden Guide Award was developed by an NGO and is given to an individual demonstrating guiding excellence in Western Australia, regardless of the type of tour or setting. This award is 'designed to encourage individual tour guides to create and deliver innovative, accurate and inspiring tours that will enhance tourism product and visitor experience' (Tourism Council of Australia, Western Australia, 2013: 1).

Australia's Northern Territory Brolga Award is similar in that it:

...recognises the personal and professional contribution, throughout their career, of a person employed in the tourism industry as a guide enhancing client experience of the tourism product. This can include site guides, tour driver/guides, multi-lingual guides, activity guides (e.g. fishing or canoeing) etc. They must have consistently contributed to the positive image of Northern Territory tourism. (Northern Territory Tourism, 2013: 1)

Both of these awards require guides to address criteria such as guiding experience, planning and research of the product, measures to ensure a high standard of interpretation and customer service and provisions for visitors with special needs (Tourism Council of Australia, 2000; Northern Territory Tourism, 2013). The National EcoGuide Award established by Ecotourism Australia (2012), is for ecotour and nature guides and as such aims to encourage excellence in more specialist guiding roles that aim to meet the principles of ecotourism. All of these awards are intended to encourage guides to achieve excellence in a range of roles, which may vary depending on the focus of the award.

As part of its package of quality assurance and continuous commitment to the professionalism of tour guiding, China offers a series of industry awards that recognises tour guides' contribution to the development of the tourism industry and encourages tour guides to constantly improve their service skills (Huang & Weiler, 2010). At a national level, there are two awards that use three criteria to assess the candidate's suitability for final nomination: first, they must demonstrate the socialist ideology and work ethics of tour guides; second, they must have strong tour guiding service skills and proficiency; and third, they must have excellent tour guiding performance levels and achievements. Huang and Weiler's (2010) study indicates that the government regards tour guides as the 'face' of the tourism industry as well as the country, and it is apparent that socialist ideology and political correctness dominate other selection criteria in the current awards of excellence schemes. While such highly politicised tour guiding policies are rare, they are not unique, an issue that was discussed in Chapter 1. Huang and Weiler contend that while China's awards of excellence appear to serve an important role as a quality assurance mechanism, their scope is fairly narrow, and without a market-oriented and research-based awards system that includes customer feedback and non-political performance-based criteria for judging excellence, the present schemes limit the potential of this mechanism to achieve quality assurance.

In summary, awards of excellence have the potential to recognise and reward advanced levels of role performance, as well as raising awareness of the importance and positive impacts of tour guiding, but do not assist in achieving minimum guiding standards. The capacity of each of the quality assurance mechanisms to achieve the three quality assurance outcomes is summarised in Table 7.1.

Implications for Research

This review reveals that research has yet to resolve issues such as what is a professional guide and how can professionalism within the tour guiding industry be achieved. The more substantial body of research on specific quality assurance mechanisms such as professional certification and licensing (Black, 2007; Calvo, 2010; Huang & Weiler, 2010; Yamada, 2011) has generally been descriptive. While it has been useful in pointing to the importance and the potential of these mechanisms to enhance the performance of tour guides with respect to the key roles that they are expected to perform, research is necessary to evaluate the efficacy of these mechanisms in achieving the three outcomes identified at the outset of this chapter.

The literature indicates that the various quality assurance mechanisms differ in what they can and cannot achieve and in the resources required to implement them. Empirical studies that monitor, assess and compare the

Table 7.1 The capacity of tour guiding quality assurance mechanisms to achieve quality assurance outcomes

| | *Quality assurance mechanisms* | | | | |
Quality assurance outcomes	*Professional associations*	*Professional certification*	*Licensing*	*Codes of conduct*	*Awards of excellence*
Awareness, appreciation and documentation of the importance, positive impacts and value-adding of tour guiding for all stakeholders including visitors and guides themselves	✓	✓		✓	✓
A minimum standard of practice for all tour guiding roles required by all guides across the industry	✓	✓	✓		
Advanced levels of performance of roles that are recognisable and rewarded	✓	✓			✓

outcomes and effectiveness of these various mechanisms with respect to tour guide performance and meeting the quality assurance outcomes would be fruitful avenues for further research. For example, what are the most effective mechanisms for influencing tour guide performance and standards? How do the different mechanisms compare in their effectiveness? Which mechanisms are most cost effective? Do some mechanisms work better in some settings, countries and tour group types than other mechanisms?

However, measuring the effects of specific mechanisms is difficult as there is often more than one mechanism in use. Ideally, research needs to compare, for example, the performance levels of guides who are members of professional associations to those who are not and guides who are certified to those who are not. Opportunities to do so – while holding other variables constant – rarely occur. Finally, many opportunities exist to apply existing models and theories to a range of different guides, countries and guiding contexts (Black & Ham, 2005; Black & Weiler, 2005; Carmody, 2013; Carmody *et al.*, 2010; Yamada, 2011).

Implications for Tour Guiding Practice

The findings from the studies that have been reviewed in this chapter and throughout the book indicate that the role of the guide is pivotal in the visitor experience and within the tourism industry. However, quality assurance and regulatory mechanisms are required to address a range of issues in the guiding industry, such as poor guiding performance, unethical practices and lack of skills and knowledge. Governments and the tourism industry should work in collaboration to support and encourage greater professionalism and performance of guides using these mechanisms. While there are, of course, many examples of high-quality guiding throughout the world, it is still important to use quality assurance as a tool to encourage and reward excellence.

To effectively develop, implement and maintain any of these mechanisms requires policy commitment and sustained allocation of resources. In selecting a mechanism, a number of issues should be considered. It needs to be recognised that each mechanism has its advantages and disadvantages, for example, some mechanisms are more appropriate for targeting specific guide roles while others can ensure quality across a range of roles. Factors such as availability of resources, which quality issues need addressing and the context of the guiding need consideration when selecting a quality assurance mechanism (Black & Weiler, 2005).

This review suggests that both professional associations and professional certification have the potential to achieve the three quality assurance outcomes, but they must be appropriately resourced by government, the tourism industry and professional associations, otherwise their capacity to meet outcomes will be limited. A combination of mechanisms appears to be an appropriate approach that would benefit all tour guiding stakeholders. Governments and the tourism industry should draw on the wealth of knowledge on existing quality assurance schemes around the world to make informed decisions about the development and implementation of appropriate mechanisms and schemes for their own guiding contexts.

Chapter Summary

This chapter has explored the issues surrounding professionalism and the process of professionalisation in the tour guiding profession. It then focused on the use of professional associations, professional certification, licensing, codes of practice and awards of excellence as mechanisms for meeting the three quality assurance outcomes: (i) raising awareness and appreciation of the importance of guiding among stakeholders, (ii) helping achieve minimum guiding standards and (iii) rewarding advanced performance of guiding roles. The following is a summary of some of the key findings in this body of literature.

This chapter reveals that each of the five mechanisms has its advantages and disadvantages and varies in its potential to achieve the three outcomes. In relation to outcome (i) – awareness, appreciation and documentation of the importance, positive impacts and value-adding of tour guiding for all stakeholders including visitors and guides themselves – this review indicates that all the mechanisms except licensing have the potential to achieve this outcome. Research also suggests that professional associations, professional certification and licensing have the potential to achieve outcome (ii) – a minimum standard of practice for all tour guiding roles required by all guides across the industry. Finally, in relation to outcome (iii) – advanced levels of performance of roles that are recognisable and rewarded – the review indicates that professional associations, professional certification and awards of excellence have the potential to achieve this outcome.

This review suggests that professional associations and professional certification are the two mechanisms that have the greatest potential to achieve all three outcomes. Professional associations can assist in meeting the outcomes as well as contributing to the professionalisation of the industry through ensuring ethical practices, continuing education, regular recertification or relicensing and monitoring of standards. While professional associations may be a cost-effective approach, there is no guarantee that they can provide all the necessary services and support as they often have limited resources. Professional certification also appears to have potential but, as with professional associations, there is limited evidence of their efficacy in achieving the three outcomes. In summary, to achieve all the quality assurance outcomes, a combination of mechanisms seems to be most appropriate and beneficial to all tour guiding stakeholders, an approach supported by a number of authors in different countries (Black & Weiler, 2005; Huang & Weiler, 2010; Yamada, 2011).

Key references

(1) Ap, J. and Wong, K.K.F. (2001) Case study on tour guiding: Professionalism, issues and problems. *Tourism Management* 22 (5), 551–563.
(2) Black, R. and Weiler, B. (2005) Quality assurance and regulatory mechanisms in the tour guiding industry: A systematic review. *Journal of Tourism Studies* 16 (1), 24–37.
(3) Black, R. and Ham, S. (2005) Improving the quality of tour guiding: Towards a model for tour guide certification. *Journal of Ecotourism* 4 (3), 178–195.
(4) Henderson, J. (2002) Creating memorable experiences for our visitor: Tourist guide licensing and training in Singapore. *Asian Journal on Hospitality and Tourism* 1 (2), 91–94.

(5) Mak, A.H.N., Wong, K.K.F. and Chang, R.C.Y. (2011) Critical issues affecting the service quality and professionalism of the tour guides in Hong Kong and Macau. *Tourism Management* 32 (6), 1442–1452.
(6) Yamada, N. (2011) Why tour guiding is important for ecotourism: Enhancing guiding quality with the ecotourism promotion policy in Japan. *Asia Pacific Journal of Tourism Research* 16 (2), 139–152.

8 Implications and Future Directions for Tour Guiding Research and Practice

Tour guiding practice has in many respects matured over the past 50 years, and in contributing to and responding to this maturation there has been a burgeoning of tour guiding research. There is greater evidence of quality as well, both outside and within the discipline of tourism studies, including theorising and applying rigorous methods to investigating and critically evaluating the phenomenon of tour guiding. Given this growth, it is challenging to summarise in a few pages the breadth and depth of all the conceptual and empirical papers on tour guides and tour guiding that have informed this book. This chapter seeks to provide some highlights, including findings from previous studies, implications for tour guiding practice and research needs and gaps. In Table 8.1, key findings are presented from the book's six thematic chapters. It must be acknowledged that there are research findings about tour guides and guiding that fall outside of these six themes and thus are not captured in these highlights. This is followed by implications for tour guiding practice that the present authors identified from their analysis of the research findings. The chapter then examines some of the many current trends both within and outside tourism that are changing the expectations and practices of tour guides and guiding, highlighting potential implications for tour guiding practice. Research needs and gaps are then presented, including emerging areas of research in tour guiding.

Research to Date: Highlights and Implications for Tour Guiding Practice

Collectively, the body of theoretical and empirical literature on tour guides and tour guiding assembled for this book offers many insights into the theory and practice of guiding. Table 8.1 highlights some of the key messages on each of the six overarching themes.

Taken as a whole, the research from the six themes covered in this book, as summarised in Table 8.1, suggests four overarching implications for tour

Table 8.1 Highlights of findings from the six key themes

Theme	Highlights
The multiple and complex roles of the tour guide	• The key roles played by guides fall into one of three spheres: instrumental (tour management); mediatory (experience management); and interpretive/sustainability (destination/resource management). Generally there has been a shift away from guides playing a largely instrumental role to playing multiple roles. • Visitors and other stakeholders agree that an array of specific guiding roles are important, but differ in their view of the relative importance and performance of individual roles. There are also differences in perceptions depending on the background of the visitors and the guiding context (e.g. location and type of tour). • In developing countries, guiding as a means of earning a living and improving one's standard of living may eclipse the performance of other roles. In protected areas, particularly in developed countries, the roles of the guide in role-modelling, managing and monitoring visitors' on-site behaviour may take precedence. • Guides can mediate or broker visitors' physical access, encounters, understanding and empathy, but most research has focused on the guide's use, or lack thereof, of interpretation to mediate understanding. The guide's role as a mediator in each of these domains can be positive as well as negative; that is, the guide can facilitate but can also constrain access, encounters, understanding and empathy. • Beyond the functional view of the roles of a tour guide that has dominated research, how tour guides play out their roles in actual practice often varies from one guide to another and from one tour group to another. As such, an individual guide can have considerable social, cultural and political agency.
Guides as interpreters, storytellers and intercultural communicators	• Communication competency of tour guides can be measured across at least three dimensions: non-verbal communication, verbal communication and the guide's traits. There may be dozens of individual competencies that make up these dimensions, and visitors and guides can perceive the relative importance and performance of each of these differently. According to the relational model of communication competence, a visitor will judge a guide's overall communication competency based on the guide's knowledge, skill and motivation. • Visitors and stakeholders view interpretation as one of the key defining roles of a quality tour guide and a distinguishing feature of a quality guided tour. Being a good interpreter is more complex and more difficult to master than other roles required of and performed by guides. Thus, interpretive guiding practice often falls short of visitors' and other stakeholders' expectations.

- Interpretive guiding involves the application of interpretation principles towards achieving predetermined outcomes aimed at benefiting visitors, other stakeholders, destinations and environments. Interpretive principles that have been found to deliver satisfaction and enhance visitor experiences include: (i) interpretation via a diversity of enjoyable communication approaches, activities and experiences; (ii) interpretation designed to promote the use of two or more senses; (iii) interpretation designed to facilitate individual and group involvement, contact or participation; (iv) communicating the relevance of an object, artefact, landscape or site to visitors; (v) communicating by way of theme development/thematic interpretation; (vi) communicating accurate fact-based information that both facilitates understanding and promotes thinking and meaning-making; and (vii) interpretation that makes people feel empathy or emotion.

- The use of drama, storytelling and narratives is pervasive in tour guiding, but individual guides vary widely in how they use these techniques as tools to enhance their communication. These and other specific interpretive guiding techniques may also need customisation to particular audiences such as visitors from non-Western cultures.

- Effective intercultural communication requires a guide to have competence in languages, the ability to explain and interpret culture, an appreciation for cultural difference and for what is and is not appropriate to communicate, interest and willingness to find common ground, social-interpersonal competence such as respect, and enough pride to act as an ambassador for his or her culture.

The contributions of tour guiding to sustainability	- Viewing tour guiding through the lens of sustainability is of benefit to destinations and all stakeholders, including visitors themselves. More travellers are now looking for experiences that are not only enjoyable and memorable but are also meaningful; that is, experiences that make a difference in their own lives and that help sustain the host environments and communities they visit. - There is evidence that tour guides contribute to sustainability by enhancing visitors' understanding and valuing of sites, communities, cultures and environments, and influencing and monitoring visitors' behaviour, en route, on-site and at destinations. - There is some, but less, evidence that tour guides can foster visitors' post-visit pro-environmental and pro-conservation attitudes and behaviours.

(Continued)

Table 8.1 (Continued)

Theme	Highlights
	• There is very little evidence that tour guides influence the social and cultural sustainability of destinations, although employing local guides has been found to be effective in some cases in enhancing positive economic, social and cultural impacts.
	• The links between tour guiding and sustainability have been most often studied in the context of nature-based and ecotour guiding, and therefore there is a greater body of evidence for tour guiding's contribution to environmental sustainability than for economic, social and cultural sustainability.
	• The antecedents of and pathways by which particular tour guiding practices contribute to the sustainability of sites, businesses, communities and destinations have been theorised but have yet to be demonstrated. There is enthusiasm for, but little evidence of, using training and quality assurance schemes to enhance the links between tour guiding and sustainability.
Visitor expectations of and satisfaction with tour guides and the guiding service	• Studies to date indicate that tour guide performance has a positive effect on visitor satisfaction and in some studies this correlation is statistically significant. More recent studies also demonstrate that satisfaction with the guiding service positively affects satisfaction with tour services and overall tour experience, although the latter finding is not consistent across all studies.
	• Some studies show that the guide's performance influences the future return of customers, differentiates a tourism operator from its competitors, and thus can benefit tourism operators through competitive advantage. The guide's performance can also be critical to the image of the destination that he or she represents. The destination's economy can also benefit, as some studies indicate that if visitors are satisfied with their guide, they are more likely to engage in shopping.
	• There are a number of specific tour guide attributes, qualities and skills that contribute to visitor satisfaction. These include clear communication and knowledge of the destination, interpersonal skills, getting the group involved in activities and interactions with tour participants, interpretation (including presentation skills and commentary) and professionalism (for example, sense of responsibility, politeness, concern for the clients, organisation and empathy).

- Attributes that are not always performed well by guides and where underperformance can lead to dissatisfaction include dealing with emergencies, honesty and ethical practices, guiding language, fostering a sense of humour, destination knowledge and friendliness.
- Guide performance is often culturally and context specific and its links to satisfaction are not always generalisable to other tour guiding contexts. There are many situational variables such as group composition, member characteristics and expectations, tour length, group cohesiveness, cultural differences, place and reasons for joining a tour that can influence visitor perceptions and satisfaction.

| Improving tour guide performance through training and education | - Guide training has much to offer as a quality assurance mechanism, in particular that it provides an avenue for anyone to meet the minimum standards needed to work as a guide. The growth and evolution of tourism globally from a service-based economy to an experience-based economy and the increasingly diverse range of roles expected of and played by tour guides are flagged as factors that have raised the urgency for tour guides to gain qualifications and expertise through training, education and professional development.
- The benefits of tour guide training and education accrue at the individual, operator and industry levels. At an individual level, training can increase guides' knowledge of relevant topics, enhance specific skills and improve a guide's employment prospects, career opportunities, level of pay and conditions of work. Training also provides an opportunity for self-evaluation, reflection and discussion. From the employer's perspective, having trained guides may help guides embrace the organisation's vision, provide a commercial advantage in terms of marketing, repeat trips, superior service and, in the long term, increased profits. At an industry-wide level, training can support and encourage professionalism, safety, customer service and informed interpretation, and can help raise standards and improve the quality of the tourism product and thus the competitive advantage of regions and destinations. |

(Continued)

Table 8.1 (Continued)

Theme	Highlights
	• There is evidence of inconsistency and inadequacy in guide training in both developed and developing countries. In developing countries, training has embraced environmental and social sustainability outcomes but tends to underemphasise interpretation. In both developing and developed countries, competency-based approaches to training have been criticised as overemphasising hard skills at the expense of the more complex elements of guiding.
	• Standardisation of training, such as a focus on core knowledge and skills, and assessment of competency together facilitate the portability of outcomes, but tend to then compromise cultural, context and individual learner relevance. Offering different levels of training from basic to advanced can encourage guides to advance their skills and knowledge and develop more professional full-time guides. Professional development and life-long learning can be facilitated by good organisational culture, but can be challenging due to the lack of monetary reward for upgrading and the remote location of many guides.
Conceptualising quality in tour guiding	• Quality assurance and regulatory mechanisms have been found to: (i) raise awareness and appreciation of the importance, positive impacts and value-adding of tour guiding for all stakeholders, including visitors and guides themselves; (ii) help develop and implement minimum guiding standards; and (iii) reward advanced performance of roles.
	• Licensing, codes of conduct and individual awards for excellence are weaker quality assurance mechanisms that achieve some of these quality assurance outcomes. All the mechanisms except licensing have the potential to achieve quality assurance outcome (i). Professional associations, professional certification and licensing have the potential to achieve quality assurance outcome (ii). Professional associations, professional certification and awards of excellence have the potential to achieve outcome (iii).
	• Professional associations and professional certification have the potential to achieve all three quality assurance outcomes but need financial support and other resources to do so. Professional associations are typically more cost effective but less certain than professional certification to achieve all quality assurance outcomes.
	• A combination of mechanisms is most appropriate and beneficial to all stakeholders.

guiding practice. Specific and more detailed implications for practice are provided in the relevant section of each chapter.

The first implication is that tourism operators, destination managers and others need to adopt a more proactive approach in marketing and conveying the importance and value of tour guides to the wider tourism industry, policymakers and the public. This includes communicating what roles they expect guides to play and being more transparent in the practices that they use to recruit, train and reward high-quality guides who can perform these roles. Acknowledgement of the importance of the guide needs to be evident in what the tourism industry both says and does, so that training, recruitment practices, professional development opportunities, levels of pay and other reward schemes convey a consistent message that quality tour guiding is central to the success of the industry. As part of this, a greater commitment is needed to collect and disseminate evidence of the outcomes of best practice guiding, with respect to not only the quality of the visitor experience but also sustainability outcomes. Governments and industry should provide support to guides to collect this evidence, including appropriate training and resourcing, so that the importance and value of guides becomes common knowledge across the industry.

Secondly, is the need to revisit tour guide training globally. Research has assembled a wealth of understanding of the roles that guides play and the standards of performance expected by visitors and others. Training needs to be informed by this body of knowledge, and needs to include not only the fundamental hard skills but also the knowledge and skills that guides require to be effective interpreters, mediators, intercultural communicators, role models and facilitators of sustainability. In developing countries, training models that work best are those where training is initiated locally and then developed as a partnership that includes educational expertise, an in-depth knowledge of tour guiding practice, a sound understanding of visitors and their expectations and an appreciation of the local context. Training approaches need to ensure the delivery of core content while maintaining the capacity to adapt to the training needs and styles of individual learners. Training needs to be accessible to guides, including those already employed in the industry, and its availability needs to be communicated. Governments should require that all guides be trained and industry needs to commit to employing only trained guides.

Thirdly, the roles and performance expectations of guides need to inform other quality assurance schemes. Minimum standards in all aspects of guiding need to be specified, embraced and enforced by industry and governments. Systems for monitoring unethical and unsatisfactory performance of guides need to be developed and resourced across the industry. Quality assurance schemes need to be in place that acknowledge good practice and reward best practice interpretation, intercultural communication and sustainability practices. Guides need to be provided with incentives for pursuing advanced levels of training, certification and performance.

A fourth and final implication from the body of research on tour guiding is that tour guides need to be developed and nurtured as independent, critical thinkers with a desire and commitment to ongoing professional development and the capacity to be self-reflective. The importance of these capacities needs to be acknowledged by both governments and industry. Tourism operators need to provide guides with opportunities for ongoing professional development including on-the-job assessment, coaching and mentoring schemes. Guides also need opportunities and incentives to update themselves with the latest findings of research on guiding, the expectations of visitors and stakeholders, trends in tourism and sustainability. Finally, governments and the tourism industry need to collaborate to support long-term employment and career progression to help professionalise the practice of tour guiding.

Trends Affecting the Future of Guiding

In addition to insights for tour guiding practice provided by previous research, current macro and micro social, political and economic influences are shaping and will shape both visitor expectations of guides and the way that guides deliver their tours. At a micro (guided tour) level, changing markets, including the growth of relatively new markets such as India and China, changing profiles and preferences of visitors who seek out guided tours (such as Gen Y onwards), changing tour guide profiles and new technologies are all likely to affect tour guides and the guided tour. At a macro (tour context) scale there are many factors that can and will affect tour guides and guiding, including increased urbanisation, social and economic changes, safety and security, health and diseases, fuel availability and prices, risk and litigation, natural and human-induced disasters, political disruptions and climate change. Some of these trends are briefly discussed here to raise awareness of these issues and highlight potential implications for tour guiding practice.

According to Yeoman (2012), with rising disposal incomes, tourists are now demanding better experiences, faster service, multiple choice, social responsibility and greater satisfaction. As visitors gain experience and confidence, their expectations may increase with respect to their involvement, control and ownership of the nature, content and quality of their travel experiences. Importantly, visitors are now more inclined to seek customisation of tour products, and some have the capacity and expectation of co-creation, that is, they actively contribute to the design and production of their own experiences (Binkhorst & Den Dekker, 2009). They may seek intellectual or emotional engagement both in planning and in the experience itself, and some seek a sense of ownership or control.

Of course, rising expectations on the part of the visitor put considerable pressure on the guide to be flexible, so the sooner that the expectations are conveyed to the guide, preferably well before the tour, the better equipped the guide can be to respond to visitors' needs.

With enhanced community consciousness about both physical and mental health and well-being, including in tourism (Filep & Pearce, 2013), it may become increasingly important for guides to develop the capacity to promote visitor health and wellness on their tours. In the first instance, guides need to be aware of visitors' health and medical needs, especially with an ageing population that is both physically and financially equipped to travel well into and beyond retirement age. Tourism operators and destinations already specialise in health and wellness tourism and experiences. However, it is not just niche markets that are health conscious, and this trend may impact many aspects of guiding from food preparation and consumption through to opportunities for physical exercise while on a tour.

Beyond this, some visitors may be actively seeking personal change and transformation, and there are now operators who promote this as part of their tours. Indeed Pine and Gilmore (2011) describe transformation as the ultimate experience. All guides need to be cognisant that, especially for longer tours, the journey for the individual participant may be an inner one as well as an outer one. In some cases, visitors may be searching for emotional engagement, personal meaning, life change or intellectual or spiritual enlightenment, and thus guides may need to develop skills as change agents. The outdoor education literature has engaged with this concept for many years and may offer insights to guides wishing to enhance their capacity to foster visitors' personal growth and development.

The advent of technology in both the marketing and the delivery of experiences is also having profound impacts throughout the tourism industry. Today's visitors are more inclined than in the past to have searched the internet and to have viewed high-quality travel documentaries pre-travel and gained considerable knowledge about destinations and their attractions, product options and pricing. As a form of value-adding, some tourism operators promote the qualifications, skills and experience of their guides to distinguish their product from their competitors and from non-guided experiences. The tour guide as a point of differentiation depends very much on both target markets and the experiences on offer, but this phenomenon is likely to grow in frequency and sophistication as the tourism industry becomes more competitive. While the use of the internet as a marketing tool makes it easier for tourism operators to convey that a guide adds value to an experience, this also increases visitors' expectations of high-quality guided experiences. Of course, it is now easier and largely cost-free for visitors to complain about their experiences including their guides. TripAdvisor and similar travel forums are more widely read and used, a trend that puts increasing pressure to deliver consistent high-quality tour guiding.

In addition to the internet, technology-assisted experiences en route and on-site are more common, ranging from highly interactive visitor centres to mobile phone apps to podcasts in the language of the visitor's choice. One consequence is the perception that technology can in some cases substitute for what tour guides previously provided, notably the one-way delivery of directional and services information, commentary, site interpretation and language translation. For example, digitised guidebooks are now available through mobile applications designed for smartphone operators such as Nokia, Apple, Google and Android (Yeoman, 2012). This underlines the need for tour guiding to be innovative and marketed as a service that adds value in ways that technology cannot. The most obvious aspects of this are that tour guiding can be interactive with both visitors and host communities, and that the experience can be changed and even customised to visitors' needs and expectations. Guides and operators can also embrace technology to enhance the delivery of guided tours, such as incorporating podcasts and smartphone apps into their tours.

Technology has also made it possible for people with a broader range of physical and even mental capacities to travel, including on guided tours. Moreover, most developed countries and some developing countries have a much greater sense of accessibility and equal opportunity in tourism than in the past, and this includes the opportunity for everyone, irrespective of ability, to enjoy the full range of guided tour experiences. At the same time, an ageing population translates to a larger proportion of both mental and physical disabilities among those who are travelling. Guides need to be trained and equipped to assist individuals with a variety of special needs, ranging from hearing difficulties, sight impairment and mobility restrictions (including the need for an aid such as a wheelchair), to learning difficulties, anxieties and stress disorders.

Increasing incidences of extreme weather events and natural disasters due to climate change, and human-induced threats such as the global financial crisis, health epidemics and even terrorism, challenge tour guides in ways they may not have been previously. As a relatively benign example, a guide is often called upon to interpret a phenomenon or site such as a battlefield, terrorist or natural disaster site to visitors with very different nationalistic, religious and political values and views. A more extreme situation, however, may be managing a tour group during a natural event (such as an attack by a wild animal), a natural disaster (such as a tsunami) or a violent incident (such as a hostage taking). Tour guides have been known to act as bodyguards, rescuers and lifesavers in such situations and may be increasingly expected to do so in a politically and socially changing world.

Finally, there is a growing expectation that guides contribute to the economic, environmental, social and cultural sustainability of communities and destinations, and this is no longer confined to specialist guides such as ecotour and nature guides. Moreover, guides may act as knowledge and capacity builders and even activists for change in host communities and at destinations. They may also be promoted as caretakers and monitors of both visitors and their behaviour, and as information trackers in relation to tourism impacts. Similar to the use of volunteer tourists who engage in data collection for the purposes of monitoring impacts and changes in natural and cultural environments, guides need to be trained, equipped and rewarded for such activities. Guided tours are already being used as a tool for change in urban areas for participants to visualise possible futures (Hansson, 2009). This type of guided experience is a form of citizen participation where people are being taken through the process of 'experiencing – understanding – taking action'. This is also happening with art tours where some guides are adopting the role of provocateur and change agent by presenting alternative viewpoints and counterculture narratives. In a similar vein, in Europe young people are employed as guide activists, guiding and facilitating groups of young people through cities using experiential activities to raise tourists' awareness of environmental and social issues and to engage them in solutions (www.touristsavetheworld.com).

Research Needs, Gaps and New Directions

There are many avenues that could be pursued in future research on tour guiding. This section begins by presenting a global perspective on tour guiding research needs, based on the collectivity of tour guiding research completed to date, building on what was introduced in Chapter 1. After presenting broad geographical, topical, theoretical and methodological perspectives on research needs and gaps, the research implications raised in each of the thematic chapters are presented. The section concludes with an overview of new and emerging research topics not covered in the previous chapters.

A global perspective on gaps in tour guiding research

Based on the authors' comprehensive search of published English-language literature to date, Chapter 1 presented an overview of tour guiding research. *Geographically*, two-thirds (66%) of the empirical research on tour guiding that reported a study location was undertaken in Australia, the United States, Europe or Asia (mainly in Chinese-speaking countries). There were 14 studies undertaken in Latin/South America. Only 10 published studies (5%) were clearly investigations across more than one country, and fewer than 10 studies were located in each of Africa, Canada, New Zealand and the Middle East. These patterns suggest that future work should be carried out and supported in and by authors from Africa, South America, the Pacific and Asia. There is also a dearth of cross-national and comparative research. Tour guiding in the context of the polar regions, rural areas and marine, coastal and inland waterways is also largely under-researched. Thus, while acknowledging that there may well be a rich body of tour guiding research and scholarship in other languages, analysis of the English-language literature suggests that research on tour guiding may be biased with respect to geographical focus.

Another bias of current research is the *tourism genre* in which tour guiding research has been undertaken. As noted in Chapter 1, nature-based tourism was the context for more than a third (35%) of the tour guiding research identified for this book, followed by heritage/cultural tourism (21%) and adventure tourism (10%). Tour guiding in the context of group/package tourism (6%) and urban tourism (5%) is relatively under-researched, and studies of tour guides and guiding in the context of business, health and wellness, sport, cultural/music, theme parks, educational/industrial sites, shopping tours, events, boat/cruise-based, street/beach-based, pro-poor, philanthropic, volunteer and dark tourism are virtually non-existent.

In addition to tourism contexts, there are a number of *market segments* relevant to tour guiding that seem to be neglected by researchers. For example, elderly visitors and those with special needs (e.g. people with disabilities such as a visual or hearing impairment) have been virtually ignored in tour guiding research. Studies of visitors from non-Western cultures are only very recent and are still largely limited to visitors from Chinese-speaking countries.

This book has reviewed studies that have drawn on a range of *disciplinary perspectives*, notably human geography, sociology, anthropology, communication/language studies and psychology. These same disciplines and newer disciplines, such as business studies (mainly consumer behaviour services and marketing), environmental studies, environmental education and heritage/nature interpretation, have added considerably to the literature and are also evident in the journals in which the researchers publish, including, of course, leisure, recreation and tourism studies. The analysis presented in Chapter 1 of the disciplinary background of those who have researched tour guides and guiding suggests minimal contribution from disciplines such as economics, political science, cultural studies, some of the business disciplines (e.g. human resource management, organisation behaviour, leadership/management), law, medicine, history, adult education and most of the physical sciences. While it was not an aim of this book to review bodies of literature that might inform future tour guiding theory, research and practice, there does appear to be opportunities to bring insights from these disciplines to the investigation of the phenomenon of tour guiding. Collaboration with researchers and scholars from other disciplines may also serve tour guiding researchers.

An analysis of *theoretical development* in tour guiding suggests that, up until the new millennium, tour guiding research could be characterised as being theoretically weak (Weiler & Kim, 2011).

While some more recent guiding literature is theory based, the development, testing and refinement of tour guiding theory have been very limited in scope. For example, Weiler and Yu (2007) identify the brokering of physical access, understanding and encounters with locals as three dimensions of cultural mediation, but these have not been explored, tested or refined beyond the context of their study. McGrath's (2007) highlighting of 'emotional access' could, for example, be a fourth dimension of guide mediation to add to Weiler and Yu's three dimensions. Some authors have suggested the application of intercultural communication and linguistics theory, but again these have received limited attention, mainly in the context of Chinese tour guiding (Dioko *et al.*, 2013; Huang, 2004; Scherle & Nonnenmann, 2008; Yu & Weiler, 2006).

A quantitative analysis of the *theories* that underpinned the 280 publications reviewed for this book was abandoned because so few authors declared or demonstrated engagement with a particular theory or theoretical framework. Those who did tended to rely on conceptual frameworks developed within tourism and tour guiding itself, such as Cohen's (1985) and Weiler and Davis's (1993) conceptual frameworks depicting the roles of a guide. In recent decades, the embedding of theory from other disciplines has been more evident, such as media and mediation theory (Chapter 2), theories of communication and intercultural communication competence (Chapter 3), theories from cognitive and behavioural psychology (Chapters 3 and 4), service quality theories (Chapter 5), competency-based training and educational theory (Chapter 6) and theories relating to professionalisation (Chapter 7).

Some tour guiding researchers have identified specific opportunities where future research could more extensively and explicitly draw on theory from other disciplines. Leadership theory in the tour guiding context has been discussed in the literature (Howard, 1998; Weiler, 1996) but has not been empirically tested. Both Weiler (1996) and Howard (1998) point to Hersey and Blanchard's (1982) leadership model and the need for further work in this area, specifically to identify the extent to which tour guides play a role in influencing tourist behaviour and attitudes, to explore appropriate leadership styles for tour guides and to develop a methodology for assessing tourists' level of readiness in relation to leadership. Place attachment (Morgan, 2009) and place identity (de la Barre, 2013) as both antecedent to and outcomes of a guided tour experience have also been highlighted as theories that lend themselves to further investigation in a tour guiding context. A number of researchers outline the merits of other specific theories, theoretical frameworks and models for future research on tour guiding (Houge Mackenzie & Kerr, 2013; Macdonald, 2006; Mason & Christie, 2003; Morgan & Dong, 2008; Weiler & Kim, 2010; Yu & Weiler, 2006).

As mentioned in Chapter 1, research on the *broader context of tour guiding* has been limited. For example, there has been no critical historical analysis of the phenomenon of tour guiding or investigations of the international context of tour guiding. A number of global trends were outlined in an earlier section of this chapter; however, no research has been undertaken on how such trends have impacted or are impacting tour guides and tour guiding.

It was noted in Chapter 1 that, collectively, tour guiding researchers draw on a relatively wide range of *data sources and research methods*, but tend to make heavy use of surveys, interviews and various forms of observation. In terms of collecting data from visitors, guides and other stakeholders, there is scope for making greater use of non-field-based survey methods such as web-based surveys. Researchers investigating tour guides and guiding have made relatively little use of case studies, ethnography, focus groups, analysis of government and industry documents, visitors' and guides' verbal narrative and written texts, web-based materials such as travel advisory sites and visual/photo analysis.

A thematic look at tour guiding research gaps

So far, this examination of research needs has taken a general and collective (non-specific) perspective of gaps in tour guiding research to date. Gaps at a thematic level are presented next, using the six themes around which this book has been written. Drawing on the 'Implications for Research' sections in each chapter, this section highlights some of the most topical areas within each of the six themes.

With regard to the roles of the tour guide, further research is needed to explore role expectations and performance within each of the three spheres (tour management, experience management and resource management) identified in Chapter 2, as well as role expectations of stakeholders other than visitors. More work is required to investigate the extent to which guides are recruited, trained and empowered to deal with variations in role expectations and performance. With the increasing and diverse number of roles that guides are expected to play, more exploration would be beneficial on the interplay between roles including role conflict. Further work is needed to explore the role of the guide beyond the guided tour experience, for example as promotional or image-building agents or as observers of the tourism industry and its impacts. Given the importance of the mediator role, researchers should consider what visitors expect and why they do or do not use tour guides as mediators, especially with respect to mediation of encounters and affect (empathy). More detailed investigation of the effectiveness of specific techniques for each of the four domains of mediation/ brokering – physical access, encounters (interactions), understanding (intellectual access) and empathy (emotional access) – is also needed. As tourism expands into new and niche areas, such as pro-poor tourism, philanthropic tourism, volunteer tourism and dark tourism, tour guiding roles may need adapting.

With changing tourism markets, more research is needed to determine how differences and changes in consumer expectations and travel experiences will impact on guide roles and communication. For example, work is needed on communication/interpretation expectations and preferences of visitors from different cultures and the applicability of interpretation principles in these contexts. In relation to interpretive best practice principles, more studies are required to explore the relationship of individual best practice principles to guiding effectiveness, that is, how and to what extent specific applications of interpretive guiding principles and practices contribute to specific outcomes such as enhancing the visitor experience. In addition, there is scope for investigating how often, how consistently and how appropriately each technique is used and the relative costs and benefits of using any one of these interpretation principles in relation to specific tourist markets.

In terms of the role of guides in sustainability, more studies are needed to evaluate the short- and long-term effects of what guides say and do on visitors' post-visit attitudes and behaviours towards the environment and towards cultural heritage, acknowledging that sustainability outcomes are likely to vary across different markets, cultures and contexts. Objective, verifiable evidence that links specific environmental messages and role-modelling practices with visitors' pro-environmental attitudes and behaviour is also needed. A valuable contribution to the literature would be studies looking at the benefits of specific guiding practices on sustainability outcomes for host populations, cultures and destinations, and in particular the extent and pathways by which tour guiding improves the economic viability and competitiveness of a business, local community or destination. This type of work is especially needed for tour guiding outside nature-based and ecotourism contexts.

A useful avenue for research would be to compare the visitor experiences and level of satisfaction between guided and non-guided tours. The correlation between tour guide performance and visitor satisfaction is an area requiring further work beyond Chinese-speaking tour guides and tour groups. Studies could be carried out using a range of cultural and ethnic guiding contexts and different types of tour groups. Other factors that could be explored would be tour guide characteristics such as leadership style and cultural background, as well as tour length and group size. The literature would benefit from studies that identify the antecedents to visitor satisfaction such as service quality, perceived value, motivation, positive and negative emotions and other aspects of a guide's performance.

As tour guide stakeholders' expectations of a quality guided experience increase, a range of quality assurance mechanisms have been developed to enhance the performance of guides with respect to their key roles. Many opportunities for research exist in relation to all the quality assurance tools including training, licensing and professional certification. In particular, work is needed on monitoring, assessing and comparing the outcomes and effectiveness of the various mechanisms with respect to tour guide performance, specific roles, communication competence, visitor satisfaction and sustainability outcomes. In terms of training, systematic testing and advancing of different conceptual training models and approaches are needed, together with longitudinal evaluation of training particularly when guides return to their workplace.

Finally, in terms of other quality assurance and regulatory mechanisms, more work is required to explore the efficacy of these mechanisms for achieving the three quality assurance outcomes: (i) raising awareness, appreciation and documentation of the importance of guides; (ii) helping to develop and implement minimum guiding standards; (iii) rewarding advanced levels of performance of roles. This work could include examining the costs and benefits of each mechanism in the context of particular tour group types, settings and countries. Finally, an important area of potential research is to explore stakeholder perspectives on what is a professional guide and how professionalism can be achieved within the tour guiding industry.

Emerging themes in tour guiding research

Finally, a selected number of existing but emerging themes in the tour guiding literature that have not been captured by the six thematic chapters in this book are reviewed in this section. These are areas that have attracted the attention of only one or a handful of researchers and offer further promise.

The first theme is the role of gender in tour guiding that has been briefly mentioned in a few studies (Meisch, 2002; Torland, 2011b) but has been explored in depth in only two studies. Lin *et al.* (2008) explored how images of female tour leaders were used by tour companies to advertise their tour products that resulted in consumers being more likely to purchase a tour than if the photos had been of male tour leaders. Modin *et al.*'s (2011) study of docents (volunteer guides) as creators of empathy in plantation house museums in the Southern United States touches on how the docent's gender influenced the affective impact of the tours.

They found that gender shaped the docent's narrative by privileging the representation of certain historical groups over others, for example the story of the White male planter over the Black slaves. However, they also suggested that the visitors' characteristics including gender may also be a key factor in shaping the historical portrayals delivered to them by the guides. Together, these factors represent a barrier to telling a more balanced, accurate and emotionally compelling story. Further studies on gender and guiding would provide valuable insights into the different personal and professional experiences of guides and how gender influences role expectations and performance, as well as the impact of the visitor's gender on the guides themselves.

This leads to a second emerging theme, that of the health, safety and well-being of the tour guides themselves. Some studies demonstrate the financial and personal risks that some guides take to ensure financial security. Studies such as those by Crick (1992) and Bras and Dahles (1999) have explored the work of informal guides. The latter study looked at street guides in Jogjakarta and beach boys in Lombok, both in Indonesia, and explored the sexual advances to female tourists in the context of them being small-scale entrepreneurs, combining several jobs in the tourism industry. These guides seek a romantic interlude that may last a few days or sometimes years, but maintain it only if it has financial rewards. Sexual encounters are not the main focus of these guides: it is the financial benefit and improved security. One of the study informants called them 'multifunctional guides' offering companionship, entertainment and sex in return for an experience with a Western woman and money.

Other authors have explored the issue of the personal well-being of tour guides from a range of perspectives. Since early 2000, there have been a number of papers (Houge Mackenzie & Kerr, 2013; Sharpe, 2005; Torland, 2011b) focusing on tour guiding and emotions, drawing on the original theory of Hochschild's (1983) emotional labour, with most studies contextualised in adventure guiding. These studies found that guides were required to fulfil a demanding set of emotional expectations from tourists and employers and they regularly engaged in strategies to help them manage these expectations. Deep acting by tour guides helped convey a sense of authenticity to tourists while promoting a feeling of achievement among the guides, leading to higher levels of job satisfaction. In contrast, surface acting in some cases resulted in negative emotions and impaired performance. The findings from these studies have important implications for guides as well as tourism operators to help reduce issues such as burnout, staff turnover and poor service quality, and the development of coping strategies. Future studies could apply other sociological and psychological theories apart from Hochschild's (1983) emotional labour theory. More quantitative studies are needed that can establish cause-and-effect relationships and produce generalisable findings. In particular, more research is needed on the links between emotional labour and visitor and organisational outcomes.

Other risks encountered by guides include sexual encounters and related sexually transmitted diseases. Fluker and Deery (2003) looked at the sexual behaviour of white-water rafting guides and Cabada *et al.* (2007) investigated Peruvian tour guides' sexual behaviour and knowledge of sexually transmitted infection (STI) prevention. While the majority of guides (65%) were sexually active during the year prior to the study, almost 42% did not use condoms and 27% reported symptoms compatible with an STI. These results are of concern because of the bridging position of tour guides between potential STI carriers in travellers and the local population (including sex workers). In a similar study, Avcikurt *et al.* (2011) explored Turkish tour guides' awareness and attitudes about HIV and AIDS and found that knowledge of HIV and AIDS varied with gender, age and work experience, but of more concern were their misconceptions about the transmission or methods of treatment and protection. Further research on guides' knowledge of and attitudes to health issues, their health status and health risks would be beneficial to guides and their employers. These issues of risk, health and safety have implications for the content of tour guide training programmes.

A third emerging theme is the economic benefits of and willingness to pay for tour guiding services including high-quality interpretive guiding. The economic benefit of tour guiding is particularly pertinent in developing countries and remote areas of developed countries where guiding can provide an important avenue of employment and economic benefits to the wider community. Little is known about visitors' willingness to pay, which tourist markets might be willing to pay more and for which aspects, roles or level of performance visitors might be willing to pay. Carver *et al.* (2003) provide a model depicting the social and economic value of interpretation, the enhancement of this value via training and certification and the theoretical relationship of these to participants' willingness to pay, but research has yet to demonstrate this relationship in a tour guiding context.

A fourth and final emerging theme that has received limited attention but which is worthy of further work is the perspectives and views of tour guides themselves. Their voice, experiences, opinions and views are critical in understanding the tour guiding industry and the life of a tour guide both professionally and personally. Aloudat (2010) highlighted the valuable role of guides as important observers of tourism destination performance. A tour guide's day-to-day involvement with the tourism process allows valuable 'ground-level' insights that are not always available to managers who are more remote from the operational levels of tourism. The guides' observations of visitors' behavioural characteristics may also offer a significant source of data for national tourism bodies in understanding market segments.

Conclusion

This book draws from the published literature on tour guiding, which in recent years has grown in both depth and breadth. The studies reviewed in this book cover a wide range of contexts in which guided tours are conducted, ranging from city streets to heritage and wildlife tourism attractions, from high-end tourist lodging establishments to national park campgrounds, and from highly developed destinations to very remote ones in both developed and developing countries. This book has largely focused on presenting, dissecting and in some cases integrating the findings from research to date based around six key themes: (i) the multiple and complex roles and role dimensions of tour guiding; (ii) the role of the guide as communicator and interpreter; (iii) tour guides' contribution to sustainability; (iv) visitor expectations of and satisfaction with their guides; (v) the training, education and professional development of guides; and (vi) mechanisms for ensuring quality in tour guiding practice. An examination of research within these six themes has revealed that the tour guide plays a pivotal role in visitors' experiences and their level of satisfaction. Guides perform a key instrumental role in the logistics and running of the tour; however, increasingly guides are required to play more and diverse roles including that of mediator and interpreter. Particularly in specialist areas such as ecotourism and nature-based tourism, and now increasingly in more generalist guiding contexts, guides are also expected to facilitate and support sustainable tourism experiences by influencing and monitoring visitor behaviour and delivering messages that influence visitors' post-visit attitudes and behaviour. To enhance the performance of tour guides, improve visitor satisfaction and contribute to sustainability, a range of quality assurance mechanisms such as training, professional certification and licensing are now being used to assist in meeting these outcomes.

In summary, the authors of this book have used the six key themes prominent in the tour guiding literature to provide an authoritative, state-of-the-art review of the scholarly literature on tour guiding theory and practice to stimulate further research on tour guiding by social scientists across a range of disciplines and to foster quality tour guiding practice. Tour guiding research, methods and findings to date have been critically examined and synthesised to help identify key theoretical learnings and empirical findings. This review has also helped to track the evolution of tour guiding theory and research over time, to identify factors that have contributed to its evolution and, in the present chapter, to consider how global trends and issues might influence tour guiding practice in the future.

By drawing on this extensive body of research, the authors have sought to provide a framework for better identifying and understanding both the major challenges and the opportunities presented by and facing tour guiding and tour guides. Most importantly, the authors have sought to build a foundation and impetus for more research that can ultimately underpin quality tour guiding practice.

Appendix: Highlights from a Selection of Tour Guide Associations

World Federation of Tourist Guide Associations (WFTGA)

The WFTGA membership is comprised of tourist guide associations, individual tourist guides (where there is no association) and affiliates such as tour operators and universities. The WFTGA executive board is elected by delegates (country representatives) at its biennial convention. Members of the executive board (EXBO) are unpaid volunteers and are all professional tourist guides. The area representatives are appointed by the EXBO and are also unpaid professional tourist guides who help the executive around the world.

The benefits for members include: links on the association's website that allow clients to find tourist guides anywhere in the world and give another profile on search engines that allows the association to showcase its work through 'Guidelines Internetion@al' – the association's web-based magazine and news events, as well as listing on Viator.com, an international booking service for tourist guides that is checked by the WFTGA for licenses and qualifications. Members can also join the association's Facebook pages with opportunities for networking and potential tour bookings. The association also organises WFTGA training events and a biennial convention to develop guide's professional skills, network and find out more about tourist guiding around the world. Guides can also become international tourist guide trainers.

Country member associations can host the biennial convention, which raises the profile of the guides in the host country and can bring financial benefits. Guides in developing countries can apply for a Jane Orde Scholarship to attend the convention and training events. Through the WFTGA there is affiliate membership of the United Nations World Tourism Organisation (UNWTO) and operational relations with the United Nations Educational, Scientific and Cultural Organisation (UNESCO) that provides opportunities for cooperation among national tour guide associations.

The WFTGA acts as a global forum for tourist guides and it markets tourist guides around the world through its website and presentations, by attending the World Travel Market and other travel fairs worldwide and through its mailings and brochures. It raises the profile of tourist guides through contacts with international organisations such as UNESCO, UNWTO, governments and authorities. On occasion, member associations can be invited to represent the association at tourism events in their own country and thus raise their profile as well. The association liaises with other organisations such as the Federation of European Tourist Guides Associations (FEG), the International Tour Managers Association (IATM), the South East Asia Tourist Guide Federation and the Arab Tourist Guide Federation. It organises and promotes the biennial convention with the host country. The association encourages best practice for tourist guides through its training courses around the world and promotes European/International Organisation for Standardisation (EN/ISO) standards for tourist guide trainers around the world. It also supports members in national and international issues such as illegal or unqualified guiding, authority or government issues, qualification and training. The federation publicises International Tourist Guide Day (ITGD) to raise the profile of its members and the tourist guide profession and has created the Cultour Card Programme for members. The association also publishes and distributes useful booklets and other publications for tourist guides.

For more information on the WFTGA see www.wftga.org

International Federation of Mountain Guide Associations (IFMGA)

The IFMGA is a worldwide association, founded by guides from Austria, France, Switzerland and Italy, and has been in existence since 1965. The association represents mountain guide associations from more than 20 countries across Europe, Asia, the Americas and Oceania, representing almost 6000 guides. The aim of the association is to maintain close ties between all mountain guides; to standardise the working regulations which govern the profession; to ensure better safety conditions for clients; and to facilitate the ability of mountain guides to work abroad, on mountains all over the globe.

To become a certified IFMGA mountain guide, highly competent guides with a high level of training are required in four different disciplines: rock climbing, ice climbing, mountaineering and ski mountaineering. IFMGA training gives a guide the ability to work on any mountain range. It takes 5–10 years to become a mountain guide, from the moment they begin serious mountaineering to the moment they receive their guide diploma. Proper training guarantees an international standard. The technical commission at the IFMGA looks to its permanent working party to study the evolution of techniques and how to improve the level of guide training.

This commission is made up of national technical heads and meets twice a year. Guides are trained via the training schemes delivered by their national associations, sometimes in collaboration with an organisation such as a school or university.

For a national mountain guide association to become a member of the IFMGA is a long process of integration, which must be backed up by national legislation. To be accepted into the IFMGA can take a new country from 5 to 15 years, or until the criteria required are fulfilled (notably the capacity of the country's association to train guides to the required level).

Experience shows that the development of standardised mountain guide activity necessary for the safety of the public is ideally supported by a legal status or strict regulations. To obtain a valid IFMGA diploma requires a very long and very intensive investment on the part of the guide. A lack of rigorous guidelines and training negatively affects the profession's development and image.

For more information on the IFMGA see www.ivbv.info

The Guild of Registered Tourist Guides (UK)

The Guild is the national professional association for Blue Badge Tourist Guides working throughout the British Isles. It was established in 1950 and is dedicated to raising and maintaining the highest professional standards of its membership. It has 700 full members and a network of regional and local associations with nearly 1000 members holding group membership. Overall, the Guild represents around 1700 guides. Its members offer guiding in 34 different languages. The Blue Badge is recognised internationally as the qualification of excellence in site and heritage interpretation, and in communication skills. Blue Badge Registered Tourist Guides are trained under the auspices of The Institute of Tourist Guiding, often in conjunction with universities or colleges of further education. Most training courses for guides last at least two academic terms and some, such as those in London, may be up to nearly two years. A wide spectrum of academic, specialist and practical training is covered as well as a core curriculum of the history, architecture and social development of the country.

The Guild is run by an executive council, elected by the membership, and salaried office staff, and provides support and advice to its members on both policy and all issues covering guide services, sites, coach operators and health and safety. The Guild acts as a lobby group for the tourist guide profession and a consultative body on guiding matters. The Guild is a member of the FEG and the WFTGA.

For more information on the Guild of Registered Tourist Guides see http://www.britainsbestguides.org/

Guiding Organisations Australia Inc. (GOA)

GOA is a not-for-profit, industry-operated, incorporated association. GOA is the national peak industry body for Australian tour guides, incorporated in January 2003. GOA is positioned as the central acknowledged authority on guiding issues, conveying verified information and endorsed by industry stakeholders. GOA members are state tour guide associations and related professional associations such as Interpretation Australia. GOA's vision is to develop a universal and cooperative tour guiding network and standard in Australia that is world's best practice.

The purpose of GOA is to represent, promote and protect the common interests of Australian tour guides and continually improve the quality of their services by:

- Providing a national forum to develop best practice and promote a high degree of professionalism for tour guides.
- Raising private, public and government awareness, locally and nationally, of the importance of the tour guide's role.
- Maintaining cooperative relationships with national, international, state and territory tourism industry organisations.

GOA provides:

- All stakeholder members and subscribers with improved information distribution possibilities.
- Guides with news of current professional development opportunities and other benefits, including exchanges, new positions and contact with other guides from diverse backgrounds.
- Commercial benefits, including discount and family offers as they occur.
- Access to government departments and tourism bodies which provide valuable consultation and referral points for the guiding sector.
- Goods and services providers with communication channels to reach a current, qualified database of guides (within privacy requirements).
- Tour guiding organisations with added value for their members. These organisations are at the centre of the industries network, and are involved in issues such as the development of tour guiding and interpretation standards and training.
- Promotion of member organisations' activities and encourages independent guides to join guiding organisations to participate in their professional development and accreditation processes.

GOA has two levels of membership. State tour guide associations within Australia make up the full members of GOA. Associate members are government departments, incorporated organisations, businesses supporting tour guiding activities and partnerships with tour guide members.

Individual guides are encouraged to take up Guides of Australia accreditation, a scheme that provides tourists with an assurance that a guide has met specific standards and has a commitment to the best practice standards outlined in the Australian Tour Guides' Code of Guiding Practice. Guides of Australia accreditation is suitable for tour guides in all sectors of the tourism industry; it encourages professional development and promotes training in all relevant skills. Accreditation provides industry recognition for guides who achieve the specified standards. It is not mandatory but is encouraged by many industry stakeholders including employers, tourism organisations and government agencies. Once accredited, the guide's name is recorded in the National Register of Accredited Tour Guides. Tour guides working in Australia are encouraged to take up membership of a state tour guide association for the benefits of networking, training and refresher courses, familiarisations, discounts and recognition.

For more information on GOA see http://www.goa.org.au/

SveGuide – Sweden's Guide Association

SveGuide is Sweden's official guide association. The organisation was established in 1983 and has around 1000 authorised guides throughout Sweden, in more than 20 local and regional organisations and associations. The guides conduct tours in Swedish, English, German and French and 30 other languages, including sign language. The organisation aims to ensure that all SveGuide guides have the relevant knowledge, education, standards and ethics to meet the required competencies. Authorised SveGuides are recognised by their badge with the SveGuide's logo. SveGuide is a member of the European Federation of Tourist Guides Association.

For more information on SveGuide see http://www.guidesofsweden.com/

Forum Advocating Cultural and Eco-Tourism Inc. (FACET)

FACET is a Western Australian-based network and information resource for people with an interest in cultural and nature-based tourism and ecotourism. The association was conceived in 1991 when it became apparent that many exciting opportunities and developments were taking place in the field of cultural tourism and ecotourism, in isolation of each other. FACET was established to advise on and promote sustainable tourism to government and industry involved in this new growth area. The forum's membership is diverse and is drawn from the tourism sector, academe, government agencies, cultural, ecological and scientific institutions and the general public. FACET's mission is to inspire and promote responsible community use of Western Australia's cultural and natural heritage through tourism.

In 1998, FACET initiated the concept and developed the FACET Golden Guide Award. The aim of the award is to recognise individual excellence in tour guiding and raise the profile of this important profession. It acknowledges the significant contribution that quality tour guides make to enriching the experience of visitors through interpreting the natural and cultural environment. The award is open to tour guides and coach captains working in the natural, cultural and heritage environments in either a paid or voluntary capacity. The award has been incorporated into the Western Australian Tourism Awards and is presented at the Western Australian Tourism Awards gala dinner and reported nationally. Good interpretation is essential for successful tour guiding, ensuring that the visitor is left with a memorable experience. FACET believes it is important to acknowledge guides who are leading the way in offering visitors an authentic and enriching experience.

For more information on FACET see http://www.facet.asn.au

References

Almagor, U. (1985) A tourist's 'Vision Guest' in an African game reserve. *Annals of Tourism Research* 12 (1), 31–47.

Aloudat, A.S. (2010) The world view of tour guides: A grounded theory study. PhD thesis, University of Bedfordshire.

Altschuld, J.W. (1999) The case for a voluntary system for credentialing evaluators. *American Journal of Evaluation* 20 (3), 507–517.

Ap, J. and Wong, K.K.F. (2001) Case study on tour guiding: Professionalism, issues and problems. *Tourism Management* 22 (5), 551–563.

Armstrong, E.K. and Weiler, B. (2002) Getting the message across: An analysis of messages delivered by tour operators in protected areas. *Journal of Ecotourism* 1 (2), 104–121.

Arnould, E.J. and Price, L.L. (1993) River magic: Extraordinary experience and the extended service encounter. *Journal of Consumer Research* 20 (1), 24–45.

Arnould, E.J., Price, L.L. and Tierney, P. (1998) Communicative staging of the wilderness servicescape. *Service Industries Journal* 18 (3), 90–115.

Arslanturk, Y. and Altunoz, O. (2012) Practice tips: Efficiency and quality perceptions of prospective tour guides. *Procedia Social and Behavioral Sciences* 62, 832–836.

Australian Tourism Export Council and Tourism Queensland (2001) *Issues for the Regulation of Tourist Guides in Australia*. Sydney: Australian Tourism Export Council.

Avcikurt, C., Koroglu, O., Koroglu, A. and Avcikurt, A.S. (2011) HIV/AIDS awareness and attitudes of tour guides in Turkey. *Culture, Health & Sexuality* 13 (2), 233–243.

Baker, D.A. and Crompton, J.L. (2000) Quality, satisfaction and behavioural intentions. *Annals of Tourism Research* 27 (3), 785–804.

Ballantyne, R. and Uzzell, D. (1999) International trends in heritage and environmental interpretation: Future directions for Australian research and practice. *Journal of Interpretation Research* 14 (1), 59–75.

Ballantyne, R., Weiler, B., Crabtree, A., Ham, S.H. and Hughes, K. (2000) *Tour Guiding: Developing Effective Communication and Interpretation Techniques* [video and workbook]. Brisbane: Queensland University of Technology.

Ballantyne, R. and Hughes, K. (2001) Interpretation in ecotourism settings: Investigating tour guides' perceptions of their role, responsibilities and training needs. *Journal of Tourism Studies* 12 (2), 2–9.

Ballantyne, R., Packer, J. and Hughes, K. (2009) Tourists' support for conservation messages and sustainable management practices in wildlife tourism experiences. *Tourism Management* 30, 658–664.

Barnhart, P.A. (1997) *The Guide to National Professional Certification Programs*. Amherst, MA: HRD Press Inc.

Barsky, J.D. (1992) Customer satisfaction in the hotel industry: Meaning and measurement. *The Hospitality Research Journal* 16, 51–73.

Beaumont, N. (1991) Ecotourism and the conservation ethic: Recruiting the uninitiated or preaching to the converted? *Journal of Sustainable Tourism* 9 (4), 317–341.

Binkhorst, E. and Den Dekker, T. (2009) Agenda for co-creation tourism experience research. *Journal of Hospitality Marketing & Management* 18, 311–327.

Black, R. (2002) Towards a model for tour guide certification: An analysis of the Australian ecoguide program. PhD thesis, Monash University.

Black, R. (2007) Certification to enhance ecotour guide performance. In R. Black and A. Crabtree (eds) *Quality Assurance and Certification in Ecotourism* (pp. 316–335). Wallingford: CABI.

Black, R.S. (in press) Guided tours. In J. Jafari and H. Xiao (eds) *Encyclopaedia of Tourism*. New York: Springer.

Black, R., Ham, S. and Weiler, B. (2001) Ecotour guide training in less developed countries: Some preliminary research findings. *Journal of Sustainable Tourism* 9 (2), 147–156.

Black, R. and King, B. (2002) Human resource development in remote island communities: An evaluation of tour-guide training in Vanuatu. *International Journal of Tourism Research* 4 (2), 103–117.

Black, R. and Weiler, B. (2002) Tour guide certification in the Australian ecotourism industry: Conception to adulthood. Paper presented at the Proceedings of CAUTHE 2002: Annual Conference of Council for Australian University Tourism and Hospitality Education, Fremantle, WA.

Black, R. and Weiler, B. (eds) (2003) *Interpreting the Land Down Under: Australian Heritage Interpretation and Tour Guiding*. Boulder, CO: Fulcrum.

Black, R. and Ham, S. (2005) Improving the quality of tour guiding: Towards a model for tour guide certification. *Journal of Ecotourism* 4 (3), 178–195.

Black, R. and Weiler, B. (2005) Quality assurance and regulatory mechanisms in the tour guiding industry: A systematic review. *Journal of Tourism Studies* 16 (1), 24–37.

Black, R. and Weiler, B. (2013) Current themes and issues in ecotour guiding. In R. Ballantyne and J. Packer (eds) *The International Handbook on Ecotourism* (pp. 336–350). Cheltenham: Edward Elgar Publishing.

Boren, L., Gemmell, N. and Barton, K. (2007) The role and presence of a guide. Preliminary findings from swim with seal programmes and land-based seal viewing in New Zealand. Paper presented at the Proceedings of the 5th International Coastal and Marine Tourism Congress: Balancing Marine Tourism, Development and Sustainability, 11–15 September, Auckland.

Bosque, I.R. and Martin, H.S. (2008) Tourist satisfaction: A cognitive-affective model. *Annals of Tourism Research* 35 (2), 785–799.

Bowen, D. (2001) Antecedents of consumer satisfaction and dis-satisfaction (CS/D) on long-haul inclusive tours – a reality check on theoretical considerations. *Tourism Management* 22 (1), 49–61.

Bowen, D. and Clarke, J. (2002) Reflection on tourist satisfaction research: Past, present and future. *Journal of Vacation Marketing* 8 (4), 297–308.

Bowie, D. and Chang, J.C. (2005) Tourist satisfaction. A view from a mixed international guided package tour. *Journal of Vacation Marketing* 11 (4), 303–322.

Bowman, G. (1992) The politics of tour guiding: Israeli and Palestinian guides in Israel and the Occupied Territories. In D. Harrison (ed.) *Tourism and the Less Developed Countries* (pp. 121–134). London: Bellhaven Press.

Bramwell, B. and Lane, B. (1993) Sustainable tourism: An evolving global approach. *Journal of Sustainable Tourism* 1 (1), 1–5.

Bras, K. (2000) Dusun Sade: Local tourist guides, the provincial government and the (re)presentation of a traditional village in Central Lombock. *Pacific Tourism Review* 4 (2/3), 87–103.

Bras, K. and Dahles, H. (1999) Pathfinder, gigolo and friend: Diverging entrepreneurial strategies of tourist guides on two Indonesian islands. In H. Dahles and K. Bras (eds) *Tourism and Small Entrepreneurs. Development, National Policy and Entrepreneurial Culture: Indonesian Cases* (pp. 128–145). Elmsford: Cognizant Communication Corporation.

Britton, S. and Clarke, W.C. (eds) (1987) *Ambiguous Alternative: Tourism in Small Developing Countries*. Suva: University of the South Pacific.

Brockelman, W.Y. and Dearden, P. (1990) The role of nature trekking in conservation: A case-study in Thailand. *Environmental Conservation* 17 (2), 141–148.

Brown, T., Ham, S. and Hughes, M. (2010) Picking up litter: An application of theory based communication to influence tourist behaviour in protected areas. *Journal of Sustainable Tourism* 18 (7), 879–900.

Bryon, J. (2012) Tour guides as storytellers – From selling to sharing. *Scandinavian Journal of Hospitality and Tourism* 12 (1), 27–43.

Buckley, R.C. (2001) Major issues in tourism ecolabelling. In X. Font and R.C. Buckley (eds) *Tourism Ecolabelling: Certification and Promotion of Sustainable Management* (pp. 19–26). Wallingford: CABI Publishing.

Cabada, M.M., Maldonando, F., Bauer, I., Verdonck, K., Seas, C. and Gotuzzo, E. (2007) Sexual behaviour, knowledge of STI, prevention and prevalence of serum makers for STI among tour guides in Cuzco, Peru. *Journal of Travel Medicine* 14 (3), 151–157.

Calvo, C. (2010) Costa Rica license certification for tour guiding. *e-Review of Tourism Research* 8 (6), 179–195.

Carmody, J. (2013) Intensive tour guide training in regional Australia: An analysis of the Savannah Guides organisation and professional development schools. *Journal of Sustainable Tourism* 21 (5), 679–694.

Carmody, J., King, L. and Prideaux, B. (2010) The Savannah Guides: A tour guiding model for regional Australia? Paper presented at the Proceedings of CAUTHE 2010: Challenge the Limits. In CAUTHE 2010 20th Annual Conference of Council for Australian University Tourism and Hospitality Education, 8–11 February, Hobart.

Carr, A. (2001) Alpine adventurers in the Pacific Rim: The motivations and experiences of guided mountaineering clients in New Zealand's Southern Alps. *Pacific Tourism Review* 4 (4), 161–169.

Carver, A.D., Basman, C.M. and Lee, J.G. (2003) Assessing the non-market value of heritage interpretation. *Journal of Interpretation Research* 8 (1), 83–92.

Casson, L. (1974) *Travel in The Ancient World.* London: George Allen and Unwin Ltd.

Chan, A. (2004) Towards an improved understanding of tour services and customer satisfaction in package tours. Paper presented at the Second Asia-Pacific CHRIE Conference and Sixth Biennial Conference on Tourism in Asia, Phuket, Thailand.

Chan, A. and Baum, T.G. (2004) The impact of tour guide performance on tourist satisfaction: A study of outbound tourism in Hong Kong. In *Tourism, State of the Art II Conference, Proceedings 27–30 June 2004* (pp. 1–15). Glasgow: University of Strathclyde.

Chang, J.C. (2006) Customer satisfaction with tour leaders' performance. A study of Taiwan's package tours. *Asia Pacific Journal of Tourism* 11 (1), 97–117.

Chang, J.C. and Chiu, C.P. (2008) Perceptions of tour providers about tipping in Taiwan. *Tourism (Zagreb)* 56 (4), 355–370.

Chang, K.C. (2012) Examining the effect of tour guide performance, tourist trust, tourist satisfaction and flow experience on tourists' shopping behavior. *Asia Pacific Journal of Tourism Research* 19 (2), 219–247.

Chittenden, H.M. (1979) *The Yellowstone National Park.* Norman, OK: University of Oklahoma Press.

Choi, H.S.C. and Sirakaya, E. (2006) Sustainability indicators for managing community tourism. *Tourism Management* 27, 1274–1289.

Christie, M.F. and Mason, P.A. (2003) Transformative tour guiding: Training tour guides to be critically reflective practitioners. *Journal of Ecotourism* 2 (1), 1–16.

Chu, T., Lin, M. and Chang, C. (2012) mGuiding (mobile guiding) – Using a mobile GIS app for guiding. *Scandinavian Journal of Hospitality and Tourism* 12 (3), 269–283.

Cohen, E. (1982) Jungle guides in northern Thailand: The dynamics of a marginal occupational role. *Sociological Review* 30 (2), 234–266.

Cohen, E. (1985) The tourist guide: The origins, structure and dynamics of a role. *Annals of Tourism Research* 12 (1), 5–29.

Cohen, E.H., Ifergan, M. and Cohen, E. (2002) A new paradigm in guiding: The *Madrich* as a role model. *Annals of Tourism Research* 29 (4), 919–932.

Cole, S. (1997) Anthropologists, local communities and sustainable development. In M.J. Stabler (ed.) *Tourism and Sustainability: Principles to Practice* (pp. 219–230). Wallingford: CAB International.

Commonwealth of Australia (1994) *National Ecotourism Strategy.* Canberra: Australian Government Printing Service.

Council of Europe, European Standardisation Committee (CEN) (2007) *Tourism Services – Requirements for the Provision of Professional Tourist Guide Training and Qualification Programmes* (pp. 1–16). Brussels: Council of Europe.

Crabtree, A. and Black, R. (2000) *EcoGuide Program Guide.* Brisbane: Ecotourism Association of Australia.

Crick, M. (1992) Life in the informal sector: Street guides in Kandy, Sri Lanka. In D. Harrison (ed.) *Tourism and the Less Developed Countries* (pp. 135–147). London: Belhaven Press.

Dahles, H. (2002) The politics of tour guiding: Image management in Indonesia. *Annals of Tourism Research* 29 (3), 738–800.

Davidson, P. and Black, R. (2007) Voices from the profession: Principles of successful guided cave interpretation. *Journal of Interpretation Research* 12 (2), 25–44.

Davies, N., Mitchell, K., Cheverst, K. and Blair, G. (1998) Developing a context sensitive tourist guide. In *Proceedings of the First Workshop on Human–Computer Interaction with Mobile Devices* (pp. 64–68). Glasgow: University of Glasgow.

de Kadt, E. (1979) *Tourism: Passport to Development?* New York: Oxford University Press.

de la Barre, S. (2013) Wilderness and cultural tour guides, place identity and sustainable tourism in remote areas. *Journal of Sustainable Tourism* 21 (6), 825–844.

Department of Resources, Energy and Tourism (2013) *Servicing Chinese Visitors: Project Description.* T-Qual Grants – Strategic Tourism Investment Grants. Australian Government, Canberra.

Dioko, L.A.N. and Unakul, M.H. (2005) The need for specialized training in heritage tour guiding at Asia's world heritage sites – Preliminary findings on the challenges and opportunities. Paper presented at the 2005 PATA Educator's Forum, Macao.

Dioko, L.A.N., Harrill, R. and Cardon, P.W. (2013) The wit and wisdom of Chinese tour guides: A critical tourism perspective. *Journal of China Tourism Research* 9 (1), 27–49.

Dolnicar, S. (2006) Nature conserving tourists: The need for a broader perspective. *Anatolia: An International Journal of Tourism and Hospitality Research* 17 (2), 235–256.

Douglas, N., Douglas, N. and Derrett, R. (eds) (2001) *Special Interest Tourism.* Milton, Queensland: John Wiley and Sons.

Eberts, M., Brothers, L. and Gsler, A. (1997) *Careers in Travel, Tourism and Hospitality.* Chicago: VGM Career Horizons.

EcoTourism Australia. (2012) EcoGuide Program. See http://www.ecotourism.org.au/ecoguide.asp (accessed 20 July 2013).

Edelheim, J.R. (2009) With the Simpsons as tour guides: How popular culture sources can enhance the student experience in a university tourism unit. *Journal of Hospitality and Tourism Management* 16 (1), 113–119.

El Sharkawy, O.K. (2007) Exploring knowledge and skills for tourist guides. Evidence from Egypt. *Multidisciplinary Journal of Tourism* 2 (2), 77–94.

Filep, S. and Pearce, P.L. (eds) (2013) *Tourist Experience and Fulfilment: Insights from Positive Psychology.* New York: Routledge.

Fine, E.C. and Speer, J.H. (1985) Tour guide performances as sight sacralization. *Annals of Tourism Research* 12 (1), 73–95.

Finlayson, A. (2000) Professionalism. *Interpscan* 27 (2), 3–5.

Fluker, M. and Deery, M. (2003) Condoms in the first aid kit: River guides, clients and sex. In T.G. Bauer and B. McKercher (eds) *Sex and Tourism. Journeys of Romance, Love and Lust* (pp. 109–118). Binghamton: The Haworth Press Inc.

Font, X. and Buckley, R.C. (2001) *Tourism Ecolabelling: Certification and Promotion of Sustainable Management.* Wallingford: CABI Publishing.

Füller, J. and Matzler, K. (2008) Customer delight and market segmentation: An application of the three factor theory of customer satisfaction on life style groups. *Tourism Management* 29 (1), 116–126.

Gardner, T. and McArthur, S. (1994) *Guided Nature-based Tourism in Tasmania's Forests: Trends, Constraints and Implications.* Hobart: Forestry Tasmania.

Gelbman, A. and Maoz, D. (2012) Island of peace or island of war: Tourist guiding. *Annals of Tourism Research* 39 (1), 108–133.

Geva, A. and Goldman, A. (1991) Satisfaction measurements in guided tours. *Annals of Tourism Research* 18, 177–185.

Giannoulis, C., Skanavis, C. and Matthopoulos, D. (2006) Environmental interpreters role in Greek ecotourism settings. Paper presented at the Conference Interpreting World Heritage, 1–5 May, San Juan, Porta Rico.

Gilg, A. and Barr, S. (2006) Behavioural attitudes towards water saving? Evidence from a study of environmental actions. *Ecological Economics* 57 (3), 400–414.

Giovannetti, J.L. (2009) Subverting the master's narrative: Public histories of slavery in plantation America. *International Labor and Working-Class History* 76 (1), 105–126.

Goffman, E. (1990) *The Presentation of Self in Everyday Life.* London: Penguin Books.

Goodwin, H. (2006) Measuring and reporting the impact of tourism on poverty. Paper presented at the Cutting Edge Research in Tourism: New Directions, Challenges and Applications, University of Surrey, Guilford.

Guiding Organisation of Australia (GOA) (2012) About GOA. See http://www.goa.org.au/index.php/about (accessed 14 August 2013).

Guild of Registered Tourist Guides (2001) *Registered Blue Badge Guides.* London: Guild of Registered Tourist Guides.

Gunnarsson, D. (2010) Showing respect. On having an ethical approach at the guided tours of a mosque on Sodermalm, Stockholm. Paper presented at the First International Research Forum on Guided Tours, 23–25 April 2009, Halmstad University, Sweden.

Gurung, G., Simmons, D. and Devlin, P. (1996) The evolving role of tourist guides: The Nepali experience. In R. Butler and T. Hinch (eds) *Tourism and Indigenous Peoples* (pp. 108–128). London: International Thomson Business Press.

Haase, C. (1996) Designing and delivering an industry driven tourism training program. Paper presented at the Ecotourism and Nature-based Tourism: Taking the Next Steps, Alice Springs, Australia.

Haig, I. and McIntyre, N. (2002) Viewing nature: The role of the guide and the advantages of participating in commercial ecotourism. *The Journal of Tourism Studies* 13 (1), 39–49.

Hall, C.M. (1995) *Introduction to Tourism in Australia.* Melbourne: Addison Wesley Longman.

Hallin, A. and Dobers, P. (2012) Representation of space. Uncovering the political dimension of guided tours in Stockholm. *Scandinavian Journal of Hospitality and Tourism* 12 (1), 8–26.

Ham, S. (2009) From interpretation to protection – Is there a theoretical basis? *Journal of Interpretation Research* 14 (2), 49–57.

Ham, S.H. (1992) *Environmental Interpretation: A Practical Guide for People with Big Ideas and Small Budgets.* Golden, CO: North American Press.

Ham, S.H. and Weiler, B. (2002) Interpretation as the centrepiece of sustainable wildlife tourism. In R. Harris, T. Griffin and P. Williams (eds) *Sustainable Tourism: A Global Perspective* (pp. 35–44). London: Butterworth-Heinemann.

Ham, S.H. and Weiler, B. (2003) Toward a theory of quality in cruise-based interpretive guiding. *Journal of Interpretation Research* 7 (2), 29–49.

Ham, S.H. and Weiler, B. (2006) *Development of a Research-Based Tool for Evaluating Interpretation.* Brisbane: Sustainable Tourism Collaborative Research Centre.

Ham, S. and Weiler, B. (2007) Isolating the role of on-site interpretation in a satisfying experience. *Journal of Interpretation Research* 12 (2), 5–24.

Hanna, S., Del Casino, J., Selden, V.J. and Hite, B. (2004) Representation as work in 'America's most historic city'. *Social and Cultural Geography* 5 (3), 459–481.

Hansson, E. (2009) Guided tours as tools for change – Taking the planning dialogue into – and in – the streets. In P. Adolfsson, P. Dobers and M. Jonasson (eds) *Guiding and Guided Tours* (pp. 63–84). Goteborg: BAS Publishers.

Harris, R. and Jago, L. (2001) Professional accreditation in the Australian tourism industry: An uncertain future. *Tourism Management* 22 (4), 383–390.

Hawkins, D.E. and Lamoureux, K. (2001) Global growth and magnitude of ecotourism. In D. Weaver (ed.) *The Encyclopedia of Ecotourism* (pp. 63–72). Wallingford: CABI Publishing.

Henderson, J. (2002) Creating memorable experiences for our visitor: Tourist guide licensing and training in Singapore. *Asian Journal on Hospitality and Tourism* 1 (2), 91–94.

Henning, G.K. (2008) The guided hike in Banff National Park. A hermeneutical performance. *Journal of Sustainable Tourism* 16 (2), 182–196.

Herodotus. (trans. De Selicourt, A.) (1972) *Herodotus the Histories.* Harmondsworth: Penguin Books Ltd.

Hersey, P. and Blanchard, K.H. (1982) *Management of Organisational Behaviour: Utilising Human Resources.* London: Prentice-Hall.

Heung, V.C.S., Wong, M.Y. and Qu, H. (2002) A study of tourists' satisfaction and post-experience behavioural intentions in relation to airport restaurant services in Hong Kong S.A.R. *Journal of Travel and Tourism Marketing* 12 (2/3), 111–133.

Hillman, W. (2003) Protectors and interpreters of the outback: A study of the emerging occupation of the Savannah Guide. PhD thesis, James Cook University. See http://eprints.jcu.edu.au/79/ (accessed 18 July 2013).

Hillman, W. (2004) Savannah Guides: Ecotour guides of outback Australia. In Proceedings of the Sociological Association of Australia 2004 Conference. From TASA 2004 Conference, 8–11 December 2004, Latrobe University, Beechworth, VIC, Australia.

Hochschild, A.E. (1983) *The Managed Heart: Commercialization of Human Feeling.* Berkeley, CA: University of California Press.

Holloway, J.C. (1981) The guided tour a sociological approach. *Annals of Tourism Research* 8 (3), 377–402.

Holloway, J.C. (1994) *The Business of Tourism.* London: Pitman Publishing.

Honey, M. and Rome, A. (2001) *Protecting Paradise: Certification Programs for Sustainable Tourism and Ecotourism.* New York: Institute of Policy Studies.

Hongying, Y. and Hui, C. (2009) Analysis of tour guide interpretation in China. In C. Ryan and H. Gu (eds) *Tourism in China: Destination, Cultures and Communities* (pp. 225–237). New York: Routledge.

Hoskins, W.L. (1986) Professional certification: An idea in search of a problem. *Business Economics* 21 (2), 15–20.

Houge Mackenzie, S. and Kerr, J.H. (2013) Stress and emotions at work: An adventure tourism guide's experiences. *Tourism Management* 36, 3–14.

Hounnaklang, S. (2004) Profiles and roles of tour guides. A comparative study between Thailand and the UK. Paper presented at the Second APAC-CHRIE Conference, Hospitality, Tourism and Foodservice Industry in Asia: Development, Marketing and Sustainability, May 27–29, Phuket, Thailand.

Howard, J. (1998) Towards best practice in interpretive guided activities. *Australian Parks and Recreation* Summer, 28–31.

Howard, J., Thwaites, R. and Smith, B. (2001) Investigating the roles of the Indigenous tour guide. *Journal of Tourism Studies* 12 (2), 32–39.

Hsu, C. (2003) Mature motorcoach travelers' satisfaction: A preliminary step toward measurement development. *Journal of Hospitality and Tourism Research* 27, 291–309.

Hsu, C.H.C. (2000) Determinants of mature travelers' motorcoach tour satisfaction and brand loyalty. *Journal of Hospitality and Tourism Research* 24, 223–238.

Hu, W. and Wall, G. (2012) Interpretive guiding and sustainable development: A framework. *Tourism Management Perspectives* 4, 80–85.

Huang, S. and Weiler, B. (2010) A review and evaluation of China's quality assurance system for tour guiding. *Journal of Sustainable Tourism* 18 (7), 845–860.

Huang, S., Hsu, C.H.C., and Chan, A. (2010) Tour guide performance and tourist satisfaction: A study of the package tours in Shanghai. *Journal of Hospitality & Tourism Research* 34 (1), 3–33.

Huang, S., Weiler, B. and Assaker, G. (2014 - online first) Effects of interpretive guiding outcomes on tourist satisfaction and behavioral intention. *Journal of Travel Research*. doi: 10.1177/0047287513517426

Huang, Y. (2004) A study of intercultural communication of professional tour guides in Yunnan. PhD thesis, La Trobe University.

Hughes, G. (1995) The cultural construction of sustainable tourism. *Tourism Management* 16 (1), 49–59.

Hughes, J. (1994) Antarctic historic sites: The tourism implications. *Annals of Tourism Research* 12 (2), 281–294.

Hughes, K. (1991) Tourist satisfaction: A guided cultural tour in North Queensland. *Australian Psychologist* 26 (3), 166–171.

Hughes, M., Ham, S.H. and Brown, T. (2009) Influencing park visitor behaviour: A belief-based approach. *Journal of Park and Recreation Administration* 27 (4), 38–53.

Hutchinson, P. and Bramwell, J. (1996) Making the change from tourism to ecotourism: Customised training the East Gippsland TAFE model. Paper presented at the Ecotourism and Nature-based Tourism Conference: Taking the Next Steps, Alice Springs, Australia.

Io, M. and Hallo, L. (2012) A comparative study of tour guides' interpretation: The case of Macao. *Tourism Analysis* 17, 153–165.

Issaverdis, J.P. (1998) *Tourism Industry Accreditation – A Comparative Critique of Developments in Australia* (p. 226). Melbourne: Victoria University, Department of Hospitality, Tourism and Marketing.

Issaverdis, J.P. (2001) The pursuit of excellence: Benchmarking, accreditation, best practice and auditing. In D. Weaver (ed.) *The Encyclopedia of Ecotourism* (pp. 579–594). Oxford: CAB International.

Jacobson, S.K. and Robles, R. (1992) Ecotourism, sustainable development and conservation education: Development of a tour guide training program in Tortuguero, Costa Rica. *Environmental Management* 16 (6), 701–713.

Jensen, O. (2010) Social mediation in remote developing world tourism locations – The significance of social ties between local guides and host communities in sustainable tourism development. *Journal of Sustainable Tourism* 18 (5), 615–633.

Johns, N., Avci, T. and Karatepe, O.M. (2004) Measuring service quality of travel agents: Evidence from Northern Cyprus. *The Service Industries Journal* 24, 82–100.

Johnson, P.C. (2001) An examination of risk within tourist experiences to the Islamic Republic of Iran. *Annals of Leisure Research* 4, 38–57.

Jonasson, M. (2011) Virtual- and live-guided tours: Exchanging experiences. *Journal of Hospitality and Tourism* 8 (2), 78–94.

Jonasson, M. and Scherle, N. (2012) Performing co-produced guided tours. *Scandinavian Journal of Hospitality and Tourism* 12 (1), 55–73.

Jones, C.B. (1999) *The New Tourism and Leisure Environment: A Discussion Paper.* San Francisco: Economics Research Associates.

Kang, M. and Gretzel, U. (2012) Effects of podcast tours on tourist experiences in a national park. *Tourism Management* 33 (2), 440–455.

Kayes, R. (2005) Coral reef tourism and conservation in Bocas del Toro: An analysis of ecotourism and its tour guide-based components. Unpublished manuscript, ISP Collection Paper 433. DigitalCollections@SIT. See http://digitalcollections.sit.edu/ (accessed 18 July 2013).

Kohl, J. (2007) Putting the ecotour guide back into context: Using systems thinking to develop quality guides. In R. Black and A. Crabtree (eds) *Quality Assurance and Certification in Ecotourism* (pp. 337–363). Oxford: CAB International.

Kohl, J., Brown, C. and Humke, M. (2001) Overcoming hurdles: Teaching guides to interpret biodiversity conservation. *Legacy* 12 (4), 19–28.

Kong, H., Cheung, C. and Baum, T. (2009) Are tour guides in China ready for the booming tourism industry? *Journal of China Tourism Research* 5, 65–76.

LeClerc, D. and Martin, J.N. (2004) Tour guide communication competence: French, German and American tourists' perceptions. *International Journal of Intercultural Relations* 28, 181–200.

Lin, C.T., Wang, K.C. and Chen, W.Y. (2008) Female tour leaders as advertising endorsers. *Service Industries Journal* 28 (9), 1265–1275.

Littlefair, C. and Buckley, R. (2008) Interpretation reduces ecological impacts of visitors to World Heritage Site. *Ambio* 37 (5), 338–341.

Littlefair, C.J. (2003) The effectiveness of interpretation in reducing the impacts of visitors in national parks. PhD thesis, Griffith University.

Lopez, E.M. (1980) The effect of leadership style on satisfaction levels of tour quality. *Journal of Travel Research* 18 (4), 20–23.

Lopez, E.M. (1981) The effect of tour leaders' training on travelers' satisfaction with tour quality *Journal of Travel Research* 19 (4), 23–26.

Lugosi, P. and Bray, J. (2008) Tour guiding, organisational culture and learning: Lessons from an entrepreneurial company. *International Journal of Tourism Research* 10 (5), 467–479.

Lustig, M. and Koester, J. (1993) *Intercultural Competence: Interpersonal Communication Across Cultures.* New York: Harper Collins.

MacCannell, D. (1976) *The Tourist: A New Theory of the Leisure Class.* London: Macmillan.

Macdonald, S. (2006) Mediating heritage: Tour guides at the former Nazi party rally grounds, Nuremberg. *Tourist Studies* 6 (2), 119–138.

Mak, A.H.N., Wong, K.K.F. and Chang, R.C.Y. (2009) Factors affecting the service quality of the tour guiding profession in Macau. *International Journal of Tourism Research* 12 (3), 205–218.

Mak, A.H.N., Wong, K.K.F. and Chang, R.C.Y. (2011) Critical issues affecting the service quality and professionalism of the tour guides in Hong Kong and Macau. *Tourism Management* 32 (6), 1442–1452.

Manidis Roberts Consultants (1994) *An Investigation into a National Ecotourism Accreditation Scheme.* Canberra: Commonwealth Department of Tourism.

Marion, J. and Reid, S. (2007) Minimizing visitor impacts to protected areas: The efficacy of low impact education programs. *Journal of Sustainable Tourism* 15 (1), 5–27.

Mason, P. (2007) No better than a band-aid for a bullet wound!: The effectiveness of tourism codes of conduct. In R. Black and A. Crabtree (eds) *Quality Assurance and Certification in Ecotourism* (pp. 46–64). Wallingford: CAB International.

Mason, P. and Mowforth, M. (1996) Codes of conduct in tourism. *Progress in Tourism and Hospitality Research* 2, 151–167.

Mason, P.A. and Christie, M.F. (2003) Tour guides as critically reflective practitioners: A proposed training model. *Tourism Recreation Research* 28 (1), 23–33.

McGrath, G. (2003) Myth, magic, meaning and memory. Mentor tour guides as central to developing integrated heritage tourism at archaeological sites in Cusco, Peru. Paper presented at the Proceedings of the 12th International Tourism and Leisure Symposium, Barcelona.

McGrath, G. (2007) Towards developing tour guides as interpreters of cultural heritage: The case of Cusco, Peru. In R. Black and A. Crabtree (eds) *Quality Assurance and Certification in Ecotourism* (pp. 364–394). Wallingford: CAB International.

Medio, D., Ormond, R.F.G. and Person, M. (1997) Effect of briefing on rates of damage to corals by SCUBA divers. *Biological Conservation* 79 (1), 91–95.

Meged, J.W. (2010) Guides' intercultural strategies in an interaction perspective. Paper presented at the First International Research Forum on Guided Tours, 23–25 April 2009, Halmstad University, Sweden.

Meisch, L.A. (2002) Sex and romance on the trail in the Andes: Guides, gender and authority. In M.B. Swain and J.H. Momsen (eds) *Gender-Tourism-Fun(?)* (pp. 172–179). Elmsford: Cognizant Communication Corporation.

Metry, M. (2000) The influences that shape the guided interpretive experience at the Jenolan Caves. Bachelor of Tourism Management (Honours) thesis, University of Technology, Sydney.

Mills, E.A. (1920) *The Adventures of a Nature Guide.* Garden City: Doubleday, Page and Co.

Ministry for Business and Labour (2013) Innoguide tourism: A European tourist guiding project. See http://www.innoguidetourism.eu/ (accessed 14 September 2013).

Mitchell, J.P. (1996) Presenting the past: Cultural tour-guides and the sustaining of European identity in Malta. In L. Briguglio, R. Butler, D. Harrison and W. Leal Filho (eds) *Sustainable Tourism in Islands and Small States: Case Studies* (pp. 199–219). London: Cassell PLC.

Modlin, E.A., Alderman, D.H. and Gentry, G.W. (2011) Tour guides as creators of empathy: The role of affective inequality in marginalizing the enslaved at plantation house museums. *Tourist Studies* 11 (1), 3–19.

Monto, R.C. and Raikkonen, J. (2010) Tour leaders in customer complaints. Paper presented at the First International Research Forum on Guided Tours, 23–25 April 2009, Halmstad University, Sweden.

Moore, S., Weiler, B., Croy, G., Laing, J., Lee, D., Lockwood, M., Pfueller, S. and Wegner, A. (2009) *Tourism-Protected Area Partnerships in Australia: Designing and Managing for Success.* Brisbane: STCRC Report.

Morgan, M. (2009) Interpretation and place attachment: Implications for cognitive map theory. *Journal of Interpretation Research* 14 (1), 47–59.

Morgan, M. and Dong, X.D. (2008) Measuring passenger satisfaction of interpretive programming on two Amtrak trains in the Midwest: Testing the expectancy disconfirmation theory. *Journal of Interpretation Research* 13 (2), 43–58.

Morrison, A.M., Hsieh, S. and Wang, C.Y. (1992) Certification in the travel and tourism industry. *Journal of Tourism Studies* 3 (2), 32–40.

Morse, M.A. (1997) All the world's a field: A history of the scientific study tour. *Progress in Tourism and Hospitality Research* 3, 257–269.

Moscardo, G. (1996) Mindful visitors: Heritage and tourism. *Annals of Tourism Research* 23 (2), 376–397.

Moscardo, G. and Woods, B. (1998) Managing tourism in the wet tropics world heritage area. In E. Laws, B. Faulkner and G. Moscardo (eds) *Embracing and Managing Change in Tourism* (pp. 307–323). London: Routledge.

Mossberg, L.L. (1995) Tour leaders and their importance in charter tours. *Tourism Management* 16 (6), 437–445.

Mykletun, R.J. (2013) IRFGT 2013: Third International Research Forum on Guided Tourism. *Scandinavian Journal of Hospitality and Tourism* 13 (3), 269–271.

Nasopoulou, T. (2011) *Ecoguiding and Problems in Protected Areas in Greece.* Greece: Guide for National Parks and Wetlands.

National Association for Interpretation (2003) Bibliography of interpretive resources. *Journal of Interpretation Research* 8 (2), 1–164.

Nature and Ecotourism Accreditation Program (2000) *Nature and Ecotourism Accreditation Program* (2nd edn). Brisbane: Nature and Ecotourism Accreditation Program.

Northern Territory Tourism (2013) Outstanding Interpretive Guide, Brolga Awards. See http://www.tourismnt.com.au/brolga-awardscategories.aspx (accessed 14 September 2013).

Novelli, M. and Hellwig, A. (2011) The UN millenium development goals, tourism and development: The tour operators' perspective. *Current Issues in Tourism* 14 (3), 205–220.

O'Neill, F., Barnard, S. and Lee, D. (2004) *Best Practice and Interpretation in Tourist/Wildlife Encounters: A Wild Dolphin Swim Tour Example.* Wildlife Tourism Research Report Series No. 25. Gold Coast, Australia: CRC Sustainable Tourism.

Oliver, R.L. (1980) A cognitive model of the antecedents and consequences of satisfaction decisions. *Journal of Marketing Research* 17, 460–469.

Orams, M.B. (1996) Using interpretation to manage nature-based tourism. *Journal of Sustainable Tourism,* 4 (2), 81–94.

Orams, M.B. and Hill, G.J.E. (1998) Controlling the ecotourist in a wild dolphin feeding program: Is education the answer? *Journal of Environmental Education* 29 (3), 33–39.

Orde, J. (2011a) *Overview of Tourist Guide Associations Worldwide.* Vienna: World Federation of Tourist Guides Associations.

Orde, J. (2011b) *Overview of the Guiding Profession Worldwide.* Vienna: World Federation of Tourist Guides Associations.

Ormsby, A. and Mannle, K. (2006) Ecotourism benefits and the role of local guides at Masoala National Park, Madagascar. *Journal of Sustainable Tourism* 14 (3), 271–287.

Oschell, C.M. (2009) The development and testing of a relational model of competence in the context of guided nature-based tourism. PhD thesis, University of Montana.

Overend, D. (2012) Performing sites: Illusion and authenticity in the spatial stories of the guided tour. *Scandinavian Journal of Hospitality and Tourism* 12 (1), 44–54.

Paaby, P., Clark, D.B. and Gonzalez, H. (1991) Training rural residents as naturalist guides: Evaluation of a pilot project in Costa Rica. *Conservation Biology* 5 (4), 542–546.

Page, S.P. and Dowling, R. (2002) *Ecotourism.* Harlow: Pearson Education Ltd.

Parasuraman, A., Zeithaml, V.A. and Berry, L.L. (1985) A conceptual model of service quality and its implications for future research. *Journal of Marketing* 49 (4), 41–50.

Parasuraman, A., Zeithaml, V.A. and Berry, L.L. (1988) SERVQUAL: A multiple-item sale for measuring consumer perceptions of service quality. *Journal of Retailing* 64 (1), 12–40.

Parasuraman, A., Zeithaml, V.A. and Berry, L.L (1994) Reassessment of expectations as a comparison standard in measuring service quality: Implications for further research. *Journal of Marketing* 58, 111–124.

Pastorelli, J. (2003) *Enriching the Experience – An Interpretive Approach to Tour Guiding.* Frenchs Forest: Pearson Education Australia.

Peake, S.E. (2007) Whale watching tour guides. Communicating conservation effectively. Paper presented at the Proceedings of the 5th International Coastal and Marine Tourism Congress: Balancing Marine Tourism, Development and Sustainability, 11–15 September, Auckland.

Pearce, P.L., Kim, E. and Syamsul, L. (1998) Facilitating tourist-host social interaction. In E. Laws, B. Faulkner and G. Moscardo (eds) *Embracing and Managing Change in Tourism* (pp. 347–364). London: Routledge.

Peel, V., Sørensen, A. and Steen, A. (2012) Unfriendly, unfunny and tyrannical: An exploratory study of the travel guidebook in the Australian print media. *Tourism Analysis* 17 (3), 299–309.

Pereira, E. (2005) How do tourist guides add value to an ecotour? Interpreting interpretation in the state of Amazonas, Brazil. *FIU Review* 23 (2), 1–8.

Pereira, E.M. and Mykletun, R.J. (2012) Guides as contributors to sustainable tourism? A case study from the Amazon. *Scandinavian Journal of Hospitality and Tourism* 12 (1), 74–94.

Pond, K. (1993) *The Professional Guide: Dynamics of Tour Guiding.* New York: Van Nostrand Reinhold.

Ponting, S.S.A. (2009) Exploring practitioner conceptualisations of professionalism and the impact of professionalisation on the work of Australian ecotour guides. PhD thesis, University of Technology Sydney.

Poudel, S. and Nyaupane, G.P. (2013) The role of interpretative tour guiding in sustainable destination management: A comparison between guided and nonguided tourists. *Journal of Travel Research* 52 (5), 659–672.

Poudel, S., Nyaupane, G.P. and Timothy, D.J. (2013) Assessing visitors preference of various roles of tour guides in the Himalaya. *Tourism Analysis* 18, 45–49.

Powell, R.B. and Ham, S.H. (2008) Can ecotourism interpretation really lead to pro-conservation knowledge, attitudes and behaviour? Evidence from the Galapagos Islands. *Journal of Sustainable Tourism* 16 (4), 467–489.

Prakash, M., Chowdhary, N. and Sunayana, K. (2011) Tour guiding: Interpreting the challenges. *Tourismos* 6 (2), 65–81.

Price, L., Arnould, E. and Tierney, P. (1995) Going to extremes: Managing service quality and its implications for future research. *Journal of Marketing* 59 (April), 83–97.

Quiroga, I. (1990) Characteristics of package tours in Europe. *Annals of Tourism Research* 17, 185–207.

Raikkonen, J. and Monto, R.C. (2010) Service failure and service recovery on a package tour – complainants perceptions on tour leaders. Paper presented at the First International Research Forum on Guided Tours, 23–25 April 2009, Halmstad University, Sweden.

Randall, C. and Rollins, R.B. (2009) Visitor perceptions of the role of tour guides in natural areas. *Journal of Sustainable Tourism* 17 (3), 357–374.

Regnier, K., Gross, M. and Zimmerman, R. (1994), *The Interpreter's Guidebook: Techniques for Programs and Presentations.* Stevens Point, WI: UW-SP Foundation Press Inc.

Reisinger, Y. and Steiner, C. (2006) Reconceptualising interpretation. The role of tour guide in authentic tourism. *Current Issues in Tourism* 9 (6), 481–498.

Roggenbuck, J. (1992) Use of persuasion to reduce resource impacts and visitor conflicts. In M. Manfred (ed.) *Influencing Human Behavior: Theory and Applications in Recreation, Tourism and Natural Resources Management* (pp. 149–208). Champaign, IL: Sagamore Publishing.

Roggenbuck, J., Williams, D.R. and Bobinski, C.T. (1992) Public-private partnership to increase commercial tour guides' effectiveness as nature interpreters. *Journal of Park and Recreation Administration* 10 (2), 41–50.

Ryan, C. and Dewar, K. (1995) Evaluating the communication process between interpreter and visitor. *Tourism Management* 16 (4), 295–303.

Salazar, N.B. (2005) Tourism and glocalisation. 'Local' tour guiding. *Annals of Tourism Research* 32 (3), 628–646.

Salazar, N.B. (2006) Touristifying Tanzania: Local guides, global discourse. *Annals of Tourism Research* 33 (3), 833–852.

Savannah Guides (2009) Protectors and interpretators of the outback. See http://www.savannah-guides.com.au (accessed 13 August 2013).

Scherle, N. and Nonnenmann, A. (2008) Swimming in cultural flows: Conceptualising tour guides as intercultural mediators and cosmopolitans. *Journal of Tourism and Cultural Change* 6 (2), 120–137.

Scherle, N. and Kung, H. (2010) Cosmopolitans of the 21st century? Conceptualising tour guides as intercultural mediators. Paper presented at the First International Research Forum on Guided Tours, 23–25 April 2009, Halmstad University, Sweden.

Scherrer, P., Smith, A.J. and Dowling R.K. (2011) Visitor management practices and operational sustainability: Expedition cruising in the Kimberley, Australia. *Tourism Management* 32 (5), 1218–1222.

Schmidt, C.J. (1979) The guided tour: Insulated adventure. *Urban Life* 7 (4), 441–467.

Sharpe, E.K. (2005) 'Going above and beyond': The emotional labor of adventure guides. *Journal of Leisure Research* 37 (1), 29–50.

Sheldon, P.J. (1989) Professionalism in tourism and hospitality. *Annals of Tourism Research* 16, 492–503.

Shephard, K. and Royston-Airey, P. (2000) Exploring the role of part-time ecotourism guides in central Southern England. *Journal of Sustainable Tourism* 8 (4), 324–332.

Sizer, S.R. (1999) The ethical challenges of managing pilgrimages to the Holy Land. *International Journal of Contemporary Hospitality Management* 11 (2/3), 85–90.

Skanavis, C. and Giannoulis, C. (2009) A training model for environmental educators and interpreters employed in Greek protected areas and ecotourism settings. *International Journal of Sustainable Development & World Ecology* 16 (3), 164–176.

Skanavis, C. and Giannoulis, C. (2010) Improving quality of ecotourism through advancing education and training for eco-tourism guides. *Tourismos* 5 (2), 49–68.

Skibins, J.C., Powell, R.B. and Stern, M.J. (2012) Exploring empirical support for interpretation's best practices. *Journal of Interpretation Research* 17 (1), 25–44.

Smith, L.D.G., Broad, S. and Weiler, B. (2008) A closer examination of the impact of zoo visits on visitor behaviour. *Journal of Sustainable Tourism* 16 (5), 544–562.

Smith, V.L. (1961) Needed: Geographically-trained tourist guides. *The Professional Geographer* 13 (6), 28–30.

Social Change Media (1995) A national ecotourism education strategy. Unpublished report, Newcastle Australia.

Spitzberg, B.H. and Cupach, W.R. (1984) *Interpersonal Communication Competence*. Beverly Hills, CA: Sage Publications.

Spitzberg, B.H. and Hurt, H.T. (1987) The measurement of interpersonal skills in an instructional context. *Communication Education* 36 (1), 28–45.

Stamation, K., Croft, D., Shaughnessy, P.D., Waples, K.A. and Briggs, S.V. (2007) Educational and conservation value of whale watching. *Tourism in Marine Environments* 4 (1), 41–55.

Steiner, C.J. and Reisinger, Y. (2004): Enriching the tourist and host intercultural experience by reconceptualising communication. *Journal of Tourism and Cultural Change* 2 (2), 118–137.

The Ecotourism Society (1993) *Ecotourism Guidelines for Nature Tour Operators*. North Bennington, VT: The Ecotourism Society.

Thomas, T. (1994) Ecotourism in Antarctica. The role of the naturalist-guide in presenting places of natural interest. *Journal of Sustainable Tourism* 2 (4), 204–209.

Tilden, F. (1977) *Interpreting our Heritage* (3rd edn). Chapel Hill, NC: North Carolina Press.

Torland, M. (2011a) Effects of emotional labor on adventure tour leaders' job satisfaction. *Tourism Review International* 14 (2/3), 129–142.

Torland, M. (2011b) Emotional labour and job satisfaction of adventure tour leaders: Does gender matter? *Annals of Leisure Research* 14 (4), 369–389.

Tosun, C., Temizhan, S.P., Timothy, D.J. and Fyrll, A. (2007) Tourist shopping experiences and satisfaction. *International Journal of Tourism Research* 9 (2), 87–102.

Toplis, S. (2000) *Evaluating the Effectiveness of the Australian Tourism Awards in Promoting Ecological Sustainability to the Australian Tourism Industry: A Victorian Perspective.* Melbourne: RMIT University, Department of Hospitality, Tourism and Leisure, School of Business.

Tourism Council of Australia, Western Australia (2000) *Western Australian Tourism Awards.* Perth, Western Australia: Tourism Council of Australia Western Australia.

Tourism Tasmania (2000) *Nature: The Leading Edge for Regional Australia.* Hobart: Tourism Tasmania.

United Nations Environment Programme Industry and Environment. (1995) *Environmental Codes of Conduct for Tourism.* Paris: United Nations Environment Programme Industry and Environment.

Valsson, S.H. (2010) Tourist guide training in Iceland – student profile, motivation and barriers to participation. Paper presented at the First International Research Forum on Guided Tours, 23–25 April 2009, Halmstad University, Sweden.

Van Dijk, P. and Weiler, B. (2009) An assessment of the outcomes of a Chinese-language interpretive tour experience at a heritage tourism attraction. *Tourism Analysis* 14 (1), 49–64.

Van Dijk, P., Smith, L.D.G. and Cooper, B.K. (2011) Are you for real? An evaluation of the relationship between emotional labour and visitor outcomes. *Tourism Management* 31 (1), 39–45.

Vereczi, G. (2007) Sustainability indicators for ecotourism destinations and operations. In R. Black and A. Crabtree (eds) *Quality Assurance and Certification in Ecotourism* (pp. 101–115).Wallingford: CAB International.

Wang, K.C., Jao, P.C., Chan, H.C. and Chung, C.H. (2010) Group package tour leader's intrinsic risks. *Annals of Tourism Research* 37 (1), 154–179.

Weaver, D. (2006) *Sustainable Tourism: Theory and Practice.* Oxford: Elsevier.

Weaver, D.B. (ed.) (2001) *The Encyclopedia of Ecotourism.* Wallingford: CABI Publishing.

Weiler, B. (1996) Leading tours, greening tourists: Applying leadership theory to guiding nature tours. *Australian Journal of Leisure and Recreation* 7 (4), 43–47.

Weiler, B. (1999) Assessing the interpretation competencies of ecotour guides. *Journal of Interpretation Research* 4 (1), 80–83.

Weiler, B. and Richins, H. (1990) Escort or expert? Entertainer or enabler? The role of the resource person on educational tours. Paper presented at the The Global Classroom: An International Symposium on Educational Tourism, Christchurch, New Zealand.

Weiler, B. and Davis, D. (1993) An exploratory investigation into the roles of the nature-based tour leader. *Tourism Management* 14 (2), 91–98.

Weiler, B., Crabtree, A. and Markwell, K. (1997) *Developing Competent Ecotour Guides: Does Training Deliver What Tourists Demand?* Adelaide: National Centre for Vocational Education Research.

Weiler, B. and Crabtree, A. (1998) *Developing Competent Ecotour Guides: Summary of Research Project Findings.* Adelaide: National Centre for Vocational Education Research.

Weiler, B. and Crabtree, A. (1999) Assessing ecotour guide performance: Findings from the field. In B. Weir, S. McArthur and A. Crabtree (eds) *Developing Ecotourism into the Millennium. Proceedings of the Ecotourism Association of Australia. National Conference 1998* (pp. 50–53). Brisbane: Ecotourism Association of Australia.

Weiler, B. and Ham, S.H. (1999) Training ecotour guides in developing countries: Lessons learned from Panama's first guide course. Paper presented at the International Society of Travel and Tourism Educators Annual Conference: New Frontiers in Tourism Research, Vancouver, Canada.

Weiler, B. and Ham, S.H. (2001) Tour guides and interpretation. In D. Weaver (ed.) *Encyclopedia of Ecotourism* (pp. 549–563). Wallingford: CABI Publishing.

Weiler, B. and Ham, S.H. (2002) Tour guide training: A model for sustainable capacity building in developing countries. *Journal of Sustainable Tourism* 10 (1), 52–69.

Weiler, B. and Black, R. (2003) Nature, heritage and interpretive guide training. In R. Black and B. Weiler (eds) *Interpreting the Land Down Under: Australian Heritage Interpretation and Tour Guiding* (pp. 21–40). Golden, CO: Fulcrum Publishing.

Weiler, B. and Yu, X. (2007) Dimensions of cultural mediation in guiding Chinese tour groups: Implications for interpretation. *Tourism Recreation Research* 32 (3), 13–22.

Weiler, B. and Smith, L. (2009) Does more interpretation lead to greater outcomes? An assessment of the impacts of multiple layers of interpretation in a zoo context. *Journal of Sustainable Tourism* 17 (1), 91–105.

Weiler, B. and Ham, S.H. (2010) Development of a research instrument for evaluating the visitor outcomes of face-to-face interpretation. *Visitor Studies* 13 (2), 187–205.

Weiler, B. and Kim, A.K. (2011) Tour guides as agents of sustainability: Rhetoric, reality and implications for research. *Tourism Recreation Research* 36 (2), 113–125.

Welgemoed, M. (1993) The professionalization of guiding to tourists. In A.J. Veal, P. Jonson and G. Cushman (eds) *Proceedings of Leisure and Tourism: Social and Environmental Change: World Congress of the World Leisure and Recreation Association* (pp. 692–695). Sydney: University of Technology Sydney.

Wells, M., Adams, A. and Wright, B. (1995) *Evaluating Interpretation: An Annotated Bibliography*. Fairfax, VI: Centre for Recreation Resources Policy, George Mason University.

Whinney, C. (1996) Good intentions in a competitive market: Training for people and tourism in fragile environments. In M.F. Price (ed.) *People and Tourism in Fragile Environments* (pp. 221–229). Chichester: John Wiley and Sons Ltd.

Whipple, T.W. and Thach, S.V. (1988) Group tour management: Does good service produce satisfied customers? *Journal of Travel Research* 27 (2), 16–21.

Widner, C.J. and Roggenbuck, J. (2000) Reducing theft of petrified wood at Petrified forest national park. *Journal of Interpretation Research* 5 (1), 1–18.

Wolf, I.D., Stricker, H.K. and Hagenloh, G. (2013) Interpretive media that attract park visitors and enhance their experiences: A comparison of modern and traditional tools using GPS tracking and GIS technology. *Tourism Management Perspectives* 7, 59–72.

Wong, A. (2001) Satisfaction with local tour guides in Hong Kong. *Pacific Tourism Review* 5 (1), 59–67.

Wong, K.K.F., Ap, J., Yeung, K. and Sandiford, P. (1999) *An Evaluation of the Need to Upgrade the Service Professionalism of Hong Kong's Tour Co-ordinators*. Hong Kong: Hong Kong Polytechnic University.

World Federation of Tourist Guide Associations. (2013) What is a tourist guide? See http://www.wftga.org/tourist-guiding/what-tourist-guide (accessed 30 August 2013) and http://www.feg-touristguides.com/cen-definitions.html (accessed 30 September 2013).

World Travel and Tourism Council (WTTC), World Tourism Organisation (WTO) and The Earth Council (EC) (1996) *Agenda 21 For The Travel and Tourism Industry: Towards Environmentally Sustainable Development*. Madrid: World Tourism Organisation.

World Tourism Organisation (WTO) (2013) Definition. Sustainable development of tourism. See http://sdt.unwto.org/en/content/about-us-5 (accessed 13 August 2013).

Xu, H.G., Cui, Q.M., Ballantyne, R. and Packer, J. (2012) Effective environmental interpretation at Chinese natural attractions: The need for an aesthetic approach. *Journal of Sustainable Tourism* 21 (1), 117–133.

Yamada, N. (2011) Why tour guiding is important for ecotourism: Enhancing guiding quality with the ecotourism promotion policy in Japan. *Asia Pacific Journal of Tourism Research* 16 (2), 139–152.

Yeoman, I. (2012) *2050 – Tomorrow's Tourism*. Bristol: Channel View Publications.

Yu, X. (2003) Conceptualising and assessing intercultural competence of tour guides: An analysis of Australian guides of Chinese tour groups. PhD thesis, Monash University.

Yu, X. and Weiler, B. (2006) Guiding Chinese tour groups in Australia: An analysis using role theory. In B. Prideaux and G. Moscardo (eds) *Managing Tourism and Hospitality Services: Theory and International Application* (pp. 181–194). Wallingford: CABI Publishing.

Zeppel, H. (2008) Education and conservation benefits of marine wildlife tours: Developing free-choice learning experiences. *The Journal of Environmental Education* 39 (3), 3–17.

Zeppel, H. and Muloin, S. (2008) Conservation benefits of interpretation on marine wildlife tours. *Human Dimensions of Wildlife* 13, 280–294.

Zhang, H.Q. and Chow, I. (2004) Application of importance-performance model in tour guides' performance: Evidence from Mainland Chinese outbound visitors in Hong Kong. *Tourism Management* 25 (1), 81–91.

Zillinger, M., Jonasson, M. and Adolfsson, P. (2012) Editorial: Guided tours and tourism. *Scandinavian Journal of Hospitality and Tourism* 12 (1), 1–7.

Index

This book is due for return on or before the last date shown below.